KU-223-661

Contents at a Glance

Table of Contents

My
Surface™

Jim Cheshire

QUE®

My Surface

Copyright © 2013 by Pearson Education, Inc.

ISBN-13: 978-0-7897-4854-6

ISBN-10: 0-7897-4854-1

Library of Congress Cataloging-in-Publication data is on file.

Printed in the United States of America

First Printing: December 2012

Trademarks

Warning and Disclaimer

Bulk Sales

Que Publishing offers excellent discounts on this book when ordered in quantity for bulk purchases or special sales. For more information, please contact

U.S. Corporate and Government Sales
1-800-382-3419
corpsales@pearsontechgroup.com

For sales outside of the U.S., please contact

International Sales
international@pearsoned.com

Editor-in-Chief
Greg Wiegand

Executive Editor
Loretta Yates

Development Editor
Todd Brakke

Managing Editor
Sandra Schroeder

Senior Project Editor
Tonya Simpson

Indexer
Ken Johnson

Proofreader
Leslie Joseph

Publishing Coordinator
Cindy Teeters

Book Designer
Anne Jones

Compositor
TnT Design, Inc.

About the Author

Jim Cheshire is a technology expert with a passion for gadgets. He has written a dozen books and many online articles on technology and is the author of many best-selling technical guides. Jim works on the Azure Application Platform and Tools team at Microsoft and was an early adopter of Windows RT.

When Jim's not writing, he spends time with his family, plays keyboards with his band, and enjoys writing music.

You can contact Jim through his website at www.JimcoBooks.com.

Dedication

This book is dedicated to my wife, Becky, and to my kids. The strength of my family is one of the greatest pleasures of my life. I love you all very much.

Acknowledgments

This book would not have been possible were it not for the small army of people at Que Publishing who work tirelessly to support me. I owe a great deal of gratitude to Loretta Yates, who always makes me feel like I'm the only author she has to deal with. Thanks also go to Todd Brakke, who did a great job of editing my work and offering creative ideas for additional content. Thanks also go to Tonya Simpson and others who worked so hard to turn the hundreds of screenshots into the high-quality work you now hold in your hands.

We Want to Hear from You!

As the reader of this book, *you* are our most important critic and commentator. We value your opinion and want to know what we're doing right, what we could do better, what areas you'd like to see us publish in, and any other words of wisdom you're willing to pass our way.

We welcome your comments. You can email or write to let us know what you did or didn't like about this book—as well as what we can do to make our books better.

Please note that we cannot help you with technical problems related to the topic of this book.

When you write, please be sure to include this book's title and author as well as your name and email address. We will carefully review your comments and share them with the author and editors who worked on the book.

Email: feedback@quepublishing.com

Mail: Que Publishing
ATTN: Reader Feedback
800 East 96th Street
Indianapolis, IN 46240 USA

Reader Services

Visit our website and register this book at quepublishing.com/register for convenient access to any updates, downloads, or errata that might be available for this book.

Introduction

Microsoft has done something quite extraordinary with the release of the Surface. Not only is this the first tablet computer Microsoft has ever developed, but the operating system (Windows RT) that runs on it is a significant departure from anything Microsoft has ever created. The result is a unique tablet that's a pleasure to use.

Scratching the Surface

Your Surface for Windows RT is made for work and play. Windows RT includes Office 2013 RT, which includes Word, Excel, PowerPoint, and OneNote. It also includes many other apps for information, entertainment, and productivity.

Here are just some of the things you can do with your Surface:

- Read news from major news outlets, sources for all your favorite topics, and even based on your own web searches.

- Get the latest weather, sports scores, travel ideas, stock quotes, and more.

- Listen to your music, discover new music, stream music, and buy music.

- Rent and purchase movies and TV shows from the Xbox Video Store.

- Access all your social networks, including pictures that are stored in the cloud on Facebook, Flickr, and SkyDrive.

- Open and edit Microsoft Office documents with full versions of Office applications.

- Watch video using Netflix, Hulu Plus, and more.

- Enhance your Surface with apps from the Windows Store.

You can do all of this in a portable tablet, and add a Touch Cover or a Type Cover, and you've got a genuine laptop replacement in a lightweight package.

Why You'll Love *My Surface*

The Surface for Windows RT is accessible to all kinds of users, and so is *My Surface*. If you're a nontechnical person, you'll find the step-by-step approach in *My Surface* to be refreshing and helpful. If you're a technical person new to Windows RT, you'll find plenty of tips and tricks to help you get the most out of your new tablet.

The book covers all the capabilities of your Surface. I show you how to get the most out of each feature using a step-by-step approach, complete with figures that correspond to each step. You never have to wonder what or where to tap. Each task shows you how to interact with your Surface using simple symbols that illustrate what you should do.

This icon means that you should tap and hold an object on the screen.

This icon means that you should drag an item on the screen.

This icon indicates that you should pinch on the screen.

This icon means that you should "reverse pinch."

This icon indicates that you need to swipe on the screen.

Along the way, I add plenty of tips that help you better understand a feature or task. I also warn you with It's Not All Good sidebars when you need to be careful with a particular task or when there are pitfalls that you need to know about. If you're the kind of person who likes to dig a little deeper, you'll enjoy the Go Further sidebars that provide a more in-depth look at particular topics.

Finally, for those of you with the paperback version of this book, you might notice that it isn't a big and bulky book. It's a handy size for taking with you when you go places with your Surface tablet. That way, you can always find the steps necessary to do what you want to do. Of course, if you prefer not to carry the book with you, you can always purchase the eBook version and read it on your Surface.

What You'll Find in the Book

Your Surface is full of surprises. The major functions are easy to discover, but some of the neater features are hidden away. As you read through this book, you'll find yourself saying, "Wow, I didn't know I could do that!" This book is designed to invoke just that kind of reaction.

Here are the things covered in this book:

- Chapter 1, "An Introduction to Surface," provides an introduction the Surface hardware and gives you a primer on Windows RT.

- Chapter 2, "Connecting to Networks," shows you how to connect to wireless networks, how you can access share resources on your network, and how you can remote into other computers on your network using your Surface.

- Chapter 3, "Using and Customizing the Start Screen," walks you through using the new Windows Start screen, including details on how you can customize the Start screen and make it uniquely yours.

- Chapter 4, "Security and Windows RT," shows you how to use user accounts and secure your Surface.

- Chapter 5, "Using Family Safety," provides a thorough view of Family Safety, a feature that makes it easy to control what family members can do on your Surface, which apps they can use, and when they are able to use the device. You also learn how you can get reports on activity that kids and other family members are engaging in.

- Chapter 6, "Backing Up Your Data," shows you how to use the unique features in Windows RT to back up your data and keep it safe from data loss.

- Chapter 7, "Searching and Browsing the Internet," covers the Bing app and Internet Explorer 10 on the Surface.

- Chapter 8, "Connecting with People," demonstrates how you can interact with friends and family on your social networks.

- Chapter 9, "Using Mail," covers the Mail app in Windows RT and explains how to send and receive email.

- Chapter 10, "Using Calendar," walks you through using the Calendar app to keep track of your appointments.

- Chapter 11, "Keeping Up to Date with News," shows you how to read news and other information from sources all over the Web from within the News app.

- Chapter 12, "HomeGroups and SkyDrive," explains how you can share data with others on your network with HomeGroups and how to use Microsoft SkyDrive to store and share files in the cloud.

- Chapter 13, "Discovering and Playing Music," provides information on using the Music app to play your own music and to browse and play music from Xbox Music.

- Chapter 14, "Watching Video," covers the Video app and Xbox Video, a service for renting and buying movies and TV shows.

- Chapter 15, "Pictures," shows you how to use the Photos app to view and manage pictures from your Surface and from social networks and other computers.

- Chapter 16, "Using Maps," walks you through using Maps, an app that provides detailed maps as well as directions.

- Chapter 17, "Creating Documents with Microsoft Word 2013," covers using Microsoft Word to create and edit documents.

- Chapter 18, "Crunching Numbers with Microsoft Excel 2013," walks you through using Microsoft Excel to create workbooks, including how you can use formulas and functions to create complex sheets.

- Chapter 19, "Presenting with Microsoft PowerPoint 2013," walks you through using Microsoft PowerPoint to create compelling presentations.

- Chapter 20, "Organizing Notes with Microsoft OneNote 2013," shows you how to use Microsoft OneNote to organize notes, synchronize them across your devices, and access them from anywhere.

- Chapter 21, "Enhancing Windows with Apps," shows you how to enhance the operation of your Surface using apps from the Windows Store, complete with some great app recommendations.

- Chapter 22, "Updating and Troubleshooting Windows RT," shows you how to update Windows RT and how to troubleshoot and repair problems that you might encounter.

Go Beneath the Surface

Now that you know what's in store, it's time to start having fun digging deeper into the Surface. You're sure to learn new things and experience the thrill of what your Surface can do, and you'll have fun doing it. Let's get started!

Learn how to use
Windows RT.

Learn about the
Surface hardware.

Master the basics
before diving in.

1

An Introduction to Surface

Congratulations on your purchase of the Microsoft Surface for Windows RT! The Surface for Windows RT is a unique device running a completely new version of Windows designed for ARM processors, the same processors that typically run in smartphones and some tablets. These ARM processors are specially designed for efficient power use, and because of that, you can expect to get many hours of use from your Surface between charges.

The uniqueness of Surface doesn't stop there. In fact, the Surface offers several brand-new technologies, including a built-in kickstand for convenient viewing and a revolutionary cover with a built-in keyboard.

The Surface Device

The Surface device's case is composed of magnesium, but it's made using a special method involving liquification of the magnesium and then *extremely* rapid cooling. The result is what Microsoft calls VaporMg (pronounced *vapor mag*), and it's extremely strong, light, and scratch-resistant.

ON FIRE

For those of you who are science buffs, you might already know that when magnesium reaches a certain temperature, it ignites and burns at an intense temperature. Because of this, some naysayers of the Surface claim that if the battery inside the Surface were to ignite, it would cause the device to ignite and burn uncontrollably. In fact, a burning battery burns at just under 600 degrees Fahrenheit, and magnesium requires a temperature of approximately 1,022 degrees Fahrenheit to ignite. You can do the math yourself, but I think you're safe.

Ports and Controls

Along the right edge of the Surface, you'll find the right speaker, a micro-HDMI video port used for outputting video to an HD display, a full-sized USB 2.0 port, a microSDXC memory card port, and a proprietary port for the Surface's power adapter.

By inserting a microSDXC card into the microSDXC slot, you can increase the memory of your Surface by up to 64GB. The microSDXC slot on the Surface is hidden behind the right side of the Kickstand.

It's Not All Good

Using microSDXC Cards

Windows RT does not enable you to easily use memory from a microSDXC card in specific ways. For example, you can't store movies that you download from Xbox Video or music that you get from Xbox Music to a memory card without taking some pretty complex steps.

For information on how you can get around this limitation, check out Paul Thurott's tip on his WinSupersite website at www.winsupersite.com/article/windows8/surface-tip-microsd-content-libraries-metro-apps-144658.

HD Video Port   **Right Speaker**   **USB Port**

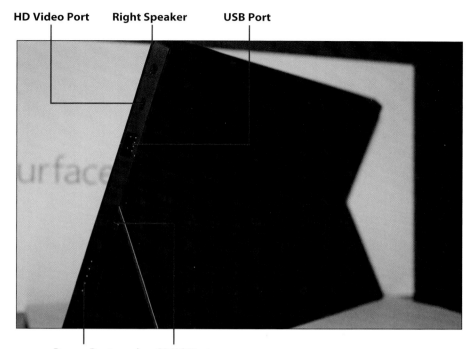

Power Port   **microSDXC Port**

On the left edge of the Surface is the left speaker, a 1/8-inch headphone jack, and the volume control. The bottom of the Surface contains the final port, a proprietary port for the Surface's unique Touch Cover or Type Cover.

The Surface's power switch is located on the top-right side of the device. If you press and release the switch, it turns off the Surface's screen. If you press and hold the switch for several seconds, it turns off the device entirely.

The Surface is also equipped with two microphones, both of which are positioned along the top edge of the device.

It's Not All Good

Powering Off

It's not recommended that you hold the power switch to turn off the Surface unless you have no other option. When you turn off the device in this way, any work you are doing is not saved, and you increase the chances of losing data.

Left Speaker   **Headphone Jack**   **Volume Control**

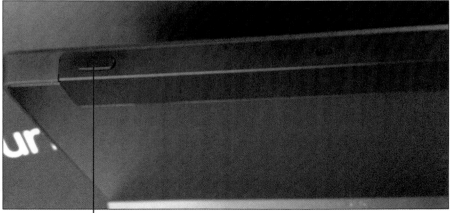

Power Button

The Kickstand

One of the features unique to the Surface is the built-in Kickstand. The Kickstand is convenient not only when you are using a keyboard with your Surface, it also perfectly positions the Surface for watching video. The Kickstand flips out from the Surface with a satisfying snap, and despite its thinness, it's tough and solid due to the VaporMg construction.

The Kickstand also is convenient when using the Surface for videoconferencing. In fact, Microsoft expects that you'll use it for that purpose, and that's why the front-facing camera in the Surface is positioned in such a way that it's aiming directly at your head when the Surface is tilted at a slight angle by the Kickstand.

Type Cover and Touch Cover

Another feature unique to the Surface is the Touch Cover and the Type Cover. These covers attach to the bottom side of the Surface using strong magnets. If you get the cover close to the bottom, the strong magnets pop it into proper position easily. When the cover is folded over the Surface's screen, the screen is automatically turned off. When the cover is folded away from the screen, the screen turns on automatically.

It's Not All Good

Covers Not Included

The Surface does not come with a cover. If you want a Touch Cover or a Type Cover, you're going to have to pay for it. The Touch Cover will run you about $120, and the Type Cover will run you about $130. Even so, I highly encourage you to buy one. It is a great addition to the Surface, especially if you plan on using Office 2013 RT apps on your device.

The truly unique thing about the Touch Cover and Type Cover is that they both double as a quality keyboard, complete with a touch pad. The Touch Cover has touch-sensitive keys that are slightly raised from the cover's surface. The Type Cover is slightly thicker and uses physical keyboard keys.

It is worth noting, however, that the Touch Cover and Type Cover only attach to the Surface at the bottom of the device. When you fold the cover over the display, it doesn't attach in any way to the top of the device. Therefore, if you hold the Surface upside down, the cover will open. I don't find it to be a problem, but it's worth mentioning.

Touch Cover

Fast Typing

I'm a pretty fast touch-typist, and I find typing on the Touch Cover to be fast and accurate.

Windows RT Basics

Windows RT is a brand-new version of the popular Windows operating system. Although it might look just like the version of Windows 8 that's running on your notebook or desktop computer, it's not the same. Windows RT is designed to run on ARM processors, while Windows 8 that you run on your notebook or desktop is designed to run on Intel processors. Is that important? Yes! You can't install software (including drivers for printers and other hardware) onto Windows RT unless that software is specifically designed for ARM processors. When it comes to the Surface for Windows RT, that means you can't install apps unless they come from the Windows Store, and unless Windows RT comes with a driver for your printer or other hardware, there's a good chance that you can't use it in Windows RT.

With all of that said, Windows RT has a huge advantage in that it is extremely power-efficient, enabling you to squeeze about 10 hours of battery life out of the device. And unlike your notebook computer, the Surface for Windows RT is capable of transitioning into a very low power state instead of going to sleep. That means that even when the device looks like it's asleep, it's still running and will notify you of appointments, new emails, and so forth.

The Start Screen

Windows RT doesn't have a Start button to get things going; instead, the Start screen is the launching point for your apps. Laid out across the Start screen are brightly colored tiles. Some of these tiles are what Microsoft calls *Live Tiles* that display useful information about the app they represent.

The Start Screen   **Live Tile**

For full information on using the Start screen, see Chapter 3, "Using and Customizing the Start Screen."

App Switching and Charms

You can have multiple apps running at the same time in Windows RT, and you can easily switch between them by swiping in from the left side of the screen. You also can display two at the same time on the screen.

More on App Switching

For full details on how app switching works in Windows RT, see "Switching Between Recent Apps" in Chapter 3.

To access settings for an app or to search within an app (or across apps), you swipe in from the right side of the screen. When you do, you'll see a series of vertical icons that you can use to interact with your apps and with Windows (Microsoft calls these *charms*).

Charms are context-sensitive. For example, if you tap the Settings charm while on the Start screen, you pull up settings for Windows, and if you tap the Settings charm while in the Music app, you pull up settings for the Music app, and so forth.

Printing from Windows RT

The Device charm is used to print in Windows RT.

Typing in Windows RT

For the most part, you type in Windows RT just as you would on any other computer. However, there are some shortcuts to make things a bit easier. For example, Windows RT has a spell checker across the entire operating system that underlines misspelled words in a red squiggly underline. Windows RT also shows suggestions while you type in many areas, and there are other minor conveniences, such as the ability to add a period at the end of a sentence by simply double-tapping the spacebar.

You can control many of these features in the General settings of your Surface.

1. From the Start screen, swipe in from the right side of the screen and tap the Settings charm.

2. Tap Change PC Settings.

3. Tap General.

4. In the Touch Keyboard section, tap Show Text Suggestions as I Type to turn off that feature.

5. Tap Add a Space After I Choose a Text Suggestion to turn off that feature.

6. Tap Add a Period After I Double-Tap the Spacebar to turn off that feature.

7. Tap Capitalize the First Letter of Each Sentence to turn off that feature.

8. Tap Use All Uppercase Letters When I Double-Tap Shift Key to turn off that feature.

9. Tap Play Key Sounds as I Type to turn off that feature.

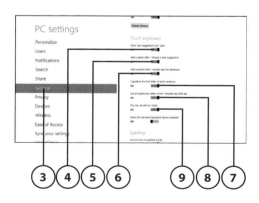

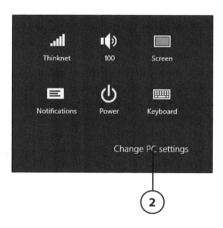

10. Swipe up to move down to the Spelling section.

11. Tap Autocorrect Misspelled Words to turn off that feature.

12. Tap Highlight Misspelled Words to turn off that feature.

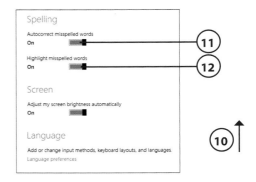

Adding Devices

You can add new devices, such as a printer, a Bluetooth headset, and so forth.

1. From the PC Settings screen, tap Devices.

2. Tap Add a Device.

3. Tap your device from the list to add it to your Surface.

Adding Bluetooth Devices

If you are adding a Bluetooth device, make sure that the device is discoverable before you tap Add a Device in step 2.

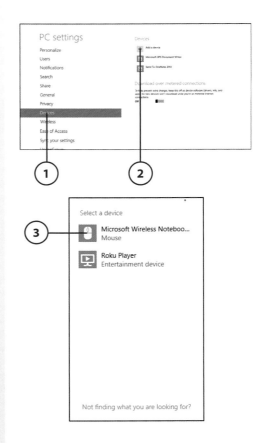

Removing Devices

If you no longer need a device that you added, you can remove the device from your Surface.

1. From the Devices PC Settings page, tap the device you want to remove.

2. Tap the - button.

3. Tap Remove to remove the device.

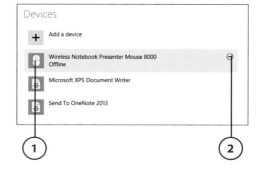

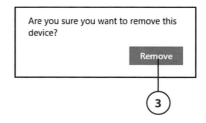

Notifications

Windows RT displays notifications in a pop-up in the upper-right corner of the screen. Notifications are displayed for calendar reminders, emails, and more. When you install additional apps from the Windows Store, these apps can also display notifications.

You can control whether notification pop-ups are displayed, whether apps can display notifications on the lock screen, and whether a sound plays when a notification is displayed. You also can specify whether individual apps are allowed to display notifications.

The Lock Screen

I cover the lock screen in the next section of this chapter.

1. From the PC Settings screen, tap Notifications.

2. Tap Show App Notifications to change the setting to Off and disable all notifications.

3. Tap Show App Notifications on the Lock Screen to change the setting to Off and disable notifications on the lock screen.

4. Tap Play Notification Sounds to change the setting to Off and disable sounds when notifications are displayed.

5. Tap the slider for an individual app to change it to Off and disallow notifications for that app.

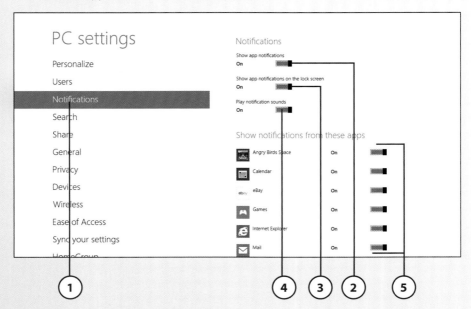

The Lock Screen

The lock screen is displayed when your Surface starts and when you turn on the display after it has been turned off. To get to the sign-in screen or the Start screen, swipe up on the lock screen or press the Esc key on your keyboard.

Signing In

For information on signing in to Windows RT, see "Securing Your PC" in Chapter 4, "Security and Windows RT."

You can customize the lock screen with one of your own pictures. You also can decide which apps are allowed to show a status on the lock screen, and choose one app to show detailed status.

1. From the PC Settings screen, tap Personalize.

2. Tap Lock Screen.

3. Tap a picture, or tap Browse to browse to one of your own pictures. A preview of the lock screen appears above the picture tiles.

4. Swipe up to reveal additional lock screen options.

5. To add an app that can display status on the lock screen, tap +.

6. Tap an app.

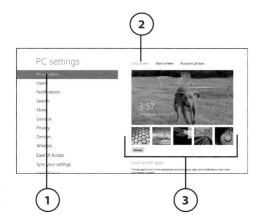

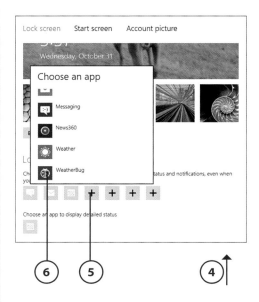

7. To change an app or remove an app from the lock screen, tap the icon for the app.

8. Tap a different app to display, or tap Don't Show Quick Status Here to remove the app's status from the lock screen.

9. To choose an app that displays detailed status on the lock screen, tap the calendar icon. (The Calendar app shows detailed status by default.)

10. Tap an app, or tap Don't Show Detailed Status on the Lock Screen to remove all detailed app statuses from the lock screen.

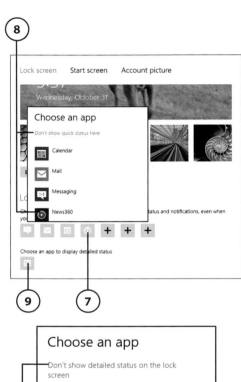

App Status

When an app shows a status on the lock screen, it consists of the app's icon and a numerical indicator showing how many notifications are available for the app. For example, the Mail app would display an envelope icon and a numeric indicator showing how many new mail messages you have.

A detailed status shows additional information. For example, if the Calendar app is selected as the app to show detailed status, you will see details on your next appointment on the lock screen.

Additional Settings

There are a few other settings in Windows RT that you should know about before we dive into the details of using your Surface.

Volume and Mute

You can control the volume of your
Surface using the volume rocker on
the left side of the case, but you also
can adjust volume by touch, including
muting the sound altogether.

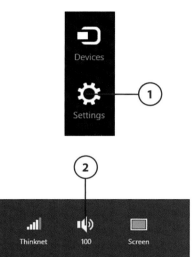

1. From the Start screen, swipe in
   from the right side of the screen
   and tap the Settings charm.

2. Tap the speaker icon.

Networks

Ignore the Network icon just to the
left of the speaker icon for now. I show
you how to join networks in the next
chapter.

3. Drag the slider down to decrease
   volume and up to increase
   volume.

4. Tap on the speaker to mute your
   Surface. Tapping it again unmutes
   it.

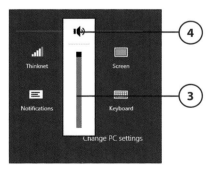

Screen Brightness and Rotation Lock

Your Surface will adjust screen brightness based on battery life and current lighting levels. However, you can adjust the brightness to your liking manually.

1. From the Settings pane, tap the Screen icon.

2. Drag the slider down to decrease brightness and up to increase brightness.

3. Tap the rotation icon to toggle the rotation lock and prevent the screen from rotating when you rotate the device.

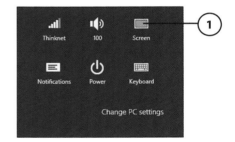

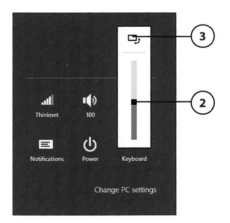

Hiding Notifications Temporarily

You might decide that you want to temporarily hide notifications. For example, if you are in a meeting for an hour and you want to make sure that your Surface doesn't pop up a notification, you can disable notifications for a specific time period.

1. From the Settings pane, tap the Notifications icon.

2. Tap a time period during which notifications are hidden.

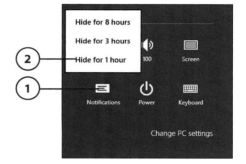

Shutting Down, Sleeping, and Restarting

If you want to shut down your Surface, put it to sleep, or restart it, you can do so from the Settings screen.

1. From the Settings screen, tap the Power icon.

2. Tap Sleep to put your Surface into a low-power sleep state.

3. Tap Shut Down to turn off your Surface completely.

4. Tap Restart to shut down and restart your Surface.

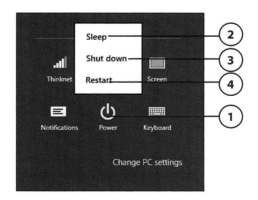

Synchronizing Settings

One of the benefits of using a Microsoft account when signing in to your Surface is that settings are synchronized across your devices. For example, if you change the background image on your lock screen on one device, that change is automatically synchronized to other computers running Windows 8 or Windows RT when you log in with that account.

You can control these synchronization settings or disable synchronization altogether.

1. From the Settings screen, tap Change PC Settings.

2. Tap Sync Your Settings.

3. To turn off synchronization of settings, tap Sync Settings on this PC to change the setting to Off.

4. To disable synchronization of personalization settings, such as the colors, background, lock screen, and your account picture, tap the Personalize slide to change the setting to Off.

5. To disable synchronization of themes, the taskbar, and other desktop settings, tap the Desktop Personalization slide to change the setting to Off.

6. To turn off synchronization of passwords and sign-in information, tap the Passwords slider to change the setting to Off.

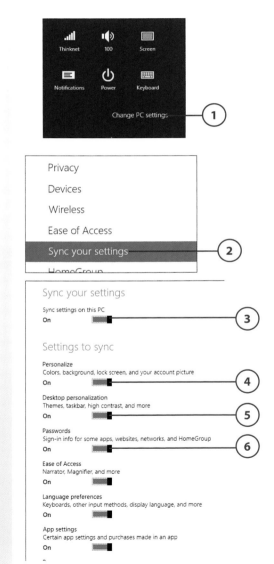

7. To turn off synchronization of accessibility settings, tap the Ease of Access slider to change the setting to Off.

8. To turn off synchronization of keyboard settings, the display language, and other language settings, tap the Language Preferences slider to change the setting to Off.

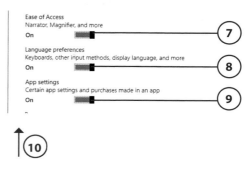

9. To turn off synchronization of app settings, tap the App Settings slider to change the setting to Off.

10. Swipe up to see additional settings.

11. To turn off synchronization of browser history and favorites, tap the Browser slider to change the setting to Off.

12. To turn off synchronization of other settings, such as File Explorer settings and mouse settings, tap the Other Windows Settings slider and change the setting to Off.

Moving On

Now that you know the basics of your Surface and Windows RT, it's time to move on to learning all that you can do with your tablet. Along the way, I show you plenty of tips and tricks, and I also warn you when it's needed.

Let's get started learning how to use your Surface!

Use Network Sharing to browse
other computers and devices.

Connect to wireless
networks.

Remote into other
computers.

2

Connecting to Networks

When you turn on your Surface for the first time, you're walked through a series of steps to get the device ready for use. One of those steps is to connect to a wireless network, and for good reason; Internet access on the Surface is an absolute necessity.

In this chapter, I show you how to connect to wireless networks, how you can share content on your Surface with other computers, and how you can even log in to other computers and remote control them from your Surface.

Wireless Networking

Your Surface supports the latest wireless networking standards, so you can connect to any wireless network you might encounter. That includes not only the wireless network in your home, but also wireless access points in public places.

Connecting to a Wireless Network

As long as a wireless network is broadcasting its name (called an *SSID*), you can connect to it easily.

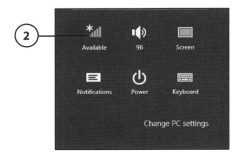

Connecting to Hidden Networks

You can connect to hidden networks as well. I show you how in the next walk-through.

1. From the Start screen, swipe in from the right side of the screen and tap the Settings charm.

2. Tap the Wireless icon to see available networks.

3. Tap a network to connect to it. (Networks are listed in order of signal strength.)

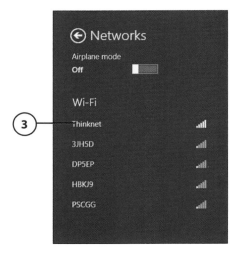

4. Tap to check Connect Automatically if you want your Surface to automatically connect to the selected network when it's in range.

Connecting Automatically

If you choose to connect to multiple networks automatically, Windows RT chooses the network to connect to based on signal strength.

5. Tap Connect to connect to the network.

6. If prompted, enter a security key to connect to the network.

7. Tap Next.

8. Tap No, Don't Turn On Sharing or Connect to Devices to turn off sharing for the network.

9. Tap Yes, Turn On Sharing and Connect to Devices to turn on sharing for the network.

Sharing

If you are connecting to a public network, you should choose to not enable sharing. However, if you are using your home network, enabling sharing will allow you to see other network devices.

I cover sharing in the "Network Sharing" section of this chapter.

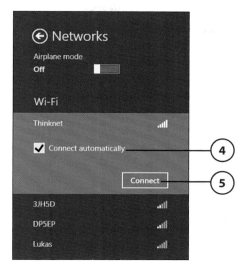

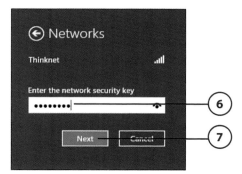

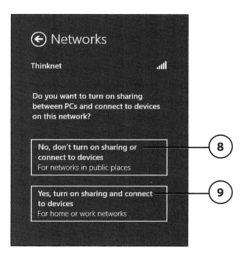

Connecting to a Hidden Network

Some wireless networks are hidden and don't broadcast their SSIDs. You can connect to these networks, but the process is a little more complex.

1. From the Start screen, swipe in from the right and tap the Search charm.

2. Tap Settings.

3. Enter **set up a connection** in the text box.

4. Tap Set Up a Connection or Network. Selecting this option takes you to the Windows desktop.

5. Tap Manually Connect to a Wireless Network.

6. Tap Next.

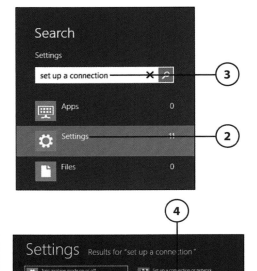

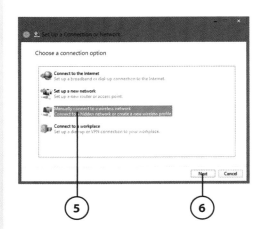

7. Enter the network name.

8. Tap Security Type and select the network's security type.

9. Tap Encryption Type and select the network's encryption type.

10. Enter the security key for the network if necessary.

Network Settings
If you don't know what settings to select for the network, check with the person who runs or administers the network.

11. Tap to select Start This Connection Automatically to automatically connect to this network when it's in range.

12. Tap to check Connect Even If the Network is Not Broadcasting to connect to a hidden network.

13. Tap Next.

14. Tap Close.

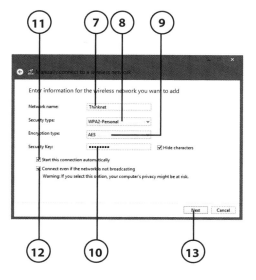

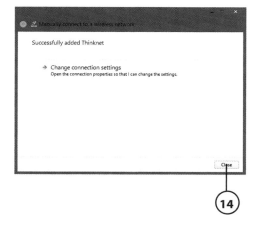

Disconnecting from a Network

If you no longer want to connect to a particular network, you can disconnect from it. If you decide to connect to the network later, you'll have to go through the process of connecting that you followed earlier in this chapter.

1. From the Settings pane, tap the Wireless icon.

2. Tap and hold on the network to which you are connected, and then release to display the context menu.

3. Tap Forget this Network to disconnect and remove the stored settings for the network.

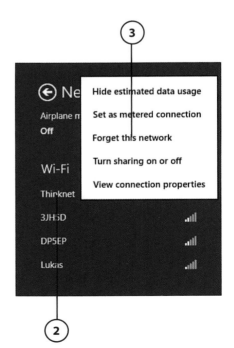

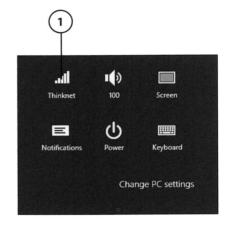

Using Airplane Mode

In some cases (such as when you are using your Surface in an airplane), you might need to turn off the wireless radio in your Surface. When this need arises, you can enable Airplane mode.

1. From the Settings pane, tap the Wireless icon.

2. Tap Airplane Mode to change the setting to On. When Airplane mode is turned on, the Wi-Fi and Bluetooth radios on your Surface are turned off.

3. Tap Airplane Mode again to turn off Airplane mode and turn on the radios again.

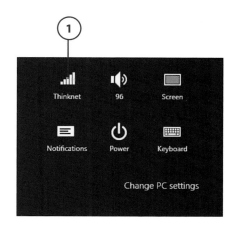

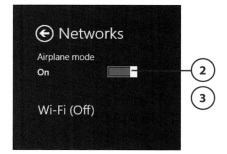

Network Sharing

Windows RT includes a network sharing feature that makes it easy for you to share files and devices (such as networked printers) with other computers on your network. For this feature to work, you must modify certain security settings on the computer. Windows RT allows you to easily enable and disable sharing.

Sharing and Public Networks

If you are connected to a public network, you should not enable sharing because it can allow others on the network to see your files and devices.

Turning Sharing On or Off

You can easily turn sharing on or off as necessary.

1. From the Settings screen, tap the Wireless icon.

2. Tap and hold on the network to which you are connected, and then release to display the context menu.

3. Tap Turn Sharing On or Off.

4. Tap No, Don't Turn On Sharing or Connect to Devices to turn off sharing.

5. Tap Yes, Turn On Sharing and Connect to Devices to turn on sharing.

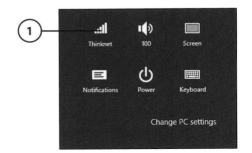

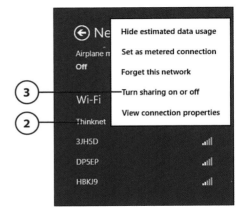

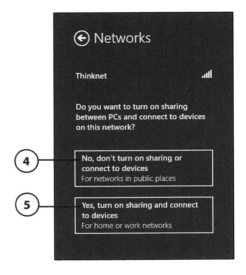

Accessing Network Resources

If sharing is turned on, you can use File Explorer in Windows RT to view resources on your network.

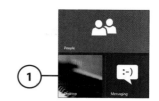

1. From the Start screen, tap Desktop.

2. Tap File Explorer on the taskbar.

3. In File Explorer, tap Network to see network resources.

4. Double-tap on a resource to connect to it.

5. Enter a username and password if prompted.

6. Tap OK to continue.

7. Browse to the network resource you're interested in.

Other Devices and Resources

In this example, I connected to another computer on my network and was able to browse the folders and files on that computer. You can use the same technique to connect to other resources and devices. For example, if you double-tap on a printer, your Surface will connect to the printer so that you can print to it.

Remoting into Other Computers

Windows RT enables you to remotely connect to other Windows computers. When you remote into a computer, what you see on your Surface is exactly what appears on the remote PC, and you can interact with that PC just as though you were using it directly.

Remote connections to other computers are established using a Remote Desktop Connection. By default, Windows does not allow remote connections, so to remote into a computer, you must first enable remote connections.

Enabling Connections on the Remote Computer

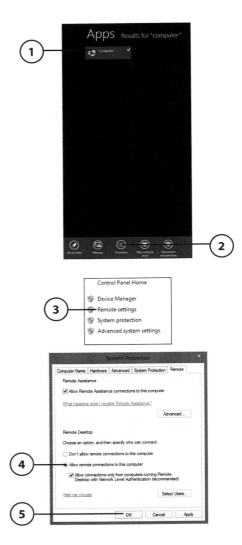

These steps should be carried out on the remote computer to which you want to connect. The computer can be running Windows XP, Windows Vista, Windows 7, or Windows 8. I show you steps for Windows 8, but the steps are almost identical on other versions of Windows.

1. From the Start screen, type **computer** on your keyboard and right-click on Computer from within the search results.

2. Click Properties.

Computer Name

In the Properties window, you'll see the computer name. Make note of it because you'll use it to connect to this computer later.

3. Click Remote Settings.

4. Click Allow Remote Connections to This Computer.

5. Click OK.

Connecting to Remote Computers

After you've enabled remote connections on your remote computer, you can connect to it from your Surface. You should carry out these steps on your Surface.

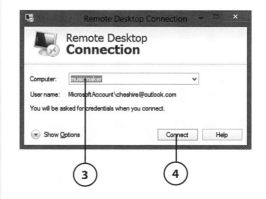

1. From the Start screen, swipe up from the bottom of the screen and tap All Apps.

2. Tap Remote Desktop Connection.

3. Enter the computer name of the remote computer.

4. Tap Connect.

5. Enter your password. If necessary, tap Use Another Account and enter a username and password.

6. Tap to check Remember My Credentials if you want Windows RT to remember your username and password.

7. Tap OK.

Use Microsoft Accounts

If you are connecting to a Windows 8 machine, you can make this process much easier by using the same Microsoft account on the remote machine that you are using on your Surface.

8. Tap Yes in the certificate errors dialog. (You can safely ignore the certificate problem in this specific case.)

9. To disconnect from the computer, tap the X in the Remote Desktop title bar.

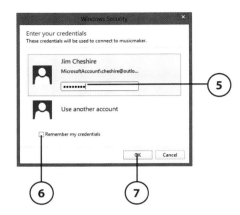

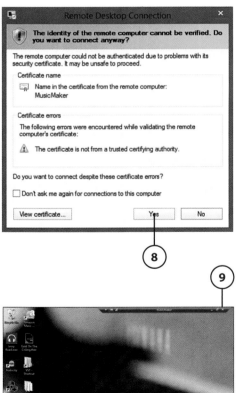

It's Not All Good

One Way

Windows RT enables you to use Remote Desktop to connect to a remote computer, but you can't use Remote Desktop on another PC to connect to your Surface. If you want to remote into a Surface, you'll have to use Surface for Windows 8 Pro.

Locate and
launch apps.

Control and
configure tiles.

Customize your
start screen.

Using and Customizing the Start Screen

Windows RT represents a significant departure from previous versions of Windows, a fact that is obvious from the moment you power on your Surface. Instead of a desktop filled with icons, the Windows RT Start screen offers a rich and colorful environment for interacting with and launching your apps.

Locating and Launching Apps

The Start screen consists of a series of tiles arranged within groups. Tiles can launch an app or link to content within an app, such as a web page in Internet Explorer.

In addition to the tiles that you see on the Start screen, many apps available in Windows RT aren't on the Start screen by default. You can launch these apps using a special All Apps view or by searching for a desired app.

Launching Apps from the Start Screen

You can easily locate an app from the start screen and launch it.

1. If necessary, swipe left or right to locate the app you would like to launch.

2. To see more of your Start screen, pinch to zoom out. (This view is called *semantic zoom*.)

3. To locate apps not represented by a tile on the Start menu, swipe up from the bottom of the screen to reveal the Command bar.

4. Tap All Apps to display the Apps screen.

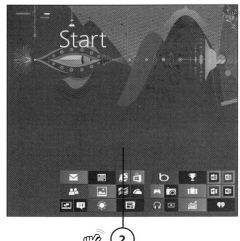

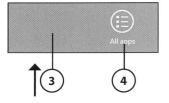

5. Swipe to locate your app.

6. You can also pinch and tap a letter to quickly scroll to apps beginning with a particular letter, or tap a name to quickly scroll to a particular app.

Returning to the Start Screen

While displaying the Apps screen, you can return to the Start screen by pressing the Windows button on your Surface (or the Winkey on your keyboard) by swiping up from the bottom of the screen and tapping All Apps, or by swiping in from the right of the screen and tapping the Start charm.

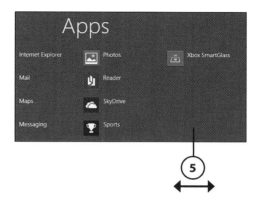

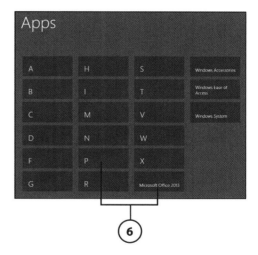

Searching for Apps

If you have any trouble finding a particular app, you can easily search for apps.

1. From the Start screen or Apps screen, swipe in from the right side of the screen, or press Winkey+C to reveal the Charms.

2. Tap Search.

3. If you aren't using a Smart Cover or Type Cover, tap inside of the textbox to open the on-screen keyboard. Enter a search phrase.

4. Apps that match your search phrase appear as you type.

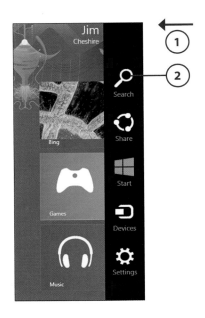

Quick Access to App Search

To quickly access the Apps screen and activate the Search charm, press Winkey+Q while on the Start screen.

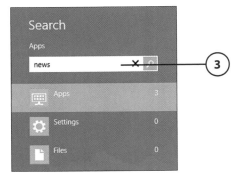

Switching Between Recent Apps

Windows Store apps are designed to take up the entire screen. When you switch back to the Start screen after launching an app, the app usually remains running even though it's no longer visible. However, you can switch back to apps that you've previously run and, in most cases, the app will resume right where you left off when you last used it.

Closing Apps

Even though multiple apps might be running at once, Windows RT controls what resources are available to apps in the background to ensure long battery life; therefore, you don't have to worry about closing apps. However, if you do want to close an app, you can. Simply activate the app, and then swipe down from the top of the screen all the way to the bottom of the screen to close it. If you're using a keyboard, Winkey+F4 closes the active app.

Switching Between Running Apps

You can switch between all the apps that are currently running.

1. Swipe from the left side of the screen.

2. Lift your finger from the screen when the thumbnail of the previous app is fully visible.

3. Repeat the process to cycle through the apps that are currently running.

Activating the Last Run App

You can switch between the Start screen and the last app that you've used by pressing the Windows button on your Surface or by pressing Winkey on the keyboard.

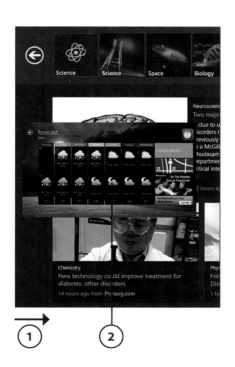

Displaying a List of Running Apps

Windows RT provides a quicker way to switch to an app of your choice when multiple apps are running at once. You can display thumbnails of the six most recently started apps along the left edge of the screen. You can then switch to an app by tapping the thumbnail.

1. Swipe from the left side of the screen until the thumbnail of another running app is visible, but don't remove your finger from the screen.

2. Drag the thumbnail of the app back to the left edge of the screen until thumbnails display along the left edge of the screen, and release your finger.

3. Tap one of the app thumbnails to activate the app.

Tip

Each subsequent press of Winkey+Tab highlights the next app in the list. Release the Winkey to switch to the highlighted app.

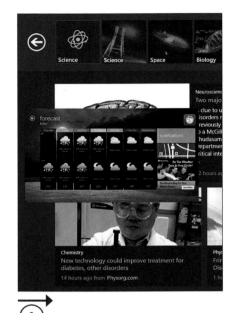

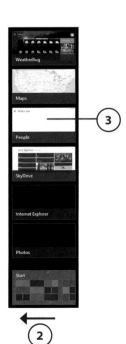

Displaying Two Apps Simultaneously

You might encounter situations in which you want to use two different apps simultaneously. For example, you might be pulling numbers from one app that you are using in a Microsoft Excel spreadsheet. In such situations, being able to display two apps on screen at the same time can be quite helpful.

Views for Multiple Apps

When displaying two apps at once, the smaller app is in *snap view* and the larger app is in *fill view*.

1. Activate the first app by either launching it from the Start screen or by switching to it as previously described.

2. Swipe from the left side of the screen just until a thumbnail of the second app appears but not so far that the entire thumbnail is visible.

3. Hold your finger on the screen until you see the separator bar.

4. Remove your finger from the screen to dock the second app next to the original app.

5. Drag the separator bar to change which app takes more space on the screen.

6. To remove one app from the screen and return to single-app mode, drag the separator bar to the edge of the screen.

Using the Keyboard for Switching Views

Press Winkey+. on your keyboard while an app is active to switch the app into snap view. Pressing Winkey+. a second time switches the app into fill view. Pressing Winkey+. a third time causes the app to fill the screen.

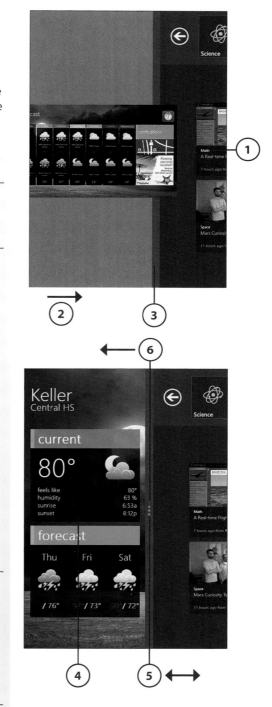

Organizing the Start Screen

After you've installed some of your own apps, your Start screen might begin to get a little unwieldy. You can bring order back to your Start screen by organizing tiles into groups.

Automatic Groups

Windows RT groups your Start screen tiles automatically, but you can rearrange these groups any way you choose.

Rearranging Tiles

You can move a tile to a new location by dragging it.

1. Tap and drag the tile up or down to release it from its current location.

2. Drag the tile to a new location. Other tiles will move to accommodate the tile you are moving. Release the tile when it is in the desired location.

3. To create a new tile group, drag the tile to a blank area at the right edge of the Start screen, and release it when a highlighted group separator appears.

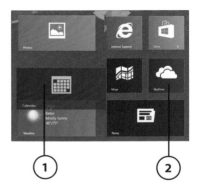

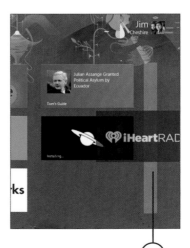

Naming Groups

Naming groups of tiles is another way of providing additional organization to your Start screen.

1. Pinch the Start screen to zoom out.

2. Tap and drag up or down on a tile in the group you want to rename to display the Command bar.

3. Tap Name Group.

4. Enter a name for your group.

5. Tap the Name button to save the name.

6. Reverse pinch to zoom in and see your newly named group.

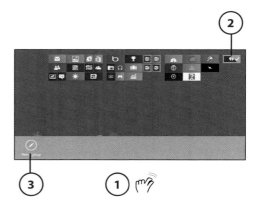

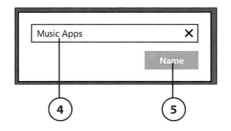

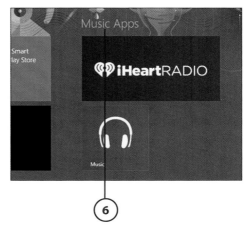

Changing or Removing a Group Name

You can also change the name of a group that you named previously, or remove the group name.

1. Pinch the Start screen to zoom out.

2. Swipe up or down on a group to reveal the Command bar.

3. Tap Name Group.

4. Type over the existing name to rename the group, or tap the X to remove the group name.

5. Tap the Name button to save the change.

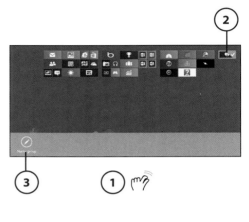

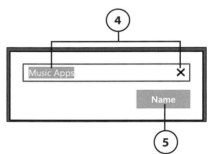

Customizing the Start Screen

There are many options available for customizing your Start screen so that it offers a personalized experience that fits your own tastes and preferences.

Changing the Start Screen Color Scheme and Background Picture

You can change the color scheme and the background picture that is displayed on your Start screen. When you change these settings, your changes are synchronized across all PCs that use your Microsoft account, assuming you have synchronization enabled. For information on synchronization of settings, see "Sync Settings" in Chapter 1, "An Introduction to Surface."

1. Swipe in from the right of the Start screen to reveal the Charms, and then tap Settings.

Tip
You can also access the Settings charm by pressing Winkey+I.

2. Tap Change PC Settings.

3. Tap Personalize if it's not already selected.

4. Tap Start Screen.

5. Tap a background picture to change the background.

6. Drag the indicator to change the color scheme.

Changes Happen Immediately
Changes to the background picture or color scheme take place immediately. You don't have to click a button to save these settings.

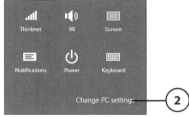

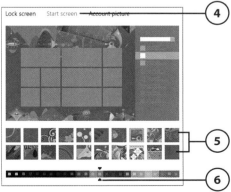

Showing Administrative Tools

Power users might want to display tiles for Administrative Tools on the Start screen. Administrative Tools consist of tools used to troubleshoot Windows and get detailed information about the system.

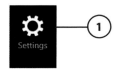

1. Swipe in from the right of the Start screen to reveal the Charms, and then tap Settings. (Remember that you can also press Winkey+I on your keyboard.)

2. Tap Tiles.

3. Tap the Show Administrative Tools slider to change the setting to Yes.

4. Tap the Back arrow to return to the Settings charm.

5. Swipe to the left to view the Administrative Tools icons on the Start screen.

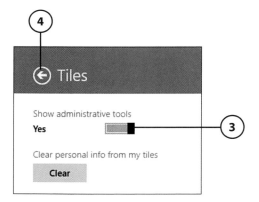

Name Your Administrative Tools

Now is a good time to give the Administrative Tools tiles a group name using the steps you learned earlier.

Removing Tiles from the Start Menu

You can remove a tile from the Start screen by unpinning it. You can unpin any tile that you no longer want displayed on your Start screen, including those that are included on the Start screen by default.

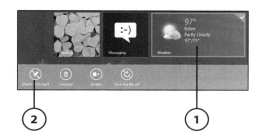

1. Swipe up or down on one or more tiles that you want to remove from the Start screen.

2. Tap Unpin from Start on the Command bar.

Pinning Apps to the Start Menu

You can pin any app to the Start menu from the Apps screen.

1. From the Start screen, swipe up from the bottom of the screen to reveal the Command bar.

2. Tap All Apps.

3. Swipe up or down on the app you want to pin to the Start screen.

4. Tap Pin to Start to pin the app to the Start screen.

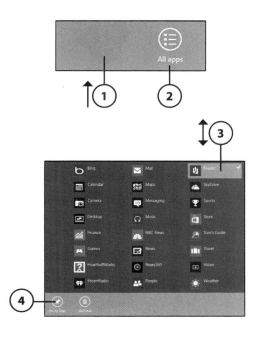

Cannot Select Pinned and Unpinned Apps

Windows RT will not enable you to select both an app that is pinned and one that is not pinned. If you select an app that is not pinned and then also select an app that is pinned, the unpinned app will be deselected automatically.

Changing Tile Sizes

Tiles can appear in two different sizes. The smaller size is approximately a square, while the larger size is the same height as the smaller size but is twice as wide. Because Windows RT uses Live Tiles (tiles that display useful information directly on the tile), making a tile larger can display more information on the tile.

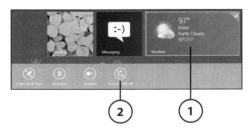

1. Swipe up or down on a tile for which you'd like to change the size.

2. If the tile is a small tile, tap Larger to make the tile a larger size.

3. If the tile is a large tile, tap Smaller to make the tile a smaller size.

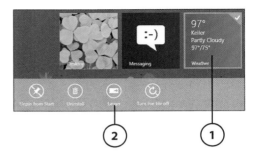

Controlling Live Tiles

Live Tiles allow for useful information to be displayed directly on a tile. For example, a weather app can display a local forecast on its tile and a news app can display news headlines on a tile. You can turn on or off Live Tile functionality.

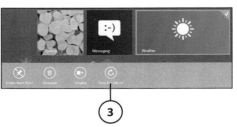

1. Swipe up or down on a tile to select it.

2. Tap Turn Live Tile Off to turn off a Live Tile.

3. Tap Turn Live Tile On to turn on a Live Tile.

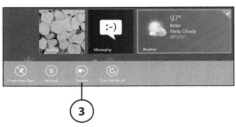

Live Tile Content

An app developer controls whether an app supports the Live Tile feature and what information is displayed on a Live Tile.

Removing Personal Information from Live Tiles

Live Tiles might display personal information that you don't want visible. For example, the Calendar app displays your next appointment on its Live Tile. If you would prefer to never have this information displayed, you can turn off the Live Tile, but if you simply would like to remove the personal information until you log off and back on again, you can do so.

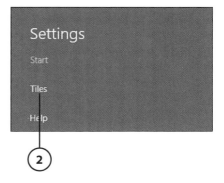

1. Swipe in from the right of the Start screen to reveal the Charms, and then tap Settings. (Remember that you can also press Winkey+I on your keyboard.)

2. Tap Tiles.

3. Tap Clear to remove personal info from all tiles.

Personal Information Restoration

After you clear personal information from your tiles, it will be removed until you log off and back on again.

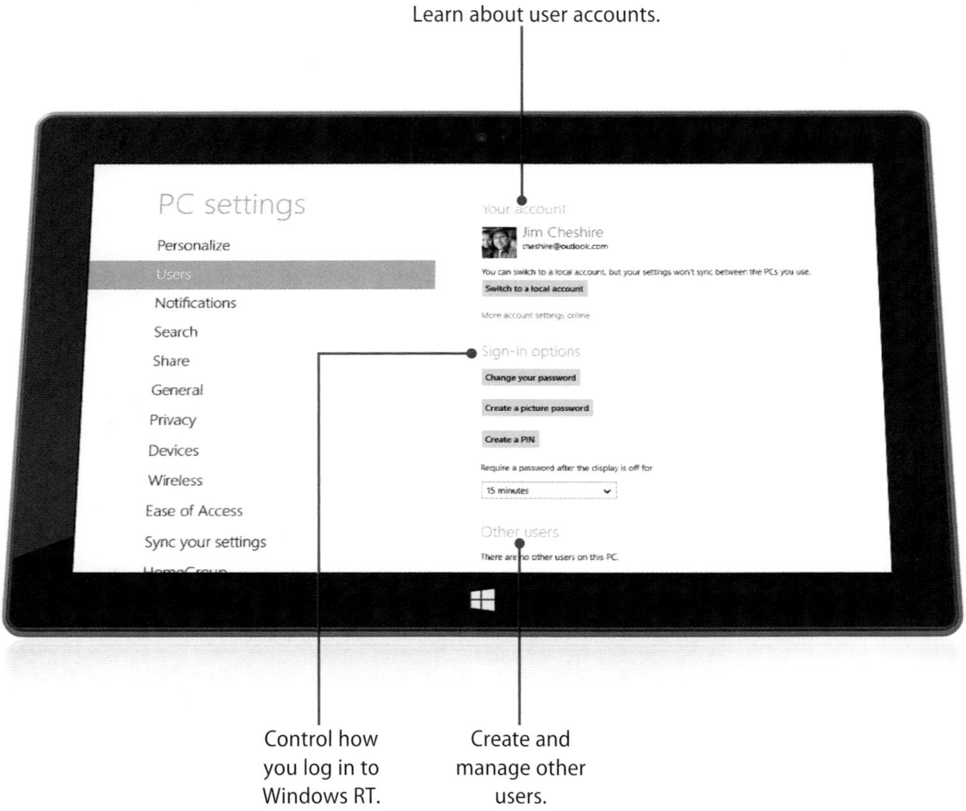

Learn about user accounts.

PC settings

Personalize

Users

Notifications

Search

Share

General

Privacy

Devices

Wireless

Ease of Access

Sync your settings

HomeGroup

Your account

Jim Cheshire
cheshire@outlook.com

You can switch to a local account, but your settings won't sync between the PCs you use.

Switch to a local account

More account settings online

Sign-in options

Change your password

Create a picture password

Create a PIN

Require a password after the display is off for

15 minutes

Other users

There are no other users on this PC.

Control how
you log in to
Windows RT.

Create and
manage other
users.

Security and Windows RT

Your Surface device is quite secure by design. All files are encrypted by default, and apps you run are isolated to their own environment and aren't allowed to access sensitive information stored on the PC. Windows RT also contains many features deep under the hood that are designed to prevent infections from viruses and other malware. It's not at all hyperbolic to say that Windows RT is the most secure version of Windows ever made.

With that said, you will still want to take steps to secure your Surface. Today's connected devices offer access to more information than ever before, and it's more important than ever to ensure that access to your PC is controlled. You also might want to let your kids play a game on your Surface without worrying that they are going to delete your emails or get access to information that should be kept private.

Securing Your PC

You secure your PC using a password. If I were to ask you what it is, you obviously wouldn't tell me (I hope), but even so, if your password is a weak one, you might as well. What do I mean by a "weak" password? I mean a password that consists of a word that appears in the dictionary or is the name of your pet, spouse, or some other word that someone might easily guess. You should protect your password vigilantly, and that means choosing one that's impossible to guess.

Creating a Strong Password

A good password would be something like this: h028w5y358j3. Believe it or not, remembering this password is pretty easy. It's simply "now is the time" on my keyboard with the spaces removed and with my fingers shifted up one row when I typed it. I use that trick often to create strong passwords.

Changing Your Password

If reading this chapter's introduction made you realize that your password needs to be stronger, you can easily change it. It's not a bad idea to change your password periodically as a security precaution.

1. From the Charms, tap Settings or press Winkey+I on your keyboard.

2. Tap Change PC Settings.

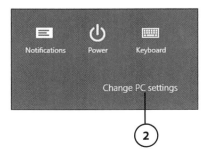

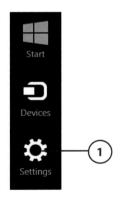

3. Tap Users.

4. Tap Change Your Password.

5. Enter your current password.

See Your Password Characters

As you enter passwords in Windows RT, dots are displayed instead of the password's actual characters. If you want to see the actual characters instead, tap and hold on the  icon at the right edge of the password field.

6. Enter your new password.

7. Reenter your new password.

8. Tap Next.

Tip

If you're using a local account, you'll need to tap Next after entering your current password and enter a password hint.

9. Tap Finish to complete the process.

Locking Your PC

When you're not using your PC, it's a good idea to lock it. When your PC is locked, your password must be entered to access the apps and information on it.

Your PC locks automatically when the screen has been off for 15 minutes, but you can also explicitly lock it immediately. (You can change the time interval for the automatic locking feature, and I'll show you how later in this chapter.)

1. From the Start screen, tap your user name.

2. Tap Lock on the menu to lock your PC.

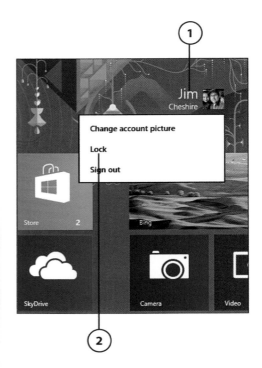

Locking Faster

You can lock your PC by pressing Winkey+L on your keyboard.

Signing Out of Your PC

You can also sign out (log off) of your PC. Signing out is similar to locking the PC except that it closes all apps you are using and completely signs you out of the PC.

1. From the Start screen, tap your user name.

2. Tap Sign Out.

Configuring Auto-Lock

You can configure Windows RT so that a password is required after a particular time period has elapsed. Doing so provides an extra level of security if you fail to explicitly log out or lock your PC.

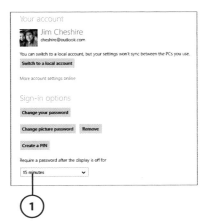

1. From the Users screen in PC Settings (refer to the previous section, "Changing Your Password"), tap the Require a Password After the Display is Off For drop-down box.

2. Select a time interval after which a password will be required. (You can also choose to always require a password or to never require a password.)

Using Picture Passwords

One of the unique features of Windows 8 (both the RT version and the Pro version) is the picture password feature. This feature enables you to use a series of gestures (taps, circles, and lines) on a picture instead of entering a password. The location, size, and direction of your gestures are all part of your picture password.

Security and Picture Passwords

It's worth mentioning that Microsoft considers picture passwords to be secure enough to allow Microsoft employees to use them on the Microsoft corporate network.

Creating a Picture Password

You can create a picture password using a picture that is included with Windows RT, or you can use one of your own pictures.

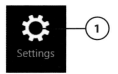

1. From the Charms, tap Settings or press Winkey+I on your keyboard.

2. Tap Change PC Settings.

3. Tap Users.

4. Tap Create a Picture Password.

5. Enter your password to confirm it.

6. Tap OK.

7. Tap Choose Picture.

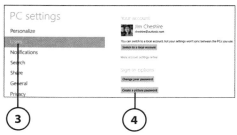

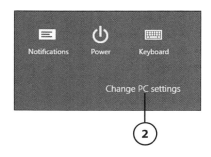

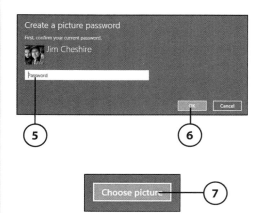

8. To change to a new folder, tap Files and select a new folder.

9. Tap the picture you'd like to use for your picture password.

10. Tap Open.

11. Drag to position the picture the way you want it.

12. Tap Use This Picture.

13. Draw three gestures on your picture using the guidelines provided.

14. Repeat your gestures to confirm them.

15. Tap Finish to complete your picture password.

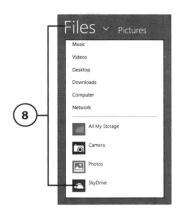

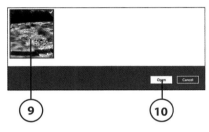

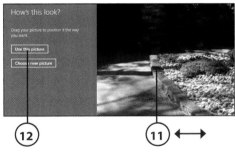

Changing Your Picture Password

If you want to change the picture that is used for your picture password, you can do so. You might also want to change the gestures used while keeping the same picture.

1. From the Users screen in PC Settings, tap Change Picture Password.

2. Enter your password to confirm it.

3. Tap OK.

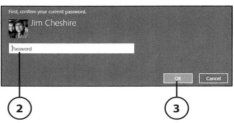

4. Tap Use This Picture to keep using the existing picture or Choose New Picture to select a new picture.

5. Enter the desired gestures for your picture password.

6. Reenter your gestures.

7. Tap Finish.

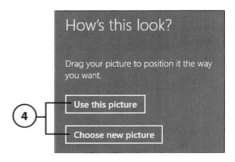

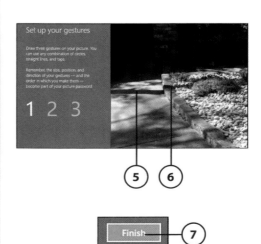

Replaying Your Picture Password

If you've forgotten the gestures you used for your picture password, Windows RT can play them back for you.

1. From the Users screen in PC Settings, tap Change Picture Password.

2. Enter your password and tap OK.

3. Tap Replay.

4. Trace the gestures that are displayed on the screen.

5. Repeat your three gestures.

6. Tap Finish.

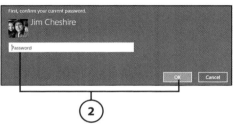

Removing Your Picture Password

You can remove your picture password, after which point you must enter your textual password when signing in.

1. From the PC Settings screen, tap Users.

2. Tap Remove to remove your picture password.

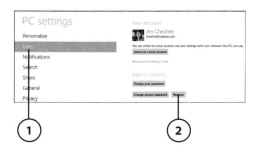

Using PINs

If you want, you can use a four-digit PIN to sign in to your Surface instead of using a password. PINs are used in addition to your textual password.

Creating a PIN

You create a PIN by entering a series of four numbers you want to use when signing in.

1. From the Users screen, tap Create a PIN.

2. Enter your password to confirm it before creating your PIN.

3. Tap OK.

4. Enter four numerals for your PIN.

5. Confirm your PIN.

6. Tap Finish.

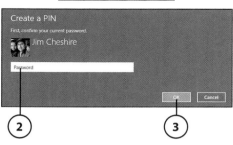

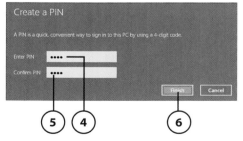

Changing a PIN

You can change your PIN easily.

1. From the Users screen, tap Change PIN.

2. Enter your password to confirm it before changing your PIN.

3. Tap OK.

4. Enter a new PIN.

5. Confirm your new PIN.

6. Tap Finish.

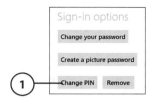

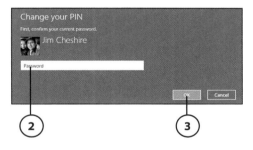

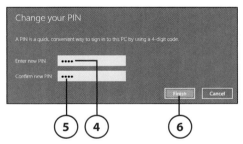

Removing a PIN

You can remove a PIN so that it can no longer be used to sign in.

1. From the Settings screen, tap Users.

2. Tap the Remove button next to the Change PIN button.

Signing in with a PIN

When a PIN is set for your account, signing in will prompt you for your PIN instead of a password.

1. Swipe up from the lock screen.

2. Enter your PIN to sign in.

It's Not All Good

If you have a picture password set, it will always be the method used to sign in when you swipe up on the lock screen. If you'd like to use your PIN, you'll need to use the method that I describe in the next step-by-step.

Using a PIN When a Picture Password Is Set

If you have a picture password set, you'll need to use these steps to use your PIN for the first time.

1. Swipe up from the lock screen.

2. Tap the Switch to Password button.

3. Tap Sign-in Options.

4. Tap the PIN keypad button.

5. Enter your PIN to sign in.

Changing Sign-in Options

When you tap Sign-in Options, you'll see various buttons depending on whether you've configured a picture password or a PIN. Tap the appropriate button to choose your sign-in option.

Managing User Accounts

User accounts are used to identify particular people using a PC. Windows not only gives each user a unique sign-in ID, but it also separates each user's data into folders that are accessible only by that user or by an administrator.

There are two types of accounts you can add; local accounts and Microsoft accounts. A local account is tied to the particular PC where it was created. A Microsoft account is tied to a particular Microsoft ID and automatically synchronizes settings and other information via the Internet.

Microsoft Accounts

If you don't already have a Microsoft account, you can find out more information by browsing to http://home.live.com.

Adding a Local Account

You can add a new local account that isn't associated with a Microsoft account. This is a convenient way of adding an account for a child or someone else who doesn't have a Microsoft account.

1. From the Users screen in PC Settings, tap the Add a User button to add a user account.

2. Tap the Sign In Without a Microsoft Account link.

3. Tap the Local Account button.

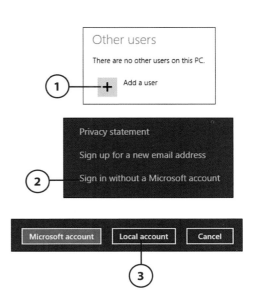

4. Enter a user name.

5. Enter a password for the new user.

6. Reenter the password to confirm it.

7. Enter a password hint. (A user can display this when signing in if he or she forgets the password.)

8. Tap Next.

9. If the account is for a child, check the box to enable Family Safety for the account.

10. Tap Finish.

Family Safety

You can find out more about the Family Safety feature in Chapter 5, "Using Family Safety."

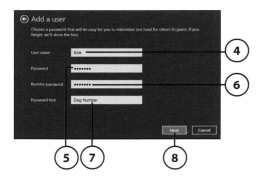

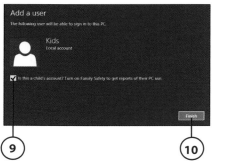

Adding a Microsoft Account

A Microsoft account enables the user to have a more consistent experience across multiple PCs. Settings made on one PC are synchronized to other PCs.

1. From the Users screen in PC Settings, tap the Add a User button to add a user account.

2. Enter the email address for the new user.

3. Tap Next.

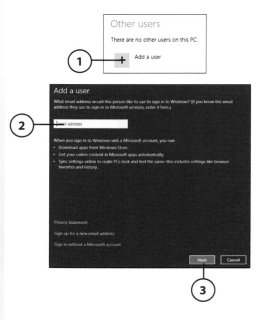

Using an Existing Microsoft Account

If the email you enter in step 2 is associated with an existing Microsoft account, you will be taken directly to step 20 while creating the account.

4. Enter an email for the Microsoft account. This can be the same email used in step 2 or a different one. (This is the email address the user will use to sign in.)

5. Enter a password.

6. Reenter the password.

7. Enter a first name.

8. Enter a last name.

9. Select a country or region.

10. Enter a ZIP code.

11. Tap Next.

12. Enter a country and phone number.

13. Enter an alternative email address in case the user loses his or her password.

14. Select a secret question.

15. Enter the answer to the selected secret question.

16. Tap Next.

17. Enter a birth date.

18. Select a gender.

19. Click Next.

20. Check the box to turn on Family Safety for the account if desired.

21. Click Finish.

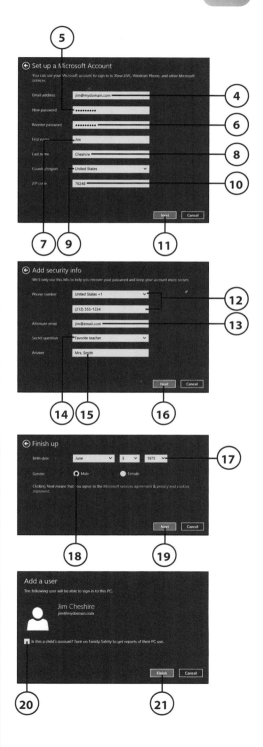

Deleting a User Account

Unfortunately, there isn't a way to delete a user account from within the Windows 8–style user interface. However, you can remove an account by using tools that are included in Windows RT for administrators of the machine. You can do so via the Apps screen, which is accessible by tapping All Apps from the Command bar.

1. From the Apps screen, tap Control Panel.

2. Tap User Accounts and Family Safety.

3. Tap Remove User Accounts.

4. Tap the account you want to remove.

5. Tap Delete the Account to delete the account.

6. Tap Keep Files to keep the user's data files or Delete Files to remove the user's data files permanently.

7. Tap Delete Account to delete the account.

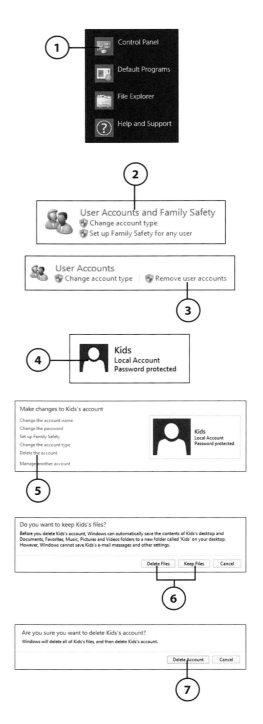

Switching Accounts

After you create a new account, you might want to switch to one of the other accounts while leaving the original account signed in. For example, you might be working on a Word document and the kids might ask to play a game. If you decide to take a break and indulge them, it's convenient to simply switch to the account used by the kids without having to close Word and sign out of your session.

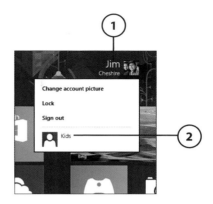

1. From the Start screen, tap your name.

2. Tap the other account from the menu.

3. Enter the password for the other account, and press Enter to sign in.

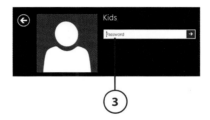

Changing from a Local Account to a Microsoft Account

If you are using a local account, you might decide at some point that you want to enjoy the advantages of using a Microsoft account instead. You can easily switch your local account to a Microsoft account.

1. From the Users screen in PC Settings, tap Switch to a Microsoft Account.

2. Enter the password for your local account.

3. Tap Next.

Moving to a Microsoft Account

When you switch to a Microsoft account, your files and settings will be transferred over to your Microsoft account so that you won't lose them.

4. Enter the Microsoft ID that you would like to use on your PC.

5. Tap Next.

6. Enter the password for your Microsoft account.

Creating a New Microsoft Account

If you don't already have a Microsoft account, you can create one by tapping on Sign Up For a Microsoft Account.

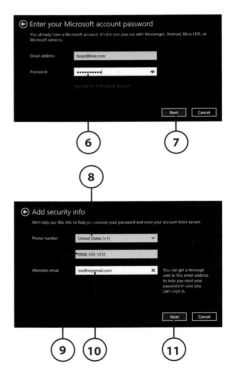

7. Tap Next.

8. Choose your geographic region.

9. Enter your phone number to be used if you forget your password.

10. Enter an alternative email address. This can be any of your email addresses. It will be used if you forget your password.

11. Tap Next.

12. Tap Finish to complete your change to a Microsoft account.

Trust Your PC

Once you switch to a Microsoft account, you'll need to add the PC to your list of trusted PCs for your Microsoft account. You can do so by tapping Trust This PC from the Users screen in PC Settings.

Switching to a Local Account

You can switch from using your Microsoft account to a local account. Before you do this, you'll want to save anything you're working on and close your applications because Windows RT requires you to log off of your computer to complete this process.

(1)

1. From the Users screen in PC Settings, tap Switch to a Local Account.

2. Enter your Microsoft account password.

3. Tap Next.

4. Enter the user name for your local user. This can be a new or an existing user.

5. Enter the password for the local account.

6. Reenter the password.

7. Enter a password hint.

8. Tap Next.

9. Tap Sign Out and Finish to complete the process and log off the PC. You will then need to log in using the local account you specified.

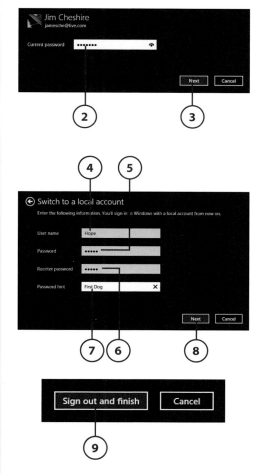

Control which
websites your
children visit.

View reports of user
activity and configure
emailing of activity
reports.

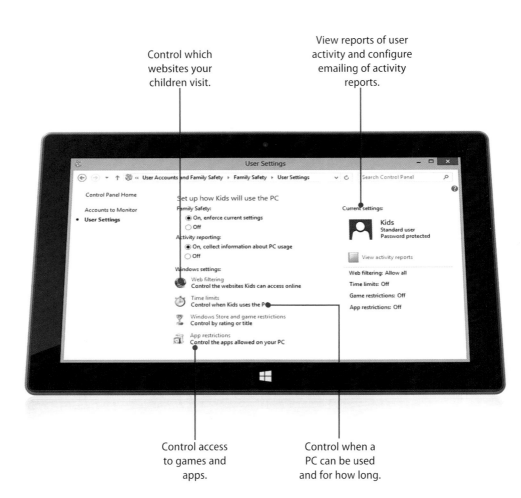

Control access
to games and
apps.

Control when a
PC can be used
and for how long.

5

Using Family Safety

Computers are quite popular with kids. They use them for playing games sure enough, but they also use them for school and many other purposes. For the past few years, my kids have used a desktop computer that sits in a common family area, but the advent of tablet PCs has made supervision of their computer use a bit trickier.

Family Safety is designed to solve that problem. Using the Family Safety feature built in to Windows RT (and other editions of Windows 8), you can easily monitor your child's use of your PC. You can even set time and other restrictions so that you can control when and how the PC is used.

It's Not All Good

Starting Fresh

Before you go down the road of configuring Family Safety, you should make sure that the list of computers you are using is tidy. Browse to familysafety.microsoft.com and make sure that your current computers are listed at the bottom of the page under Your Devices. You can edit the list from account.live.com. If you want to add a PC, browse to account.live.com from that PC and click the link to trust the PC you are using.

Configuring Family Safety

As you saw in Chapter 4, "Security and Windows RT," when you create a user, you are provided with the option to enable Family Safety for the user. However, you can enable and disable Family Safety for any user on your PC at any time.

Enabling and Disabling Family Safety for a User

If you need to enable or disable Family Safety for a user, you can do so easily.

1. Swipe in from the right side of the Start screen and tap Search.

2. Tap Settings so that your search will apply to PC settings.

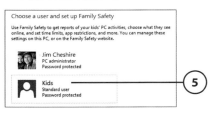

Keyboard Shortcut for Settings Search

You can press Winkey+W on your keyboard to search for PC settings.

3. Enter **family** into the search box.

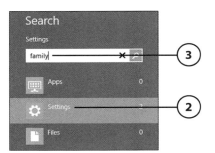

Faster Search

You can search for Family Safety more quickly by simply typing **family** from the Start screen. As soon as you start typing, the Search pane appears automatically.

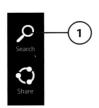

4. Tap Family Safety in the search results.

5. Tap the user for whom you'd like to configure Family Safety.

6. Tap On, Enforce Current Settings to enable Family Safety for the user.

7. Tap Off to disable Family Safety for the user.

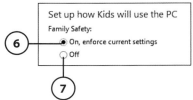

Configuring Activity Reporting

Family Safety can collect detailed information on what a user does while using a PC. You can turn this type of reporting on or off for a user.

1. From the Family Safety screen, tap the user account to access the user's User Settings screen.

2. Tap On, Collect Information About PC Usage to enable activity reporting.

3. Tap Off to turn off activity reporting.

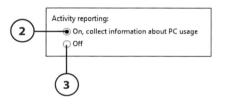

Viewing Activity Reports

You can view activity reports on users from the Family Safety applet in Control Panel and from Microsoft's Family Safety website. Activity reports show when each user used the PC, what apps they used, websites they visited, and much more.

Viewing Activity Reports from Control Panel

You can view some details of a user's activity from Control Panel as long as the user has an account on your PC.

1. From the Family Safety applet in Control Panel, tap the user for whom you're interested in reviewing activity.

2. Tap View Activity Reports.

3. Tap a link to get details on a particular type of usage.

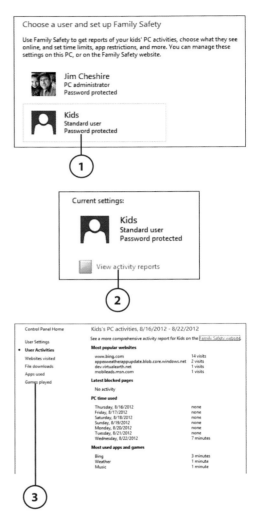

It's Not All Good

You Only See What Happened Here

The information you see in the activity report displayed in the User Activities screen contains only the activities that the user performed on the PC you're using. If the user account is a Microsoft account and that user used another PC, you won't see that activity unless you visit Microsoft's Family Safety website online. I show you how to do that next.

Viewing Activity Reports from the Family Safety Website

You can visit Microsoft's Family Safety website to view activity reports for all PCs and all users you are monitoring.

Determining Whom You See

When you visit the Family Safety website, you can see any account that you created on any of your PCs.

1. Open a web browser and browse to familysafety.microsoft.com.

2. Log in with your Microsoft account password.

3. Tap View Activity Report next to the user you're interested in.

4. View information on the Summary tab to see websites, searches, apps, downloads, and usage times for the user.

Viewing More Information

A View All link appears next to each category in the activity report. Clicking this link enables you to view even more information about the user's activities.

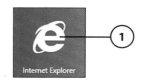

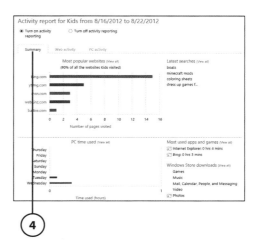

5. Tap the Web Activity tab to see information about websites that the user visited.

6. Tap the triangle next to a site to see details on pages visited on that site.

7. Enter a date range and tap Show Activity to filter on dates.

8. Check the Show Sites Accessed by Non-Browser Apps to see sites that were accessed by apps from the Windows Store.

9. Tap a filter icon and tap a filter to view specific entries.

10. Tap a column header to order results by that column.

11. Tap the PC Activity tab to see usage times and activities for the user.

12. Expand a section to see more details.

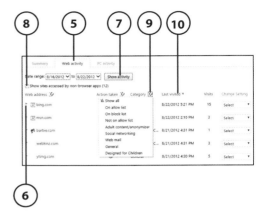

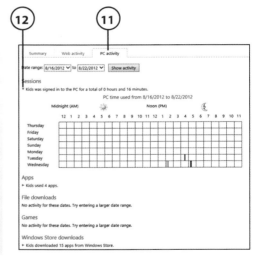

Using Web Filtering

Web filtering provides a way for you to gain some control over which websites a child is allowed to visit. In the most basic sense, web filtering enables you to set one of four different levels of automatic protection, but you can also configure specific sites that a user is allowed to visit, and you can also block one or more sites.

Just as with other Family Safety features, you can use Control Panel on your PC or the Family Safety website to configure Web Filtering. (Control Panel is available on the Apps screen after tapping All Apps on the Command bar.)

Enabling Web Filtering from Control Panel

Before you can configure any settings for Web Filtering, you must turn it on for the user. Web Filtering is configured on a per-user basis.

1. From the Family Safety applet in Control Panel, tap the user you would like to configure.

2. Tap Web Filtering.

3. Tap Kids Can Only Use the Websites I Allow to enable Web Filtering.

4. Tap Set Web Filtering Level.

5. Select a web restriction level from the list.

6. Check the Block File Downloads box if you want to prevent the user from downloading any files.

Committing Control Panel Changes

When you make changes to Family Safety settings in Control Panel, those changes are reflected on the website as well. However, to commit the changes, you must either close Control Panel or switch to another Family Safety setting.

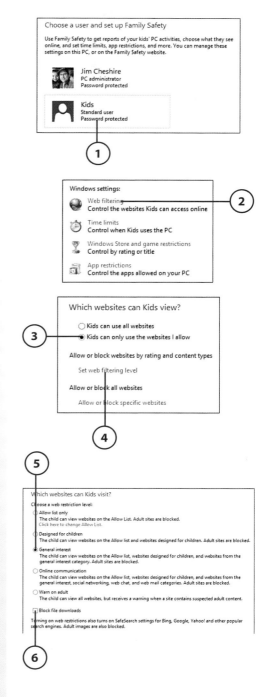

Enabling Web Filtering from the Family Safety Website

You can also enable Web Filtering from the Family Safety website at familysafety.microsoft.com.

1. From the Family Safety site, tap Edit Settings for the user you would like to configure for Web Filtering.

2. Tap Web Filtering.

3. Tap Turn On Web Filtering.

4. Select a filtering level for the user.

5. Check the Block File Downloads box if you wish to prevent the user from downloading files.

6. Tap Save to save your change.

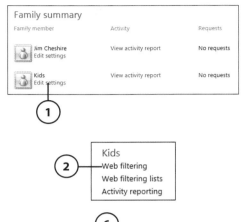

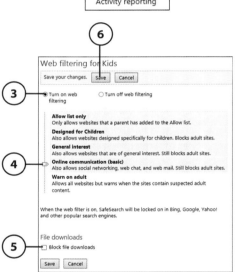

It's Not All Good

No Shortcut to Supervision

Family Safety is quite effective at blocking most inappropriate content, but as with any technology, it isn't perfect. Even with Web Filtering enabled, there's a chance that your child may access content that you consider inappropriate. The activity reporting in Family Safety can help you to identify when this happens, but there's really nothing better than keeping a parental eye on what your kids are doing.

Modifying the Web Filter List from Control Panel

Web Filtering lists enable you to take a more explicit approach to filtering websites. You can block all sites except for those that you explicitly add to an Allow list, or you can add specific sites to a Block list to block them.

1. From the Web Filtering view for the user, tap Allow or Block Specific Websites.

2. Enter a site that you would like to allow or block.

3. Tap Allow to allow the site, or tap Block to block the site.

4. To remove a site from the Allowed or Blocked list, tap the site and then tap Remove.

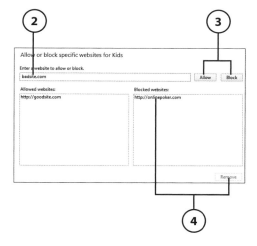

What Gets Blocked or Allowed

When you add an entry to the Web Filter list, it applies to all subdomains of the site you add. For example, if you add a filter that blocks www.badsite.com, Family Safety will block anything on the badsite.com domain. That means that pics.badsite.com, www.badsite.com, and news.badsite.com will all be blocked.

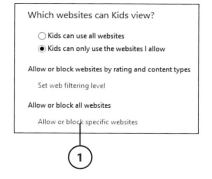

Modifying the Web Filter List from the Website

You can also modify the Web Filter List from the Family Safety website at familysafety.microsoft.com.

1. From the Settings page for the user, tap Web Filtering Lists.

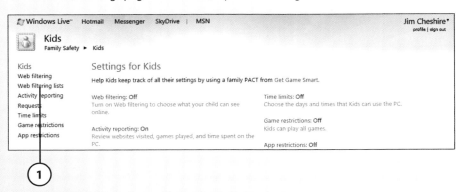

2. Enter a web address that you want to block or allow.

3. Select whether you want to block or allow the site for this user only, for all children, or for everyone.

4. Click Allow to allow the site or Block to block the site.

5. To remove a site, check the Remove box next to the site you want to remove.

6. Tap Save to save your changes.

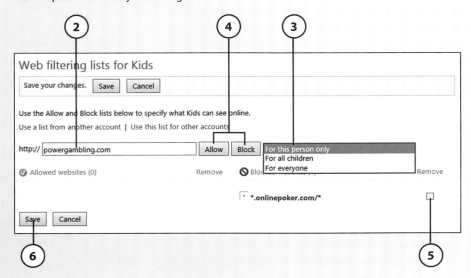

It's Not All Good

Cannot Modify Filtering Settings

There isn't a way to modify settings for a site. If you want to change the scope of the filtering rule that you set in step 3, you'll have to remove the site and add it back with the new scope.

Blocking Sites from the Activity Report

You can also block users from a site directly from the Activity Report. This is useful in cases where you happen to notice that a user has visited a questionable site and you want to prevent future visits.

1. From the Web Activity report, click the Change Setting drop-down.

2. Select Block for This Person Only to block the site only for the current user.

3. Select Block for Everyone to block the site for all users whose Family Safety settings you control.

4. Tap Save to save your changes.

Using Time Limits and Curfews

You can control how long a user can use the PC each day. You also can control a time range that the user is allowed to use the PC.

As with other settings, you can set time limits and curfews via either the Control Panel or the Family Safety website.

Setting Time Limits and Curfews from Control Panel

You can configure time limits and curfews from the User Settings screen in Control Panel.

1. From the User Settings screen for the user, tap Time Limits.

2. Tap Set Time Allowance.

3. Tap Kids Can Only Use the PC for the Amount of Time I Allow to enable time limits.

4. Use the Hours and Minutes dropdowns for Mon-Fri and Sat-Sun to set the time limits for the user.

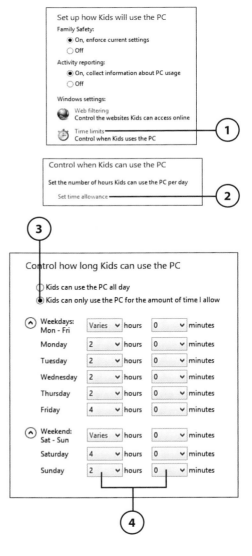

5. To configure when the user can use the PC, tap Curfew.

6. Tap Kids Can Only Use the PC During the Time Ranges I Allow.

7. Tap and drag to highlight the times and days that the user should not be allowed to use the computer.

8. Tap and drag over a disallowed area to remove the highlight and allow the time.

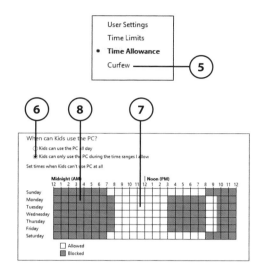

Setting Time Limits and Curfews from the Website

You can also configure time limits and curfews from the Family Safety website at familysafety.microsoft.com.

1. From the user's Settings page on the Family Safety website, tap Time Limits.

2. Tap the Turn On checkbox to turn on time limits.

3. Using the Hours and Minutes drop-downs for Mon-Fri and Sat-Sun, set the desired time limits for the user.

4. Tap Save to save your changes.

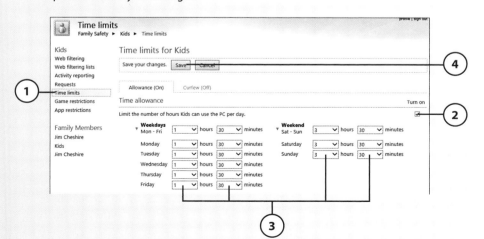

5. To configure when the user can use the PC, tap the Curfew tab.

6. Tap the Turn On checkbox to enable curfews.

7. Tap and drag to highlight areas where the user should not be allowed to use the PC.

8. Tap and drag on a highlighted area to remove the highlight and allow the user to use the PC during that period.

9. Tap Save to save your changes.

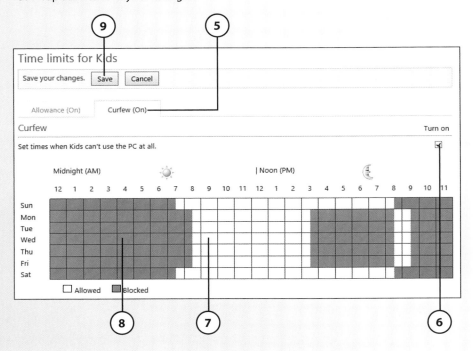

Configuring Windows Store and Game Restrictions

Windows Store and game restrictions enable you to control the games that a user can download from the Windows Store and the games that the user can run on a PC. You can control which games a user can see in the Windows Store and play on the PC based on a rating system (using the ESRB at www.esrb.org by default), and you can also set specific restrictions for games that are already installed.

Configuring Windows Store and Game Restrictions from Control Panel

You can configure Windows Store and game restrictions from the Control Panel.

1. From the Settings screen for the user, tap Windows Store and Game Restrictions.

2. Tap Kids Can Only Use Games and Windows Store Apps I Allow to enable restrictions.

3. Tap Set Game and Windows Store Ratings.

4. Tap Allow Games with No Rating to allow the user to play a game that hasn't been rated by the ESRB.

5. Tap Block Games with No Rating to prevent the user from playing any games without ratings.

6. Tap the maximum ESRB rating that the user can play from the list of ratings.

Visibility of Blocked Games in the Windows Store

Any game that is restricted due to the settings you have selected will be invisible to the user in the Windows Store. If the user has already downloaded a game that is restricted by your settings, he or she will still see it on the PC but will be unable to play it.

Blocked visibility only applies to games. Nongame apps that are blocked will still be visible in the Windows Store, but the user will not be able to install them without asking for permission.

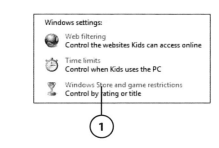

Windows settings:

Web filtering
Control the websites Kids can access online

Time limits
Control when Kids uses the PC

Windows Store and game restrictions
Control by rating or title

1

2   **3**

Control which games and Windows Store apps Kids can use

○ Kids can play all games and view all Windows Store apps
◉ Kids can only use games and Windows Store apps I allow

Allow or block games and Windows Store apps by rating

Set game and Windows Store ratings

Maximum allowed rating: ADULTS ONLY, including unrated games

Allow or block any game on your PC by name

Allow or block specific games

Always blocked: None
Always allowed: None

4

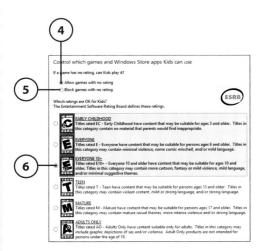

Control which games and Windows Store apps Kids can use

If a game has no rating, can Kids play it?

◉ Allow games with no rating
○ Block games with no rating

Which ratings are OK for Kids?
The Entertainment Software Rating Board defines these ratings.

EARLY CHILDHOOD
Titles rated EC - Early Childhood have content that may be suitable for ages 3 and older. Titles in this category contain no material that parents would find inappropriate.

EVERYONE
Titles rated E - Everyone have content that may be suitable for persons ages 6 and older. Titles in this category may contain minimal violence, some comic mischief, and/or mild language.

EVERYONE 10+
Titles rated E10+ - Everyone 10 and older have content that may be suitable for ages 10 and older. Titles in this category may contain more cartoon, fantasy or mild violence, mild language, and/or minimal suggestive themes.

TEEN
Titles rated T - Teen have content that may be suitable for persons ages 13 and older. Titles in this category may contain violent content, mild or strong language, and/or strong humor.

MATURE
Titles rated M - Mature have content that may be suitable for persons ages 17 and older. Titles in this category may contain mature sexual themes, more intense violence and/or strong language.

ADULTS ONLY
Titles rated AO - Adults Only have content suitable only for adults. Titles in this category may include graphic depictions of sex and/or violence. Adult Only products are not intended for persons under the age of 18.

5

6

7. Tap Allow or Block Games to explicitly block or allow a game regardless of rating.

8. Tap User Rating Setting to allow or block a game based on the allowed rating level for the user.

9. Tap Always Allow to allow the game regardless of the allowed rating level for the user.

10. Tap Always Block to always block the game.

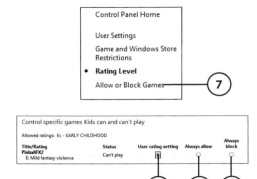

It's Not All Good

Only Rated Games Visible

Only those games that are rated by the configured rating system are listed in Control Panel. If you want more control over which games the user is allowed to play, you'll need to visit the Family Safety website.

Configuring Store and Game Restrictions from the Website

You can also configure Windows Store and game restrictions from the Family Safety website at familysafety.microsoft.com.

1. From the user's settings on the Family Safety website, tap App Restrictions.

2. Tap Turn On App Restrictions.

3. Expand Windows Store Apps.

4. Check an installed app to block the user from using the app.

5. Uncheck an installed app to allow the user to use the app.

6. Tap Save to save your changes.

Blocking Specific Nongames

Notice that the Family Safety website enables you to block any installed app while Control Panel will only allow you to control access based on the rating system.

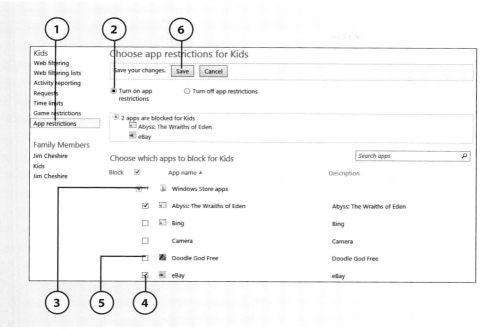

Changing the Rating System from Control Panel

By default, Family Safety uses the ESRB rating system when enforcing game restrictions. However, you can change to a different rating system if you choose.

ESRB Is Best for United States

The ESRB is the best choice for United States users. Other rating systems are typically used for other countries.

1. From the Family Safety applet in Control Panel, tap Rating Systems.

2. Select the desired rating system.

3. Tap Accounts to Monitor to commit your change.

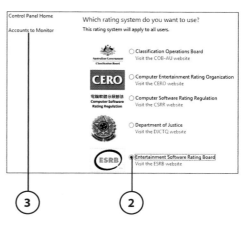

Changing the Rating System from the Website

You can also change the rating system from the Family Safety website.

1. From the Game Restrictions screen, tap Use a Different Game Rating System.

2. Tap a new rating system to use.

3. Tap Save to save your changes.

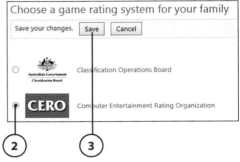

Rating System Choice Applies to All Users

The selected rating system will apply to all users you manage. You cannot use different rating systems for different users.

Handling Requests

If you've blocked access to a website or an app using Family Safety, the blocked user can request access. You can grant or deny this request from the PC the child is using or from the Family Safety website.

Responding to a Request from the User's PC

You can approve or deny a request directly from the user's PC.

1. Have the user ask for permission.

2. Have the user tap My Parent Is Here.

3. Enter your password.

4. Tap Yes.

5. Tap Allow to allow the user.

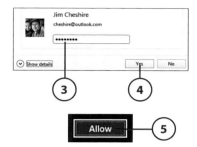

Responding to a Request from the Website

If you are not available when the user requests access, you can review the request and allow or deny it from the Family Safety website.

Web Requests

Requests that you see in Family Safety are generated by the user tapping Send Request when requesting access to a blocked app or website.

1. From the user's Settings screen on the Family Safety website, tap Requests.

2. Select a response for each request. You don't have to reply to all requests.

3. Tap Save to save your changes.

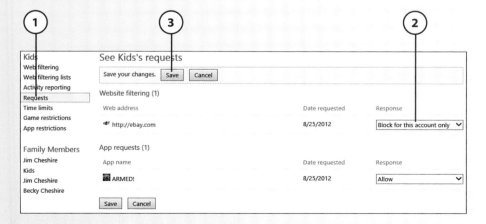

Managing Users in Family Safety

The Family Safety website at familysafety.microsoft.com lists all users for whom you've enabled Family Safety while signed in with your Microsoft account. Users are added by adding them to Family Safety on one of your PCs as you did earlier in this chapter.

Only from the Website

You can only manage users from the Family Safety website. The following procedures cannot be completed from within Control Panel on your PC.

You can add a new parent or make an existing user a parent from the Family Safety website. (Parents are authorized to respond to requests from users, view activity reports, and otherwise manage a user's Family Safety settings.) You can also remove users or link multiple users to one user account.

Adding a New Parent

If you would like to give another adult permission to respond to Family Safety requests and that user doesn't have an account on one of your PCs, you can add their account from the Family Safety website.

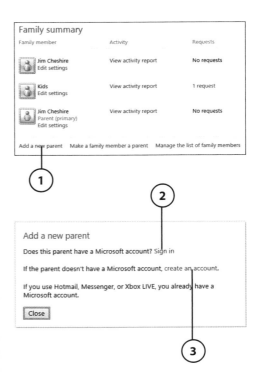

1. From the Family Safety website, tap Add a New Parent.

2. If the parent has a Microsoft account, tap Sign In and sign in with the parent's Microsoft account password to add the parent. (Make sure to enter the information for the user you're making a parent and not your Microsoft account information.)

3. If the parent doesn't have a Microsoft account, tap Create an Account to create a new Microsoft account and add the parent.

Making an Existing User a Parent

You can make an existing user a parent so that he or she can manage other users on your Family Safety account.

1. From the Family Safety website, tap Make a Family Member a Parent.

2. Select a user from the drop-down.

3. If the user already has a Microsoft account, tap Sign In and enter the user's Microsoft account information.

4. If the user doesn't have a Microsoft account, tap Create an Account and enter the information to create a new Microsoft account.

Linking Accounts

If you have different accounts on different PCs and you'd like to manage them as one account, you can link the accounts. For example, suppose my son Bobby has an account on one of my PCs under the name Bobby and another account on another PC under the name Robert. By linking the two accounts, I can manage them in Family Safety as one account.

1. From the Family Safety website, tap Manage the List of Family Members.

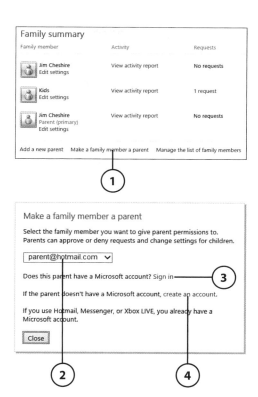

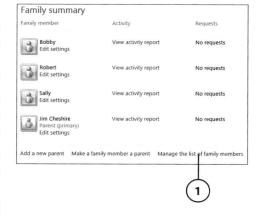

Linked Accounts Require Separate PCs

You cannot link accounts on the same PC. Accounts that you link must be on separate PCs.

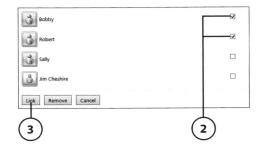

2. Tap the checkbox for the users you would like to link.

3. Tap the Link button.

4. Select the account you would like to use for the linked accounts.

5. Tap Link.

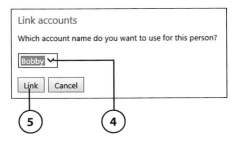

It's Not All Good

Once you link accounts, you will no longer see the separate accounts. You will only see the account you chose as the account to use for the linked accounts. There is also no way to unlink accounts once you link them.

Configuring Email Notifications

By default, you will receive weekly email notifications regarding the activities of those users you manage in Family Safety. You also will receive emails daily when users you manage have made requests to use or view content blocked by Family Safety settings.

The Family Safety website enables you to configure the emails that Family Safety sends you.

Changing Frequency of Request Emails

You can modify when you receive emails detailing user requests. You can also unsubscribe from emails so that you won't receive them.

1. From the Family Summary screen, tap Edit Settings for a parent.

2. In the Email Notifications section, tap Request Frequency.

3. Tap Immediately to receive emails immediately when requests are made.

4. Tap Daily Per Child to receive a daily email when requests are made.

5. Tap Off to unsubscribe from Family Safety request emails.

6. Tap OK.

Changing Activity Report Email Settings

You can control which users you receive a summary for regarding PC activity. You can also unsubscribe from activity reports.

1. In the Email Notifications section of the Settings screen for a parent, tap Activity Report Frequency.

2. Tap Weekly and select the users for whom you'd like to receive activity reports.

3. Tap Off to unsubscribe from activity reports on all users.

4. Tap OK.

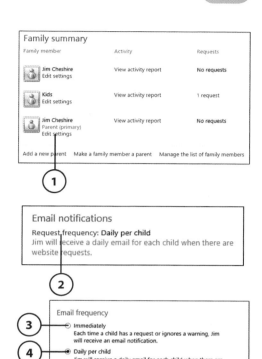

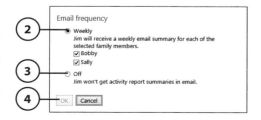

Restore your files when
bad things happen.

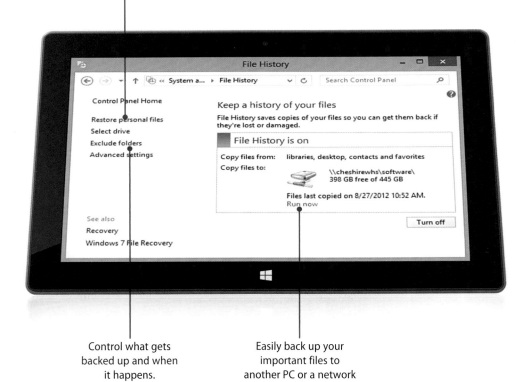

Control what gets
backed up and when
it happens.

Easily back up your
important files to
another PC or a network
drive.

Backing Up Your Data

Your Surface uses a solid-state hard drive. That means that it has no moving parts and, because of that, it's faster and more mechanically reliable than a traditional hard drive. However, solid-state drives don't even approach 100% reliability. That means that the chances of losing data stored on your Surface at some point is higher than you might think. Because most of us store irreplaceable data on our PCs these days (things such as priceless photographs), the importance of a good backup strategy simply cannot be overstated.

Configuring and Starting File History

File History is a feature in Windows RT that makes it easy to automatically save backups of critical files to an external drive or a network drive. If something happens to damage your critical files, you can easily restore them from the backed-up source.

It's Not All Good

File History Is Not a Full System Backup

File History backs up only your personal data files; it doesn't back up system files. If you want to back up folders that exist outside the folders backed up by File History, you'll need to add those folders to a library in Windows RT and File History will back them up.

For more information on using Libraries in Windows RT, see Chapter 12, "HomeGroups and SkyDrive."

Starting Your First Backup

You start your first backup by opening File History in Control Panel and pointing it to a removable drive.

Quickly Backing Up to a Removable Drive

When you insert a removable drive, such as a USB thumb drive, Windows RT displays a notification asking you to tap to choose what to do when the removable drive is inserted. If you tap that notification, you can then choose to use the drive to back up your files in one step.

Note that the option to use the drive for File History backups appears only if File History is turned off when the drive is connected.

1. Make sure that you either have a USB thumb drive or another removable drive plugged in to your PC.

2. Press Winkey+W and enter **File History** into the search box.

3. Tap File History in the search results.

4. Tap Select Drive from the File History screen.

5. Select a drive from the list.

6. Tap OK to choose the drive for File History.

7. Wait until the first backup of your files is complete before you remove the drive.

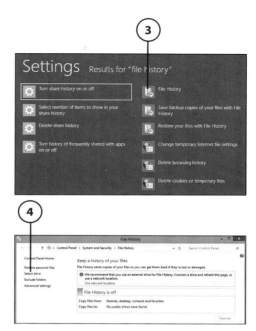

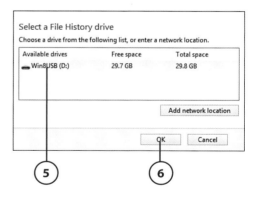

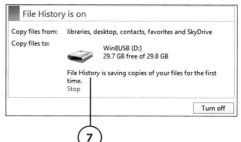

Selecting a Different Drive

After you've set up File History for the first time, you can change to a different drive for your backups. For example, you might want to back up to another machine on your network.

1. From File History in Control Panel, tap on Select Drive.

2. Select a drive from the list if your desired drive appears.

3. To add a network location for backup, tap Add Network Location.

4. Browse to the network location or enter a network path.

5. Tap Select Folder.

6. Tap OK to confirm the new drive.

7. Tap Yes to move your previously backed up files to the new drive; otherwise, tap No.

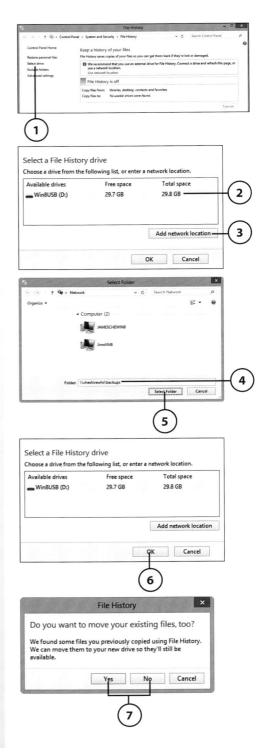

8. If a backup already exists on the selected drive and you want to use it, select the backup.

9. Tap OK.

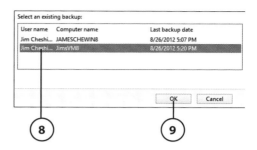

Unavailable Drives

File History is designed to accommodate situations where a backup drive becomes unavailable. If you unplug a removable drive, shut down a PC that you're backing up to, put your PC to sleep, and so on, File History will recognize that and will quietly wait until the drive is available again. When it sees the drive again, it will pick up right where it left off.

Excluding Folders

You might want to exclude some folders from being backed up. For example, if you have temporarily saved some videos to your Videos library, you might want to exclude them from being backed up to save space in your backup drive.

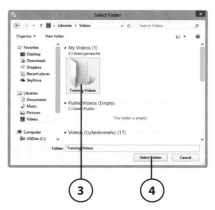

1. From File History, tap Exclude Folders.

2. Tap Add.

3. Select the folder you want to exclude.

4. Tap Select Folder.

5. Tap Save Changes.

Choosing When Backups Happen

By default, your backups happen once per hour. You can change how often backups occur so that they occur more frequently or less frequently.

1. From File History, tap Advanced Settings.

2. Tap the Save Copies of Files drop-down and select a time interval for backups.

3. Tap Save Changes.

Backups Only When Changes Happen

File History backs up a file only if the file has changed since the last time it was backed up.

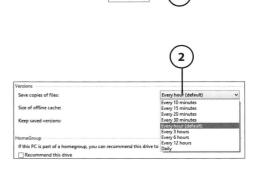

Controlling Local Disk Usage

If your backup drive isn't available, File History still stores backups of files that change. It does so by using a portion of your local drive to store file changes in a cache. When the backup drive is available again, File History uses this cache to transfer backups made while the backup drive was unavailable.

By default, File History uses 5% of disk space on your local drive for caching. You can change how much disk space is used on the local drive for caching.

1. From the Advanced Settings screen, tap the Size of Offline Cache drop-down.

2. Choose a percentage of disk space that your backup cache should use on the local drive.

3. Tap Save Changes.

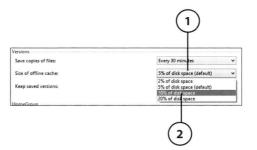

Controlling How Long Backups are Kept

By default, File History saves your backups forever; however, this can quickly fill up your backup drive. You can control how long File History saves backups.

1. From the Advanced Settings screen, tap the Keep Saved Versions drop-down.

2. Choose a new value to set how long File History keeps your backups.

3. Tap Save Changes.

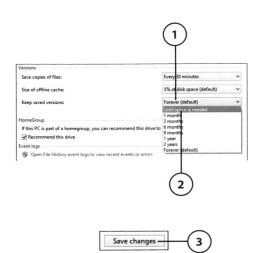

Recommending a Drive to Your HomeGroup

If you are a member of a HomeGroup, you can recommend drives that you add to File History. When you do, other members of your HomeGroup can easily configure their machines to back up to the drive by accepting the recommendation you've sent.

HomeGroup Coverage

For more information on HomeGroups, see "Using HomeGroups" in Chapter 12.

---

1. Select a drive for your File History that you'd like to recommend to others in your HomeGroup.

2. In File History in Control Panel, tap Advanced Settings.

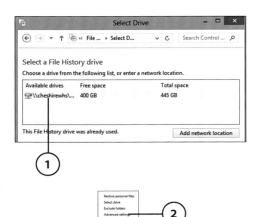

3. Check the Recommend this Drive checkbox.

4. Tap Save Changes.

5. In File History on the other user's computer, tap the Enter Your Credentials link and enter a username and password to connect to the drive.

6. If a current backup exists that you want to use, check the checkbox.

7. Tap Turn On to turn on File History.

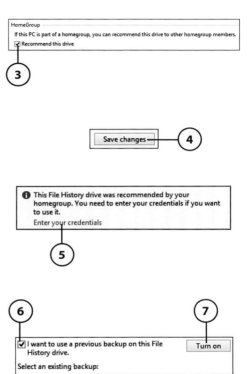

Restoring Files

File History makes it easy to locate the backed-up copies of your files and restore them. You can restore files to the same folder where they were located when File History backed them up, but you can also choose to restore files to a different location if you prefer.

Restoring Files to the Original Location

You can browse your backed-up files and easily restore one or more of them to the original file location.

1. From File History, tap Restore Personal Files.

2. Double-click on a folder to browse files inside the folder.

3. Tap the up arrow to go back to the parent folder.

4. Select a previous path from the drop-down to quickly navigate to that path.

5. Tap the Gear icon, and then tap the View menu to change the view.

6. Tap Previous Version to see an earlier version of backed-up files.

7. Tap Next Version to see later versions of backed-up files.

8. Select one or more files or folders, and tap Restore to restore them to the original location.

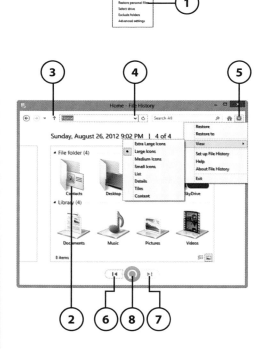

Resolving File Conflicts

If you attempt to restore a file to your local drive and that file already exists in the same location, File History enables you to overwrite the existing file, skip the file restore, or view information about the original file and the backed-up file so that you can decide what you'd like to do.

1. Tap Restore to restore one or more existing files.

2. Tap Replace to overwrite the existing file or files.

3. Tap Skip to skip the file or files.

4. Tap Compare Info for Both Files if only one conflict exists or Let Me Decide for Each File if multiple conflicts exist to compare the files and select those that you want to keep.

5. Check a location to keep all files in that location. (Files from the backup are listed on the left.)

6. Check individual files to keep specific files.

7. Check Skip to skip all files that have the same date and size.

8. Tap Continue to perform the actions you selected.

Resolving Conflicts

File History tries to help you resolve conflicts by bolding differences in file attributes. If one version of a file has a larger file size than another, File History displays the larger size in a bold font. If one file has a later date than another, the one with the later date appears bolded.

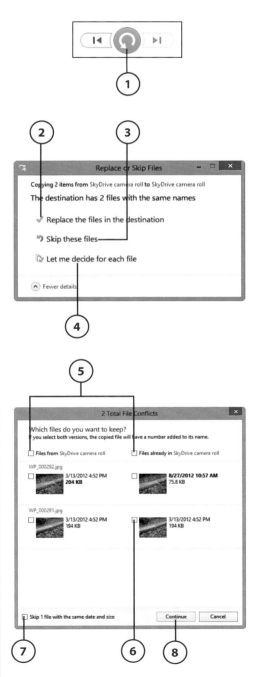

Restoring to a Different Location

If you'd like to restore files to a location other than their original location, you can easily do that. This is useful in cases where you want an additional copy of a file on your local machine or if you want to restore files to a USB thumb drive or another removable device.

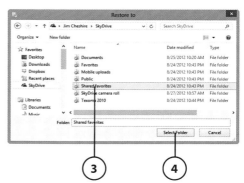

1. Select the files or folders you want to restore.

2. Tap and hold on one of the files to show the context menu, and tap Restore To on the context menu.

3. Select a location where you'd like to restore the files or folders.

4. Tap Select Folder to restore the files.

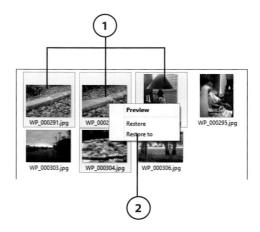

Cleaning Up Files

By default, File History saves your backed-up files forever. In many cases, you will want to keep all versions of your files, but if you have files that change often, keeping all versions might mean that your backups use more disk space than you'd like. Fortunately, you can clean up backed-up files so that you can free disk space on your backup drive.

Performing a Clean Up

When you clean up file versions, you can specify to clean up files older than a certain time frame, or you can clean up all versions except the most recent version. In no cases will cleaning file versions remove the latest version of a file.

1. From the Advanced Settings dialog in File History, tap Clean Up Versions.

2. Select an option from the Delete Files drop-down. By default, a cleanup will remove all files older than one year, but you can modify that as desired.

3. Tap Clean Up to delete the file versions in the backup as per your selection.

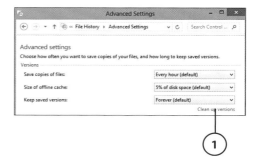

File History Might Not Find Files to Delete

If File History cannot find any files in your backups that are old enough to be deleted given your selected timeframe, it will notify you and ask you to choose a shorter period of time.

It's Not All Good

Grab a Snack

If your backups are on a network location, it could take quite a while for File History to parse through your files and clean things up. Start the process, and then go grab a snack.

Troubleshooting File History

If you see error messages that don't provide enough detail for you to figure out what went wrong, or if you notice that files you expect to be backed up aren't getting backed up, you can view detailed logs from the Windows Event Viewer.

Viewing File History Event History

You can view details of all File History events in the Windows Event Viewer.

1. From the Advanced Settings screen in File History, tap the Open File History Event Logs link.

2. If prompted, enter your password for User Account Control.

3. Select an event to see more details about it.

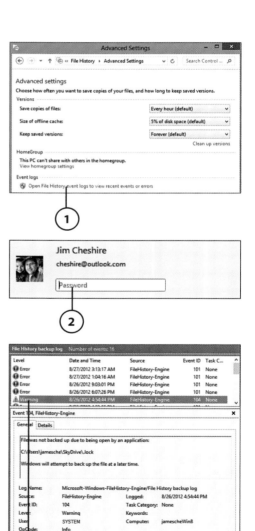

>>>Go Further

FILE HISTORY EVENTS

File History will likely log plenty of events that make no sense to you. Don't worry about them. The Event Viewer logs are really intended to be used by advanced users. However, if you do see an error that looks serious and you need more information on it, a search of Microsoft's Knowledge Base at support.microsoft.com might give you the information you need.

Use frequent site and
favorite tiles.

Visit your favorite
websites.

Search the Internet
with Bing.

Searching and Browsing the Internet

The Internet is a wonderful source of information, and your Surface makes it a pleasure to explore that information in many ways. In this chapter, I show you how you can search the Internet using the Bing app and how you can browse the content that you find using Internet Explorer, both in the new Windows 8–style interface and on the Windows Desktop.

Using the Bing App

You can search the Internet by browsing to your favorite search engine and entering a search term, but you can get a better experience by using the Bing app.

Exploring the Bing App

The Bing app offers a few unique and interesting features that make it easy to explore interesting information on the Internet in addition to search functionality.

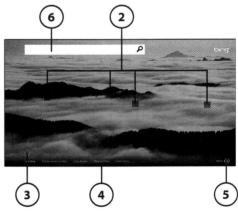

1. From the Start screen, tap the Bing tile to launch the Bing app.

2. Tap the image to see hot spots that you can tap for more information on the image.

3. Tap the information icon to see information about the image.

4. Tap a trending search topic to see search results on that topic.

5. Tap More to see a complete list of trending search topics.

6. Tap inside the search box to enter a search term.

7. Enter a search term, or tap a recent search or suggested search.

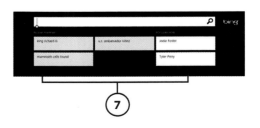

Searching in the Bing App

The Bing app displays search results in a user-friendly and helpful way. Not only do you get the kind of search results you're used to, but results will also provide deep links to specific pages within common websites.

1. Enter a search term in the textbox.

2. Tap a search result to go to that page.

3. Tap a deep link to go to a particular part of a website.

4. Tap the Bing logo to return to the Bing app's home screen.

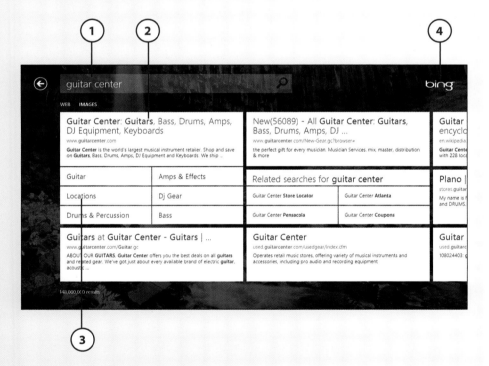

Filtering Search Results

The Bing app uses Microsoft's SafeSearch technology to allow you to filter search results so that you can restrict adult content from showing up in the results.

1. Swipe in from the right side of the screen and tap Settings.

2. Tap SafeSearch.

3. Tap the desired setting to filter your search results.

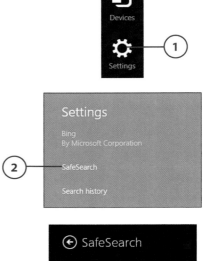

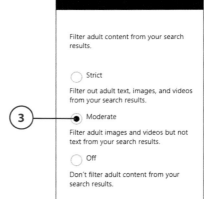

It's Not All Good

SafeSearch Isn't Family Safety

SafeSearch is effective at filtering out adult content, but it's equally easy for the person doing the search to change SafeSearch settings so that they don't block adult content. If you want more secure protection for your children, make sure to use Family Safety. I cover Family Safety extensively in Chapter 5, "Using Family Safety."

Controlling Search History

The Bing app keeps track of your search history so that you can easily return to a set of search results. If you want, you can disable this functionality so that the Bing app no longer stores your search history.

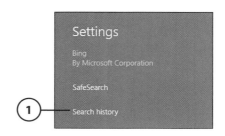

1. From the Settings pane, tap Search History.

2. Tap the Keep Search History slider to set it to Off.

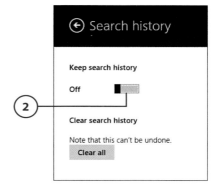

Clearing Search History

You can clear your search history so that no one can see what you've been searching for. For example, if you've been searching for the perfect birthday gift for your spouse, you can easily clear the evidence of your search.

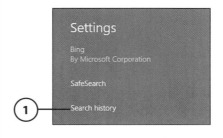

1. From the Settings screen, tap Search History.

2. Tap the Clear All button to delete all search history from the Bing app.

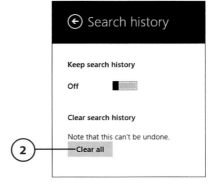

It's Not All Good

Clearing History

When you clear history, it only clears history from the Bing app. If you've gone to Bing.com in your web browser and searched the Internet, that search history is not cleared by clearing search history in the Bing app.

Browsing Sites with Internet Explorer

Your Surface comes with Internet Explorer 10, the latest version of Microsoft's web browser. Internet Explorer 10 is designed to work well with all modern websites, and it's also designed to be fast and powerful.

There are actually two different versions of Internet Explorer on your Surface. One runs in the new Windows 8 style, and the other runs on the Windows Desktop. One of the main reasons why there are two versions is because any add-ons that you might have with Internet Explorer in the past won't work on the Windows 8–style version, so the Desktop version is available for compatibility. Another reason is that compatibility mode (a special mode that fixes rendering problems with some websites) isn't available in the new version of Internet Explorer.

It's Not All Good

Websites and Touch

In my experience, some websites just don't work well with touch. Menus might not activate correctly, and other parts of the site might not work correctly.

Opening a Site in the Windows 8–Style Internet Explorer

The Windows 8–style version of Internet Explorer provides a full-screen experience for viewing websites.

1. From the Start screen, tap the Internet Explorer icon.

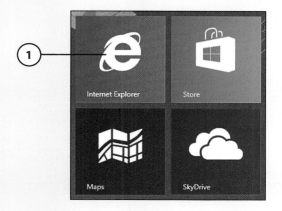

2. Tap inside the textbox and enter a website address.

3. Tap a frequently visited site to navigate to the site.

4. Tap a favorite site to navigate to the site.

Favorites and Frequent Sites

You learn much more about working with IE favorites and frequently visited sites later in this chapter, in the section, "Favorites and Frequent Sites."

---

5. Tap a link to follow it.

6. Reverse pinch to zoom in on a page.

7. Pinch to zoom out on a page.

8. Double-tap to quickly zoom in on part of a page.

9. Double-tap again to zoom out.

10. Swipe up from the bottom of the screen, and tap Back to go to the previously viewed page.

11. Tap Refresh to reload the current page.

12. Tap Forward to move to the next page in your history.

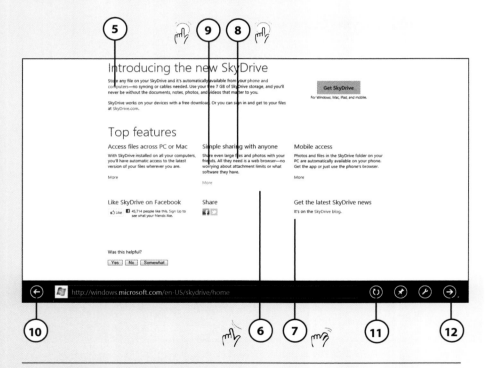

Moving Forward

The Forward button is active only if you've tapped the Back button to go back in your browsing history.

Viewing a Site in Desktop Internet Explorer

In rare cases, you might have a problem viewing a website in the Windows 8–style version of Internet Explorer. You might want to try viewing a page in the Desktop version of Internet Explorer if you see errors on a page, parts of a page aren't visible, and so forth.

1. While viewing a web page, tap the Page Tools button.

2. Tap View on the Desktop.

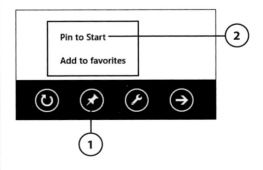

Pinning Web Pages to the Start Screen

If you find a particular useful web page, you might want to pin a link to that page to the Start screen so that you can access it quickly.

1. While viewing the page that you want to pin to the Start screen, tap the Pin Site button.

2. Tap Pin to Start.

Searching a Web Page

You can search for a particular word or phrase on a web page.

1. While viewing the web page you want to search, tap the Page Tools button.

2. Tap Find on Page.

3. Enter a search term. All occurrences of the term are highlighted in yellow and the currently selected occurrence is highlighted in blue.

4. Tap Next to select the next occurrence.

5. Tap Previous to select the previous occurrence.

6. Tap Close to close the Find pane.

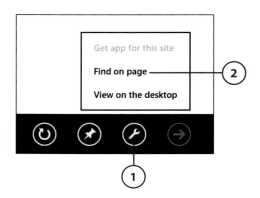

Setting the Zoom Level

You might find that increasing the zoom level in Internet Explorer makes it easier to read websites. On the other hand, if you have excellent vision, you can always decrease the zoom level to fit more content on the screen.

1. While viewing Internet Explorer, swipe in from the right of the screen and tap Settings.

2. Tap Internet Options.

3. Drag the Zoom slider to the right to increase the zoom level.

4. Drag the Zoom slider to the left to decrease the zoom level.

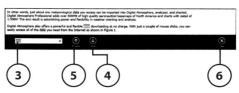

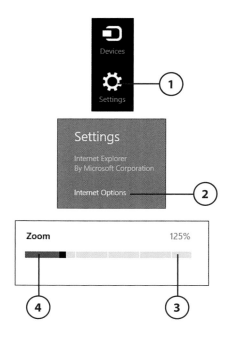

Using Flip Ahead

Flip Ahead is a new feature in Internet Explorer designed to make some web pages easier to navigate. Perhaps you are viewing a long news article that spans across several pages. By enabling the Flip Ahead feature, you can switch between pages in the article by swiping instead of tapping a link to move between pages.

1. From the Internet Explorer Settings, tap the Turn on Flip Ahead slider to enable Flip Ahead.

2. While viewing a page that is part of a series of web pages, swipe left to move to the next page in the series.

3. Swipe right to move to the previous page in the series.

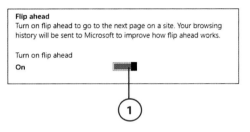

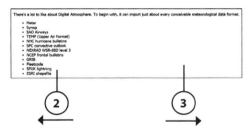

It's Not All Good

A Work in Progress

For Flip Ahead to work correctly, Internet Explorer must be able to recognize the current page as part of a series of pages. Microsoft is still perfecting this process, so when you turn on Flip Ahead, your browsing history is sent to Microsoft so that they can use it to help make the feature better. (No personally identifying information is sent to Microsoft.)

Disallowing Location Services

Some websites will request to use your current location to provide you with a more customized experience. When this happens, you'll be prompted. You can, however, configure Internet Explorer so that sites are not allowed to ask you for your location at all.

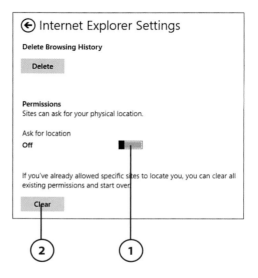

1. From Internet Explorer Settings, tap the Ask for Location slider to move it to the Off position.

2. To clear any previous permissions to use your location, tap the Clear button.

Using Tabs

Tabs enable you to have multiple web pages open at the same time. You can easily switch between tabs, open new tabs, and close tabs as desired.

It's Not All Good

Tabs Aren't Shared Between Windows 8–Style and Desktop

Tabs that you open in the Windows 8–style version of Internet Explorer are not shared with the Desktop version. Therefore, if you open a series of tabs and then choose to view a site in the Desktop version of Internet Explorer, you won't see your tabs when you switch to the Desktop version.

Opening a Link in a New Tab

You can open a link on a page in a new tab. This is a convenient way to follow links on a page you're viewing while making it easy to return to the original page.

1. While viewing a page, tap and hold on the link you want to open in a new tab.

2. Tap Open Link in New Tab.

3. Swipe down from the top of the screen.

4. Tap the icon for the new tab that you've just created to activate the tab and view the page.

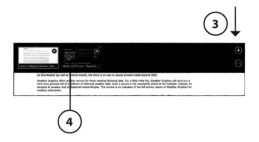

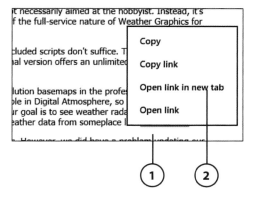

Creating a New Blank Tab

You can add a new blank tab if you want to enter a URL for a new site without closing the current site.

1. Swipe down from the top of the screen.

2. Tap New Tab to create a new tab.

3. Tap the address bar to enter the URL to open in the new tab.

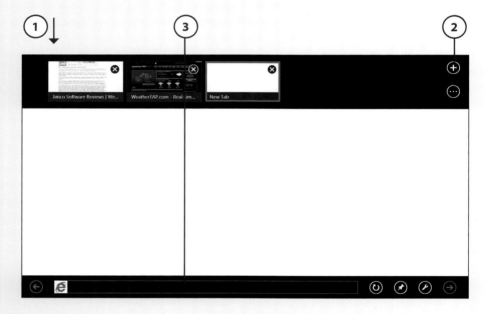

Closing a Tab

You can close individual tabs if you no longer wish to leave them open.

1. Swipe down from the top of the screen.

2. Tap Close on the tab or tabs that you want to close.

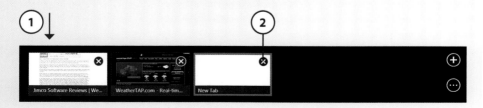

Opening an InPrivate Tab

InPrivate mode is a special mode of Internet Explorer. When you are browsing in InPrivate mode, Internet Explorer does not save your history, it doesn't save any temporary files while visiting websites, and it doesn't save any cookies. In other words, when you close an InPrivate tab, no evidence remains on your tablet that you visited the sites you visited while InPrivate mode was active.

Keep Things Private

I frequently use InPrivate mode when I'm browsing the Internet looking for gift ideas for my wife. By using InPrivate browsing, my wife won't find any clues about her gift if she happens to use my Surface to browse the Internet.

1. Swipe down from the top of the screen.
2. Tap the Tab Tools button.
3. Tap New InPrivate Tab.
4. Tap inside the address bar and enter a URL to browse privately.

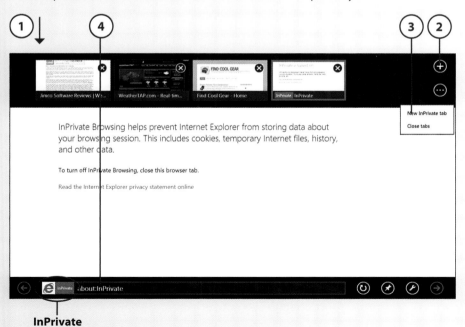

InPrivate

Ensuring You're InPrivate

When you are browsing using InPrivate mode, a blue InPrivate indicator appears in the address bar and at the bottom of the tab's icon.

Favorites and Frequent Sites

Favorites make it easy to return to your favorite website. Internet Explorer also keeps track of the sites you visit so that you can easily return to them.

Favorites Shared Between Desktop and Windows 8 Style

Unlike tabs, favorites are shared between the Windows 8–style version and the Desktop version of Internet Explorer. If you add a favorite in one, the favorite is also added to the other.

Adding a Favorite

You can add a favorite while viewing a web page.

1. While visiting the page that you want to add as a favorite, swipe up from the bottom of the screen.

2. Tap the Pin Site button.

3. Tap Add to Favorites.

Browsing to a Favorite Page

You can quickly browse to a favorite page by tapping the page's tile in Favorites.

1. Tap inside the address bar in Internet Explorer.

2. Swipe to the left if necessary to scroll to your desired favorite page.

3. Tap the tile for the page to quickly navigate to the page.

Opening a Favorite in a New Tab

You can also open a favorite page in a new tab.

1. Tap and hold on the tile for your favorite to display the context menu.

2. Select Open in New Tab to open the favorite in a new tab.

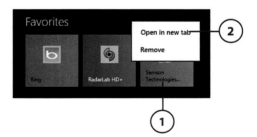

Deleting a Favorite

If you decide you no longer want a favorite, you can remove it from the Favorites list.

1. Tap and hold on the tile for the favorite you'd like to delete to display the context menu.

2. Select Remove to delete the favorite.

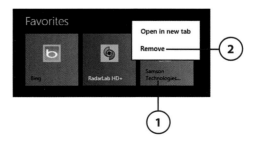

It's Not All Good

Editing Favorites

There isn't a way to edit favorites in the Windows 8 style. To edit your favorites (for example, to change the URL for a favorite), you must use the Manage Favorites interface in the Desktop version of Internet Explorer, and because that dialog isn't really designed well for touch, my preference is to delete the existing favorite and create a new favorite that points to the correct page.

Visiting a Frequent Site

Internet Explorer keeps track of sites that you visit often and provides tiles so that you can quickly return to one of those sites.

1. Tap inside the Internet Explorer address bar.

2. Tap a tile for a frequent site.

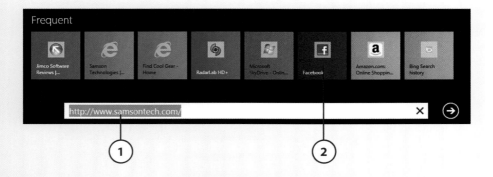

Opening a Frequent Site in a New Tab

You can open a frequently visited site inside a new tab.

1. Tap inside the address bar in Internet Explorer.

2. Tap and hold on a frequent site's tile to display the context menu.

3. Tap Open in New Tab to open the site in a new tab.

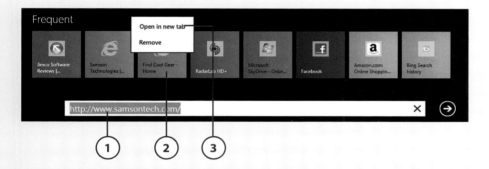

Deleting a Frequent Site Tile

You can remove the tile for a frequently visited site.

1. Tap inside the address bar in Internet Explorer.

2. Tap and hold on a frequent site's tile to display the context menu.

3. Tap Remove to delete the frequent site's tile.

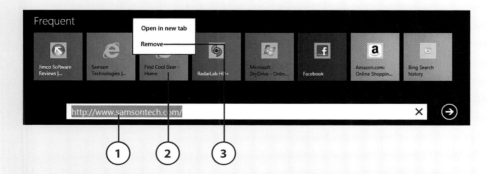

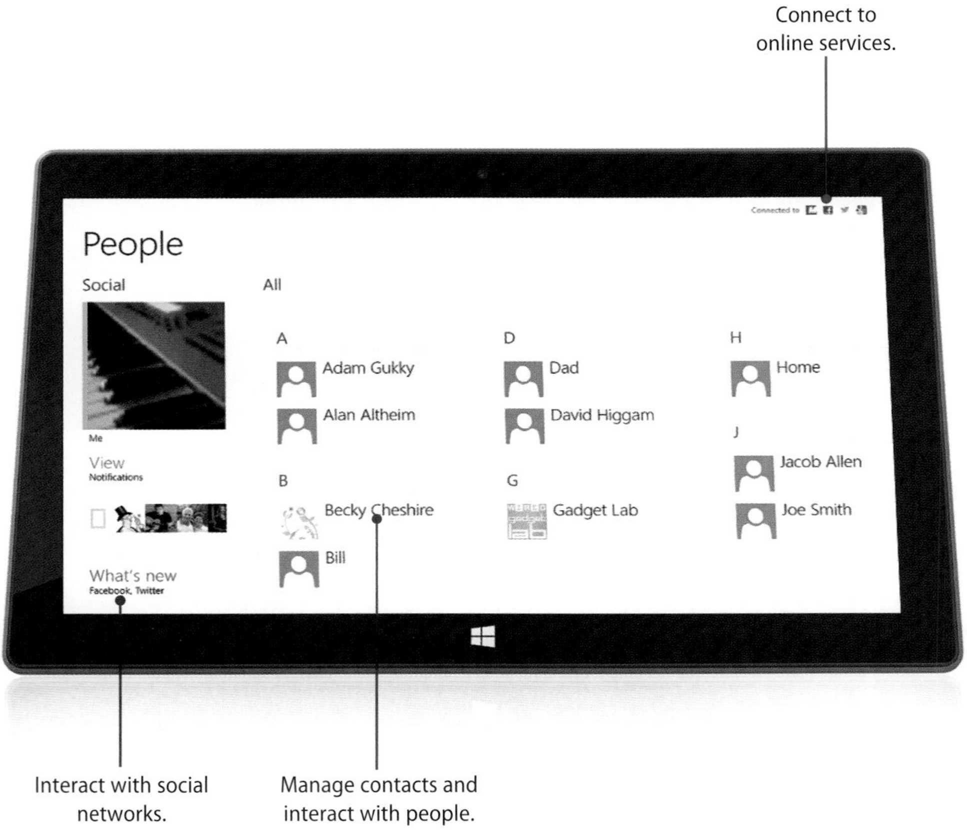

Connect to
online services.

People

Social

All

Me

A
Adam Gukky
Alan Altheim

B
Becky Cheshire
Bill

View
Notifications

What's new
Facebook, Twitter

D
Dad
David Higgam

G
Gadget Lab

H
Home

J
Jacob Allen
Joe Smith

Connected to

Interact with social
networks.

Manage contacts and
interact with people.

Connecting with People

Social is everywhere. Even if you're not all that in to Twitter, Facebook, or other social media services, chances are you still have a core group of friends and family with whom you interact. Windows RT is packed with features that make interacting with friends and family easy and convenient.

Working with Contacts

Before you can connect with your friends and family on Windows RT, you need to add them as contacts. There are several ways to go about doing that. You can manually add each person, but you also can let Windows RT automatically add your contacts from Facebook, Hotmail, Google, LinkedIn, and other websites.

Contacts in the Cloud

Cloud is the buzzword of the day, and for good reason. By using contacts from Hotmail, Facebook, Google, or another such service in the cloud (which really just means that it's on the Internet), you'll be able to maintain only one copy of your contacts. When you update a contact in one place, the update is automatically available everywhere else that contact is shared.

Adding Contacts from the Cloud

Contacts in Windows RT are managed using the People app. The People app can pull in your contacts from just about any website where your contacts are stored.

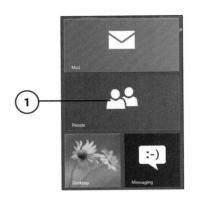

1. From the Windows RT Start screen, tap the People app.

People App Live Tile

By default, the People app is a Live Tile that might look different from the one pictured here, which has its Live Tile functionality disabled.

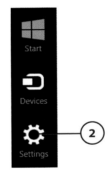

2. While in the People app, swipe in from the right side of the screen and tap the Settings charm.

3. Tap Accounts.

4. Tap Add an Account.

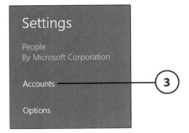

5. Tap an account.

6. Enter any information the service requires (if necessary) and tap Connect.

7. If asked, enter your login information for the service.

Adding Services

Some services ask for your username and password before you see the Connect button. Others ask for your username and password after you tap Connect.

It's Not All Good

How Long?

After you configure a connection with one of your services, you might need to wait for several minutes before the People app synchronizes with the service and updates its content. I have noticed that Facebook is particularly slow, sometimes taking up to 10 minutes to synchronize.

Changing Contact Sort Order

You might notice that, by default, the People app sorts your contacts by first name. If you'd prefer, you can change it so that your contacts are sorted by last name.

1. From the Settings bar in the People app, tap Options.

2. Drag the slider to On to sort your contacts by last name.

3. Drag the slider to Off to sort your contacts by first name.

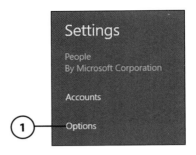

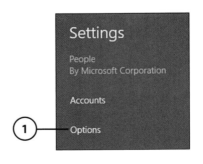

Filtering Your Contacts

You can filter your contacts so that only those contacts from the services you choose are displayed.

1. From the Settings bar in the People app, tap Options.

2. Check a service to include contacts from the service in your contacts list.

3. Uncheck a service to hide contacts from that service.

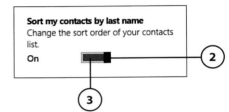

Linking Contacts

If you add contacts from more than one service, you might have some contacts that appear twice in your list. In most cases, Windows RT is smart enough to display duplicate contacts as one contact, but if the name is slightly different, you might need to manually link duplicates.

1. Tap one of the contacts you want to link from your list of contacts.

2. Swipe up from the bottom of the screen and tap Link.

3. Windows RT will suggest a contact to link in some cases. Select the contact if it's correct, or tap Choose a Contact to select a contact to link.

4. Choose one or more contacts to link to the contact that you selected from your list in step 1.

5. Tap Add.

6. Tap Save to save the linked contacts.

Linked Contacts

When you link two or more contacts, your contact list displays one contact entry for the contacts that you select to link together. Contact information for that single entry will be consolidated from all of the linked contacts.

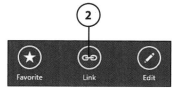

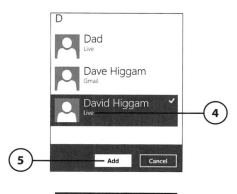

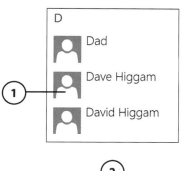

Making a Contact a Favorite

Tiles for your favorite contacts are displayed to the left of your contact list so that you can access them easily. You can easily set a contact as a favorite.

1. Tap a contact that you want to make a favorite.
2. Swipe up from the bottom of the screen.
3. Tap Favorite.

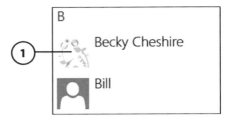

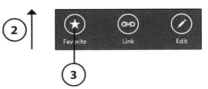

Removing a Favorite

You can easily remove a favorite by tapping the Favorite button again.

Pinning Contacts to the Start Screen

If you have a contact that you interact with often, you can pin the contact to the Start screen.

1. Tap a contact.
2. Swipe up from the bottom of the screen.
3. Tap Pin to Start.
4. Enter a name to display on the tile on your Start screen.
5. Tap Pin to Start.

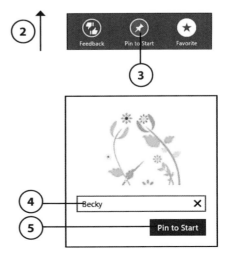

Why Pin?

You might be wondering why you would want to pin a contact to your Start screen. As you go through the rest of this chapter and see all that ways in which you can interact with people in Windows RT, it should become obvious how convenient pinning is for your frequent contacts.

By the way, if you change your mind and want to unpin a contact from your Start screen, go through the same steps and tap Unpin from Start.

Creating a New Contact

You can create new contacts on your Surface. When you create a contact, you can choose an online service for the contact. Any device that synchronizes with the selected online service will have access to the contact that you create.

1. From the People screen, swipe up from the bottom of the screen.

2. Tap New.

3. Select the service for the account.

4. Enter the contact's information.

5. Tap the plus sign to add a new field, such as a new phone number or a business address.

6. Tap Save to save the new contact.

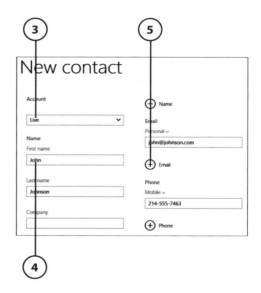

Contacts Are Not Local

It's important for you to realize that when you add a contact on your Surface, that contact isn't specific to your Surface. You are actually adding an online contact for the service you select, and that contact will be available to all devices that use the service, not just your Surface.

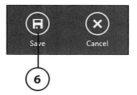

Deleting a Contact

You can delete a contact from the contact list in the People app. Deleting a contact removes the contact from all devices that synchronize with the service that originally contained the contact.

1. From the People screen, tap the contact you'd like to delete.

2. Swipe up from the bottom of the screen.

3. Tap Delete.

4. Tap Delete to confirm that you want to delete the contact.

It's Not All Good

Take Care When Deleting Contacts

Contacts in Windows RT come from one or more online services. If you delete a contact from your Surface, you are actually deleting the contact from the online service, and if you have other computers or devices (such as your smart phone) that use the same online service for contacts, the contact will be removed from those devices as well.

Removing All Contacts from a Service

As you've seen, when you add a connection to Twitter, Gmail, Facebook, or another service, any contacts for that service are added to your contact list. If you want to remove those contacts from your Surface, you can simply remove the connection with the service containing the contacts.

1. From the People app, tap any of the service icons in the upper-right corner.

2. Tap the account that you want to remove.

3. If the account settings include a Remove Account button, tap it to remove the account.

4. If the account settings do not include a Remove Account button, tap the Manage This Account Online link.

5. In the web page for the account, tap the Remove This Connection Completely link.

6. Tap the Remove button to confirm the removal of the service.

Editing a Contact

You can edit a contact in cases where information has changed or where you want to add additional information for a contact.

1. Tap a contact that you would like to edit.

2. Swipe up from the bottom of the screen.

3. Tap Edit.

4. If the contact is a linked contact, select the contact that you would like to edit from the pop-up menu.

5. Edit the contact's existing information, if necessary.

6. To add additional information, tap a plus sign.

7. Select the information you'd like to add, and enter it.

8. To change the name for a field, tap the current field name and select a new name from the list.

9. To delete a value in a field, tap inside the field, and then tap the X to delete the value.

10. Tap Save to save the contact.

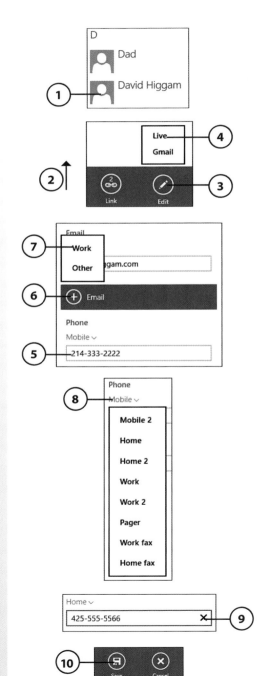

Contacting Someone from the People App

There are various ways that you can contact someone while viewing their information from within the People app.

Options for Contacting People

The communication options available to you in the People app vary based on the contact information available for a particular person.

1. Tap a contact to view the contact's details.

2. To send an email to the contact, tap Send Email to send email to the address that is displayed for the contact.

3. To send an email to an alternative email address, tap the down arrow and tap one of the contact's other email addresses.

4. To send a message to the contact, tap Send Message.

5. To send a message using an alternative service, tap the down arrow to select the desired service.

Using Email

If you'd like detailed information on how to use the Email app in Windows RT, see Chapter 9, "Using Mail."

6. To call a contact, tap the Call button.

7. To call an alternative number for the contact, tap the down arrow and select a number to call.

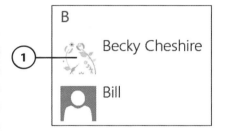

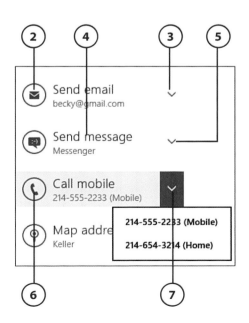

Social Networking

Windows RT integrates social networking so that you can easily post to social networks, see what's new with your friends and family, and get notified when someone interacts with you on a social network.

Posting to Social Networks

The People app provides a quick and easy interface for posting to social networks to which you connect.

1. From the People app, tap the Me tile to access your profile screen.

2. Tap the down arrow to select a social network if desired.

3. Enter a status update.

4. Tap Send to post to your social network.

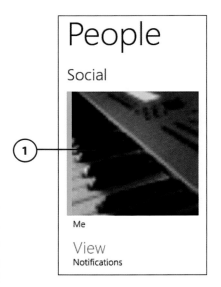

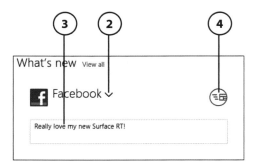

Viewing Updates on Social Networks

You can view all of your status updates, comments, and other interactions with people on your social networks.

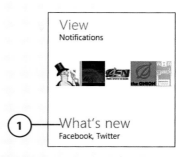

View
Notifications

1 — What's new
Facebook, Twitter

1. From the People app, tap What's New.

2. Swipe left and right to see more.

3. Tap Favorite on a tweet to mark it as a favorite.

4. Tap Undo Favorite to unmark a tweet as a favorite.

5. Tap Like on a Facebook post to like it.

6. Tap Unlike on a Facebook post to unlike it.

7. Tap the Twitter icon to see the tweet in Internet Explorer.

8. Tap the Facebook icon to see the post in Internet Explorer.

9. Tap Retweet to retweet a tweet.

10. Tap a tweet, or tap Reply to tweet a reply.

11. Tap a Facebook post, or tap Comment to comment on a post.

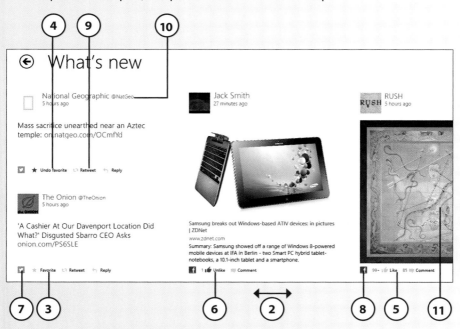

Icons in What's New

The icons that you see on the What's New page aren't chosen at random. These are the profile pictures of the people who have recently posted on your social networks.

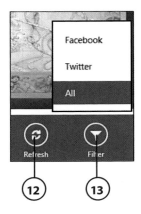

12. Swipe up from the bottom of the screen, and tap Refresh to refresh updates.

13. Swipe up from the bottom of the screen, and tap Filter to choose which social networks are displayed.

Sharing Content with People

Windows RT enables apps to share content using what Microsoft calls a *sharing contract*. Any app that implements this feature shows up on the Share charm. By default, Internet Explorer, the People app, and the Mail app allow for sharing of content, but you can add more apps from the Windows Store.

Sharing App Content with Social Networks

Windows RT makes it easy to share information with social networks. In this example, I show you how you can share a website with a social network, but sharing works the same way for any app that supports it.

Share Part of a Web Page

If you'd like to share part of a web page rather than a link to the page, select the content you want to share before sharing. Only the content you select will be shared.

1. From a web page in Internet Explorer, swipe in from the right side of the screen and tap the Share charm.

Shortcut Key for the Share Charm

You can press Winkey+H to quickly access the Share charm.

2. Tap People.

3. Tap the arrow and choose one of your connected social networks.

4. Enter a message you'd like to include with your post.

5. Tap Send.

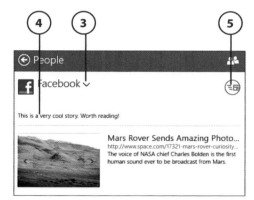

It's Not All Good

Cannot Share from Desktop Apps

You can only share from Windows Store apps. If you are viewing a website in Internet Explorer on the desktop, you will be unable to share the site using the Share charm.

Emailing App Content to Contacts

The Share charm also makes it easy to email information from an app to one or more contacts. Again, this example demonstrates sharing a web link, but other apps enable you to share additional types of information.

1. From the Share pane, tap Mail.

2. Enter one or more email addresses.

3. Enter a message for your email.

4. Tap Send to send the email.

Easily Share with Email

When you share something with an email contact, that contact is added to a shortcut list of email addresses that appears at the top of the Share pane. The next time you want to share something with that contact, you can tap his or her email address in the shortcut list and an email is automatically addressed to the contact.

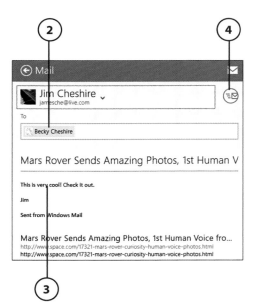

Listing Share Apps in Alphabetical Order

When you access the Share pane, the apps that you use most often when sharing are listed at the top of the list by default. You can turn off this feature so that apps are listed in alphabetical order instead.

1. From the PC Settings screen, tap Share.

2. Tap the Show Apps I Use Most Often at the Top of the App List slider to change the setting to Off.

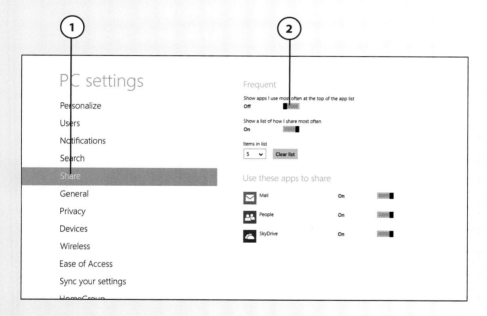

Clearing the List of Often-Shared Choices

As I mentioned earlier, when you share an item using email, the email address of the person with whom you shared the item appears on a shortcut list at the top of the Share pane. This shortcut list is populated as you share items, showing the ways in which you share most often so that you can access them quickly. You can clear this list if you want.

1. From the PC Settings screen, tap Share.

2. Tap Clear List to clear the list of often-shared methods.

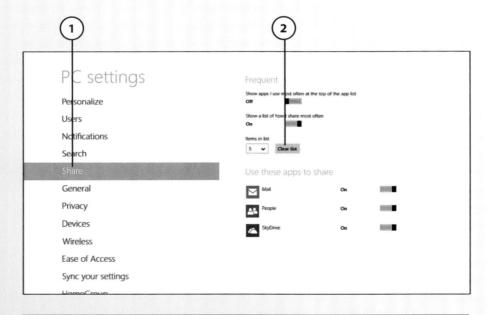

Controlling the Number of Entries on the Shortcut List

You can control how many entries appear on the shortcut list in the Share pane. Select the desired number of items from the Share settings screen. By default, five items are displayed.

Disabling the Often-Shared Shortcut List

You can turn off the often-shared shortcut list if you don't want to list ways you share most often in the Share pane.

1. From the PC Settings screen, tap Share.

2. Tap the Show a List of How I Share Most Often slider to change the setting to Off.

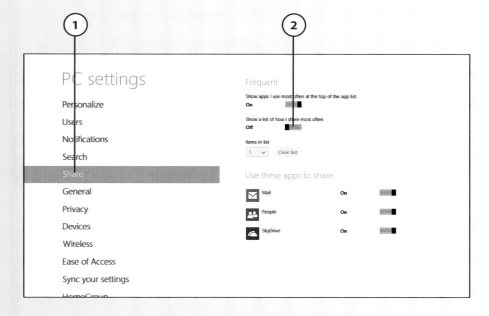

It's Not All Good

Disabling the Shortcut List Clears the List

When you disable the often-shared shortcut list, it clears items from the list. If you reenable the list, you will start fresh again and new shortcuts are added as you share additional items.

Using the Messaging App

The Messaging app enables you to send messages to people in your contact list. As with other social apps, you can connect the Messenger app to online services to add to the people with whom you can connect.

You add accounts to Messenger using the same methods described earlier in this chapter in the "Adding Contacts from the Cloud" section. The Messenger app can connect to Facebook and to Windows Messenger services.

It's Not All Good

Limit on Accounts

Even though Windows RT enables you to connect other accounts to your Surface (such as LinkedIn), you cannot add these accounts to the Messaging app. The Messaging app supports only Windows Messenger and Facebook because these are the only two services that provide a chat type of service.

Sending a Message

You can send messages to any of your contacts from either Facebook or Windows Messenger. You can even send a message to a contact who is currently offline, and your message is automatically delivered the next time the contact is online.

1. From the Start screen, tap Messaging to launch the Messaging app.

2. Tap New Message.

3. Select the contact to whom you would like to send a message.

4. Tap Choose.

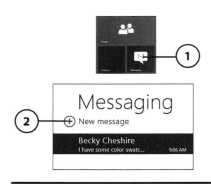

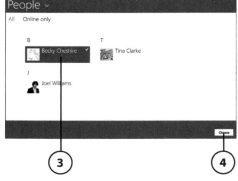

5. Tap inside the message textbox and enter your message.

6. Tap Enter to send your message.

Replying to Messages

You can reply to a message using the same steps described in steps 5 and 6.

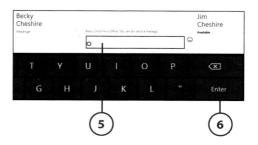

Sending a Message from a Different Account

If you are in a conversation with a contact and that contact has a connection with you via another online service, you can switch the conversation to the other online service and continue it there. For example, you might start a conversation on Windows Messenger and finish the conversation on Facebook Chat.

1. Before replying to a message, swipe up from the bottom of the screen and tap Switch.

2. Tap the service you would like to use to send your message.

3. Enter and send your message.

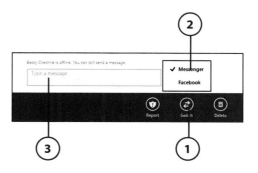

Switch Not Available

The Switch button is visible only if you are messaging with a contact who is connected to you through both Windows Messenger and Facebook Chat.

Inviting a Friend to Message with You

If you would like to chat with a friend on the Messaging app and that friend doesn't have an account for Windows Messenger or Facebook, you can invite the friend to create a Microsoft account so that you can chat with him or her in Messaging. Once the contact creates a Microsoft account, you will be able to chat with him or her using the Messaging app.

1. While in the Messaging app, swipe up from the bottom of the screen.

2. Tap Invite.

3. Tap Add a New Friend.

4. Enter an email address for the person you would like to invite. Microsoft sends an invitation to join Windows Messenger to this email address.

5. Tap Next.

6. Tap Invite to send the invitation.

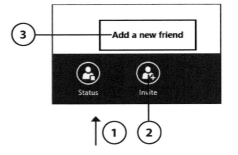

Making Yourself Unavailable

There might be times when you don't want to be disturbed by incoming messages. In those situations, you can temporarily disable messaging services. When you do this, you are signed out of the Windows Messenger service on the PC you are using.

Status Only Impacts Windows Messenger

When you change your status or availability in Messaging, it only impacts your status in Windows Messenger. It doesn't affect your status in Facebook chat.

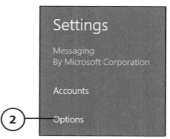

1. While in the Messaging app, swipe in from the right side of the screen and tap Settings.
2. In the Settings pane, tap Options.
3. Tap the Send/Receive Messages slider to change the setting to Off.

Offline Status

You will need to turn on messaging services to send messages again.

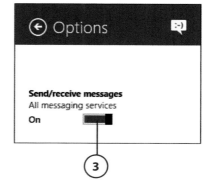

It's Not All Good

Confusion with Multiple PCs

If you have multiple PCs and you are signed on to more than one with the same Microsoft account, your status might not be accurately reflected when you make yourself unavailable. For example, if you are signed in and available on two PCs and you make yourself unavailable on one of them, your friends will still see you as being available if your status on the other PC is available.

It's important that you keep this in mind when changing your status; otherwise, your friend might send you a message that arrives on a PC you don't typically use, and when he or she doesn't get an answer, you'll appear to be ignoring the message.

Changing Your Status

You can change your status and choose whether you want to appear to be available for messaging while still remaining connected to the Windows Messenger service.

1. While using Messaging, swipe up from the bottom of the screen and tap Status.

2. Tap Invisible to make yourself appear to be offline.

3. Tap Available to make yourself appear to be online.

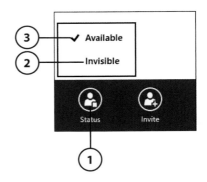

Deleting a Conversation

You can delete a conversation when you are finished sending and receiving messages.

1. Tap the conversation you want to delete.

2. Swipe up from the bottom of the screen and tap Delete.

3. Tap the Delete button.

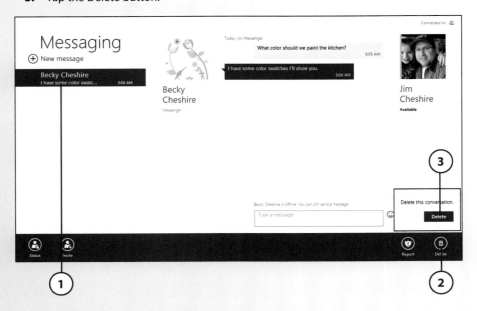

Reporting a Hacked Account

If you receive a message from a friend and you don't believe that your friend sent the message, your friend's Microsoft account might have been compromised. You can help your friend by reporting to Microsoft that the account might have been hacked.

1. While viewing the conversation with the friend whom you believe has been hacked, swipe up from the bottom of the screen and tap Report.

2. Tap the Let Us Know button.

Report Button Not Visible

The Report button is visible only for Windows Messenger contacts. If you don't see the Report button, tap the Switch button and switch to the Windows Messenger service.

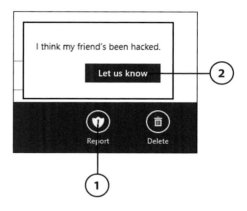

TELLING WHEN HACKING HAPPENS

When should you be suspicious about a friend's account being hacked? It's actually not easy, and there aren't any tried-and-true rules. If you get a message from a friend out of the blue and the content of the message seems uncharacteristic, like a website URL without any further message, that's a sign that your friend's account might have been hacked. You also might get a message asking for personal information or asking for money to help a friend in crisis. It's a good idea to call your friend to verify such requests.

The bottom line is that you should be suspicious of anything that doesn't seem right, and that suspicion shouldn't be limited to chat messages. It's a good rule of thumb to apply to all information you get from the Internet.

>>>Go Further

Organize email
in folders.

Attach files to
your email.

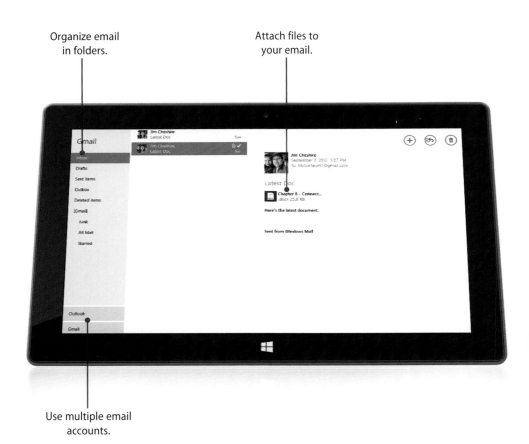

Use multiple email
accounts.

Using Mail

Like many Windows Store apps, the Mail app that comes with Windows RT seems simple at first glance, but as you dig into it, you soon realize that it is a feature-rich and powerful app for managing your email. It has the capability to connect to online services, so it's simple to keep your email synchronized across all of your devices.

Adding and Managing Email Accounts

If you sign in to your Surface using your Microsoft account, the Mail app automatically configures itself for your Microsoft email. You can easily add your other email accounts as well. You do so by tapping the Settings charm and then tapping Accounts to get to the Accounts page.

Adding a Hotmail Account

You can add your Hotmail.com, Live.com, or MSN email account to the Mail app.

1. From the Mail app, swipe in from the right side of the screen and tap Settings, or press Winkey+I on your keyboard.

2. Tap Accounts from the Settings pane.

3. Tap Add an Account in the Accounts pane.

4. Tap Hotmail.

5. Enter your username.

6. Enter your Password.

7. Tap Connect.

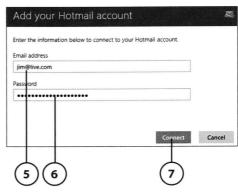

Adding an Outlook Account

Outlook accounts are used for Exchange servers, Office 365 email accounts, and Outlook.com accounts.

1. From the Accounts pane, tap Add an Account.

2. Tap Outlook.

3. Enter your email address.

4. Enter your password.

5. If you are required to enter a server address or domain name information, tap Show More Details.

6. Enter your mail server's address.

7. Enter your domain name.

8. Enter your username.

9. Tap Connect.

10. If your network administrator requires it, your PC might need to be made more secure. If so, tap Enforce These Policies to perform the necessary configuration.

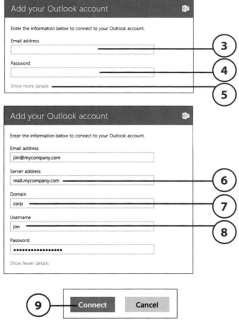

Adding a Google Account

You can add a Google account so that you can read your Gmail in the Mail app.

1. From the Accounts pane, tap Google.

2. Enter your email address.

3. Enter your password.

4. Check the checkbox to include contacts and calendars.

5. Tap Connect.

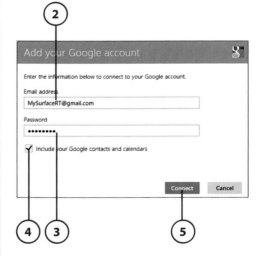

Including Contacts and Calendars

Even if you don't want to synchronize any of your Google contacts or calendars, I recommend that you check the checkbox to do so anyway. You can always turn off synchronization for contacts and calendars if you don't want it activated (I show you how later in this chapter), but if you don't check the box, you must manually add your Google account to the Calendar and People apps later.

Adding a Custom Account

If you have your own domain name and you want to add email for that account, you can do that easily.

1. From the Accounts pane, tap Other Account.

2. Enter your email address.

3. Enter your password.

4. Tap Connect.

5. If Email is unable to successfully configure your account, it will ask for additional information that is usually obtained from your email provider. Enter your username.

6. Enter your incoming mail server address.

7. If your incoming mail server doesn't support SSL, uncheck the SSL box.

8. Change the incoming mail server port number if necessary.

9. Enter the outgoing email server address.

10. If your outgoing server doesn't support SSL, uncheck the SSL box.

11. Change the outgoing mail server port number if necessary.

12. If your outgoing server doesn't require authentication, uncheck the authentication check box.

13. If your outgoing server does use authentication and the username and password are the same as the incoming server's, check the Use the Same Username and Password to Send and Receive Email checkbox.

14. Tap Connect.

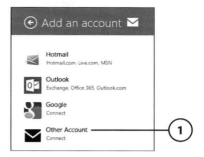

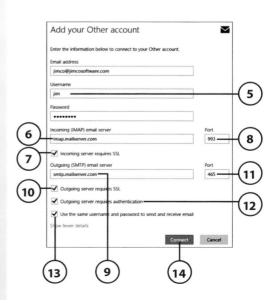

It's Not All Good

IMAP Only

Some email providers only provide what's known as POP email. The Mail app requires that you use IMAP email, and that's not the same as POP. If your email provider doesn't provide IMAP email, you're better off going with a Hotmail or Gmail account. POP is an old method of using email, and IMAP is far superior.

Outgoing Email Port

If you uncheck the box to use SSL for outgoing mail, the Mail app changes the port to 25 automatically. Port 25 is the port typically used for SMTP (outgoing) email, but many Internet providers block that port from being used. If you are using port 25 and you are unable to send email, try changing the outgoing port to port 587.

Setting When and How Much Email Is Downloaded

By default, the Mail app downloads new emails as they arrive on the mail server and downloads all email from the last two weeks. You can modify how often Email downloads email and how much email it retrieves as well.

1. From the Accounts pane, tap an account to change the settings for the account.

2. Tap the Download New Email drop-down and select how often new email should be downloaded from the server.

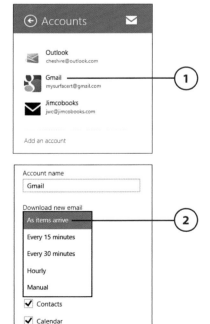

3. Tap the Download Email From drop-down and select how much email you want to download.

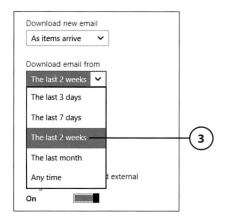

4. Drag the Automatically Download External Images slider to Off if you don't want the Mail app to automatically download images in emails.

Changes Apply Immediately

When you change the settings for an email account, the change is applied immediately. There is no OK button or anything like that. Once you've made the changes you want to make, you can just click outside the Account Settings pane to return to the Mail app.

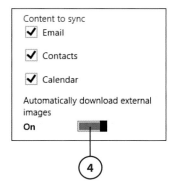

Manually Syncing Email

You can force a manual email sync by swiping up from the bottom of the screen and tapping the Sync button.

Renaming an Account

The Mail app chooses a name for accounts that you add based on the type of account. You can easily change the name to something more descriptive.

1. From the Accounts pane, tap an account to change the settings for the account.

2. Enter a new value for the Account Name.

Choosing What to Sync

You can sync email, contacts, and calendars from accounts that you add in the Mail app. (Note that not all of these are available for every service.) However, you don't have to sync all three of these. You can pick and choose what to sync from each account that you add.

1. From the Accounts pane, tap an account to change the settings for the account.

2. Check Email to sync email from the account.

3. Check Contacts to sync contacts from the account.

4. Check Calendar to sync calendars from the account.

Contacts and Calendars

Contacts are synchronized with the People app and calendars are synchronized with the Calendar app. The People app is covered in Chapter 8. The Calendar app is covered in Chapter 10.

Changing an Account Password

If you're a security-conscious computer user, you will likely want to change your passwords on a regular basis. Once you change your password for an account that you use in the Mail app, you'll need to change the password that the Mail app uses so that you can still synchronize with the account.

1. From the Accounts pane, tap the account you want to change.

2. Scroll to the bottom of the Settings pane and enter your new password.

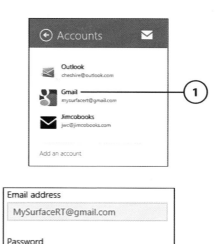

Controlling Account Email Notifications

By default, you won't see notifications when new email arrives in your inbox; however, you can enable notifications if you wish. Each of your email accounts has its own notification setting, so you can decide which accounts you want to see notifications for and which ones you don't.

1. From the Accounts pane, tap the account you want to change.

2. Scroll to the bottom of the Settings pane.

3. Drag the Show Email Notifications for This Account slider to the On position to turn on notifications.

4. Drag the Show Email Notifications for This Account slider to the Off position to turn off notifications for the account.

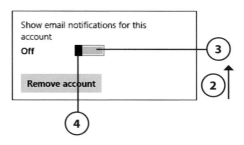

Removing an Account

If you decide you no longer want to synchronize with an account, you can remove the account from the Mail app.

1. From the Accounts pane, tap the account that you would like to remove.

2. Scroll to the bottom of the Settings pane.

3. Tap Remove Account.

Don't Fear Removal

Don't worry about removing an account—you can always add it back again. Because the Mail app uses cloud technology, it's really just a viewer for email that is stored on a server on the Internet. If you remove an account, it simply removes the Mail app's capability to view that account. It doesn't actually delete any email or anything like that.

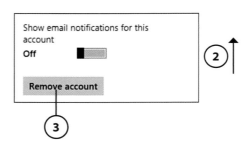

Reading and Organizing Email

The Mail app uses tabs to separate your email accounts. When you tap one of your accounts in the Mail app, you see the folders available for that email account as well as the email messages in the selected folder.

Reading an Email

The Mail app supports HTML emails as well as plain text emails. HTML is the technology used to create websites, and emails created in HTML can contain pictures along with richly formatted text.

1. Tap the desired account.

2. Tap a folder that contains your email.

3. Tap an email from the list to view the email in the reading pane.

Unread Emails

Folders show the number of unread messages in the folder immediately to the right of the folder name. Unread emails in the email list have a bolded subject line.

4. Swipe up and down to scroll in the reading pane.

5. If necessary, you can also swipe right and left to view wider emails.

6. Tap a link in email to launch your web browser and navigate to the link.

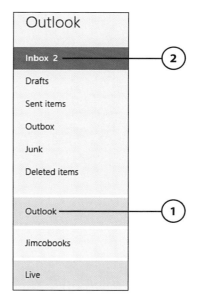

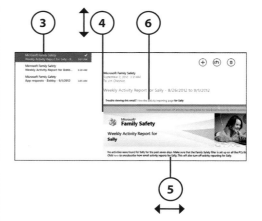

Viewing or Saving Email Attachments

Email attachments must be downloaded to your PC before you can view them.

1. Select an email that includes an attachment. Emails with an attachment display a paperclip icon.

2. Tap the attachment to download it to your PC.

3. When the download has finished, tap the attachment again.

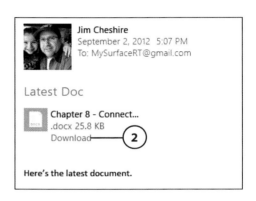

4. Tap Open to open the attachment with the app associated with the file type of the attachment.

5. Tap Open With to open the attachment with a different app.

6. To save the attachment, tap Save.

7. Browse to the location where you want to save the file.

8. Enter a name for the file.

9. Tap Save.

Using SkyDrive for Attachments

As you'll learn later in this chapter, when you send mail with an attachment, you can choose to use SkyDrive for the attached files. If a sender chooses to use SkyDrive, the email actually doesn't include any attachments. Instead, it includes links to the files on the Internet.

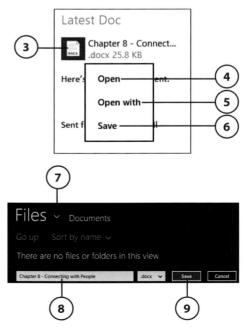

Marking Emails Read or Unread

When you view an email, it is marked as read for you automatically. You can mark one or more emails read or unread in one step without displaying the email.

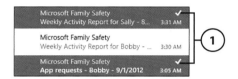

1. Select one or more emails. You can select multiple email messages by swiping left on each message you want to select. (Swiping left on a selected message deselects it.)

2. Swipe up from the bottom of the screen.

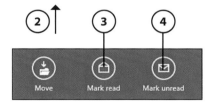

3. Tap Mark Read to mark all selected emails read.

4. Tap Mark Unread to mark all selected emails unread.

Tip

You will see the Mark Read button when one or more emails you've selected are unread. You will see the Mark Unread button when one or more emails you've selected have already been read.

Moving Emails to Another Folder

Most email services enable you to create folders so that you can more easily organize your email messages. You can then use the Mail app to move emails to another folder.

1. Select one or more emails you'd like to move to another folder.

2. Swipe up from the bottom of the screen.

3. Tap Move.

4. Tap the folder where you'd like the email to be moved.

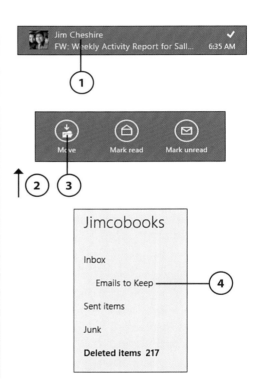

It's Not All Good

Cannot Create Folders in Email

You cannot create new folders from within the Mail app. To create new folders, you must log in to the online account for your email provider and create the folders there. If you are using an email account provided by your Internet service provider, check to see whether they offer web-based access to email using a web browser.

It's Not All Good

No Rules

Many email applications enable you to create rules that run against incoming emails. You can use these rules to move emails that fit certain criteria into folders automatically. The Mail app does not have this functionality, so if you want to move messages into a different folder, you'll have to do so manually.

Deleting Email Messages

You can delete one or more email messages. When you delete emails, they are moved to the Deleted Items folder. If you delete emails from within the Deleted Items folder, they are deleted permanently.

1. Select one or more email messages that you want to delete.

2. Tap the Delete button at the top of the currently selected email message.

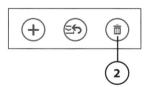

Deleting with the Keyboard

You can also press the Delete key or Ctrl+D on your keyboard to delete email messages.

Undeleting Email Messages

If you've unintentionally deleted one or more mail messages and you'd like to restore them, you must move them out of the Deleted Items folder.

1. Tap the Deleted Items folder.

2. Select one or more email messages to undelete.

3. Swipe up from the bottom of the screen.

4. Tap Move.

5. Select the folder where you'd like the messages moved.

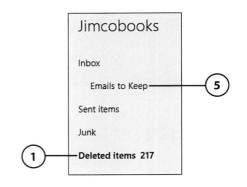

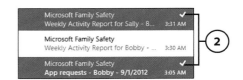

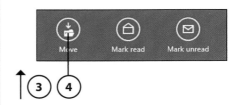

Pinning a Folder to the Start Screen

There is a Mail tile on the Start screen that launches the Mail app. If the Mail app is already running when you tap the Mail tile, it opens to the same folder you were in during your last email session. If the Mail app is not already running, it launches into the inbox of your first email account.

You might want a tile on the Start screen that will open the Mail app and show you the contents of a specific folder immediately. You can do that by pinning the folder to the Start screen. You can do this for any folder in any account.

1. Tap the account that contains the folder you want to pin.

2. Tap the folder that you want to pin to the Start screen.

3. Swipe up from the bottom of the screen.

4. Tap Pin to Start.

5. Change the name that will display on the pinned tile if you wish.

6. Tap Pin to Start.

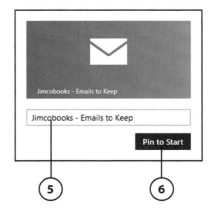

It's Not All Good

Not a Live Tile

The Mail tile on the Start screen is a live tile. However, when you pin a mail folder to the Start screen, it doesn't create a live tile, so you won't see previews of emails displayed on the tile that you pin.

Composing and Sending Email

The Mail app provides tools for basic editing of email messages. You can also attach files to an email and share parts of an email with someone easily.

Creating a New Email Message

You can create a new, blank email message.

1. Tap an account to select the account to be used to send the email.

2. Tap the + button in the upper-right corner of the Mail app.

3. To enter email addresses with the keyboard, tap inside the To or Cc box and start typing. Multiple email addresses should be separated by a semicolon.

Entering Email Addresses

As you enter email addresses, you will see a pop-up of people that are in your contact list. You can choose one from the list by tapping on it.

---

4. To enter email addresses by touch, tap the + button to the right of a textbox and select someone from your contact list.

5. Tap Show More to enter an email address that should be blind copied or to set the priority of the email message.

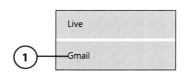

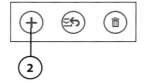

6. Tap and enter a subject for your email.

7. Tap and enter your email message. Note that Email automatically creates hyperlinks as you enter web addresses.

8. Spelling errors are underlined with a red, squiggly line. Tap the word to see a menu of corrections.

9. Tap a correctly spelled word from the list to change the misspelled word.

10. Tap Add to Dictionary to add the word to your dictionary so that it won't be marked as misspelled again.

11. Tap Ignore to ignore the spelling error for this mail message only.

12. Tap Send to send your mail message.

13. Tap Close to close your message and be given the option of saving or deleting the draft you've created.

Drafts

See the section called "Saving Email Drafts," later in this chapter, for details on how you can use email drafts.

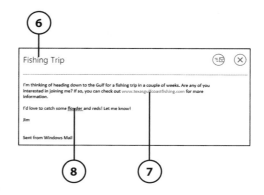

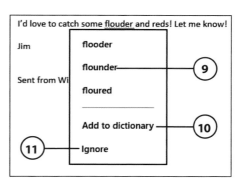

Replying to Email

You can reply to the sender of an email, reply to everyone who received the email, or forward an email to someone else.

1. With the email message selected, tap Respond.

2. Tap Reply to respond only to the sender of the email.

3. Tap Reply All to respond to everyone who received the message, except for those who were blind copied.

4. Tap Forward to forward the email message to someone else.

5. If forwarding a message, enter a recipient's email address. Otherwise, enter email addresses of anyone else whom you'd like to receive the message.

6. If forwarding the message, enter your message text.

7. Tap Send.

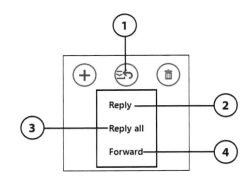

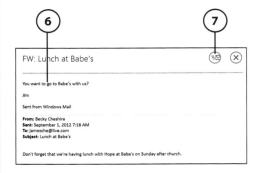

Formatting Text in an Email

You can apply special formatting to text when creating email messages.

1. Select text in your email message to which you'd like to apply formatting.

2. Swipe up from the bottom of the screen.

3. Tap Bold, Italic, or Underline to format the text as you wish.

4. Tap More for more options, such as creating lists.

5. To change the font typeface or size, tap Font.

6. Tap a typeface and size for the selected text.

7. To change text color, tap Text Color.

8. Tap the desired color for the text.

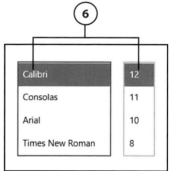

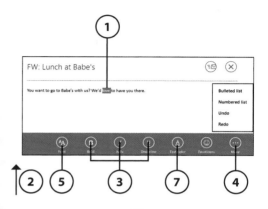

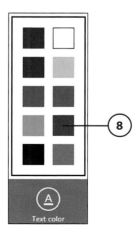

Adding Emoticons to Email

You can add emoticons, such as :), while entering your text. However, the Mail app will not convert these to emoticon images. If you'd prefer to use emoticon images instead, you can.

1. Tap where you'd like the emoticon to be added.

2. Swipe up from the bottom of the screen and tap Emoticons.

3. Tap an emoticon category.

4. Tap the desired emoticon image to insert it.

Identifying Emoticons

If you don't know what an emoticon is, you can tap and hold on it to see a description. If you release your finger while still over the emoticon, it will add that emoticon to your message. If you don't want to add the emoticon to your message, drag your finger off the emoticon before releasing.

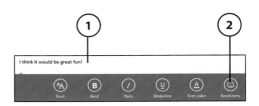

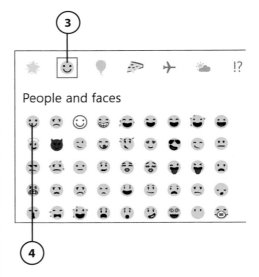

Attaching Files to an Email

You can attach files to an email. When you attach files, you have the option of using SkyDrive if you want. (SkyDrive is free online storage that Microsoft provides with your Microsoft account. For more information on SkyDrive, see Chapter 12, "HomeGroups and SkyDrive.")

1. While composing your mail message, swipe up from the bottom of the screen.

2. Tap Attachments.

3. Navigate to the folder that contains the file or files you'd like to attach.

4. Tap one or more files that you'd like to attach to your message. (If you unintentionally select a file, tap it again to unselect it.)

5. Tap Attach.

6. To send your attachment using SkyDrive, tap Send Using SkyDrive Instead.

7. To revert to sending the file as a non-SkyDrive attachment, tap Send Using Basic Attachments Instead.

Why Use SkyDrive?

When you use SkyDrive for your attachment, the recipient of your email doesn't have to download the attachment unless he or she chooses. Instead, a link to the attachment is provided in the email. The recipient can decide to download the attachment or open the attachment using that link.

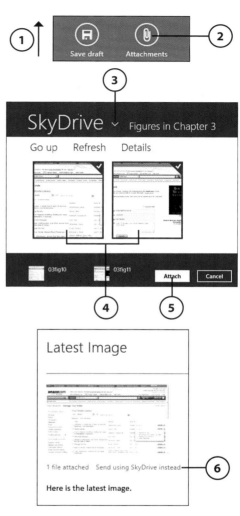

Saving Email Drafts

If you'd like to save an email you are writing so that you can finish it later before sending it, you can save a draft.

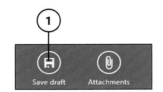

1. To save a draft and continue working on your email now, swipe up from the bottom of the screen and tap Save Draft.

2. To save a draft and close the email message so that you can continue it later, tap Close.

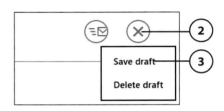

3. Tap Save Draft.

Continuing a Saved Draft

You can continue an email that you saved earlier.

1. Tap the email account that you used when creating the email draft.

2. Tap the Drafts folder.

3. Tap the email draft that you'd like to continue.

4. Tap Edit to continue composing the email.

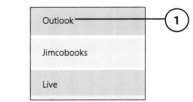

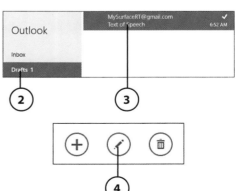

Using an Email Signature

You can enter a signature for your email account that will be automatically added to the end of all your email messages sent from that account.

1. From the Accounts pane, tap the account for which you'd like to use an email signature.

2. Drag the Use an Email Signature to Yes.

3. Enter your desired email signature in the textbox.

Email Signatures

Because email signatures are individually set for each account, you can choose to have a different signature for each of your accounts. You also can use a signature with some accounts and not with others.

Synchronize with
online calendars.

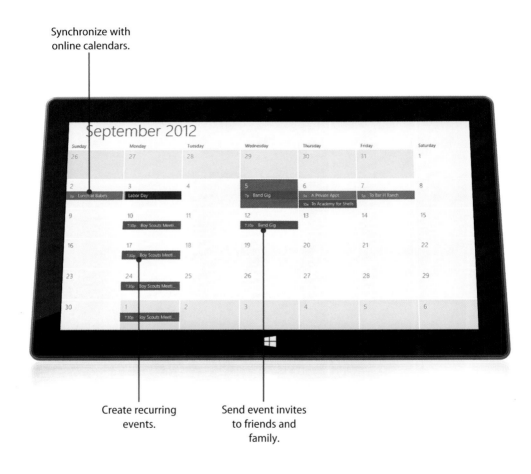

Create recurring
events.

Send event invites
to friends and
family.

Using Calendar

There's nothing new about a calendar on your computer, but there is something new about Calendar on your Surface. As with other apps on your Surface, Calendar is a cloud-enabled app that makes it easy to keep track of multiple calendars in one place.

Connecting Calendars

In my house, we use several calendars. I have a work calendar on my company's Exchange server, my wife keeps a family calendar in Gmail, and I keep my own Windows Live calendar. Fortunately, I don't have to re-create all the appointments in all of these calendars on my Surface. Instead, I simply connect all these calendars to the Calendar app, and all my appointments are immediately available to me.

You can add your Hotmail, Windows Live, MSN, Exchange, Office 365, Outlook.com, or Google calendar to the Calendar app.

Adding a Hotmail Calendar

You can add a calendar from your Hotmail.com, Live.com, or MSN account.

1. From the Settings pane of the Calendar app, tap Accounts.

2. Tap Add an Account.

3. Tap Hotmail.

4. Enter your Hotmail email address.

5. Enter your Hotmail password.

6. Tap Connect.

Microsoft Account Added Automatically

To use the Calendar app, you must enter an email and password for your Microsoft account. The calendar for that account is added automatically to the Calendar app.

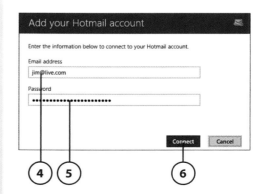

Adding an Outlook Calendar

You can add a calendar from your company's Exchange server, Office 365, or Microsoft's Outlook.com account.

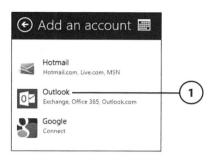

1. From the Add an Account pane (refer to "Adding a Hotmail Calendar"), tap Outlook.

2. Enter your account email address.

3. Enter your account password.

4. If you need to provide additional details such as a mail server address or additional credentials, tap Show More Details.

Outlook Details

You will need to check with your administrator or hosting provider to know what information you need to provide to connect to your Calendar.

5. Enter your email server address.

6. Enter your domain name.

7. Enter your username.

8. Tap Connect.

9. If your company requires it, tap Enforce These Policies to make your PC more secure.

Adding a Google Calendar

You can synchronize your Google calendar with the Calendar app.

1. From the Add an Account pane (refer to "Adding a Hotmail Calendar"), tap Google.

2. Enter your Google email address.

3. Enter your password.

4. Tap Connect.

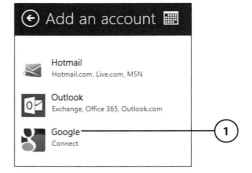

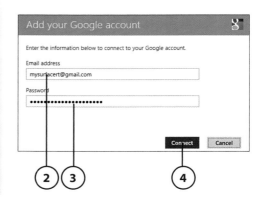

Viewing Calendars

You can choose which calendars to display in Calendar, the color used for each calendar, and which view you'd like to see for your events.

Hiding a Calendar

By default, after you connect a calendar to the Calendar app, events from that calendar are displayed. If you don't want to see events from a particular calendar, you can hide it.

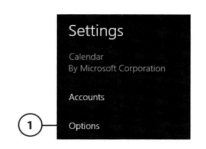

1. From the Settings pane, tap Options.

2. Each of your calendars is listed here. Drag the Show slider for the calendar you want to hide to the left to hide the calendar.

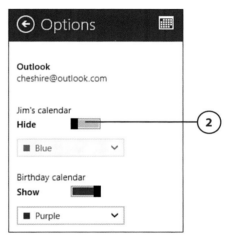

Birthday and Holiday Calendars

Note that the Calendar app automatically displays a birthday calendar and a holiday calendar. The birthday calendar displays an event when one of your contacts has a birthday.

Changing a Calendar's Display Color

The Calendar app chooses a different color for each calendar that you connect. This makes it easy to tell at a glance which calendar contains a specific event. You can customize the color used for each of your calendars.

1. From the Options pane, tap the color drop-down for the calendar you want to change.

2. Tap the desired color for the calendar.

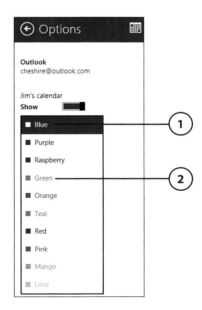

Viewing Events in Month View

By default, Calendar displays events in Month view. From this view, you can see an entire month of events in a single view.

1. If you're not already in Month view, swipe up from the bottom of the screen and tap Month to switch to Month view.

2. Swipe right to see previous months.

3. Swipe left to see future months.

4. Tap an event to see additional details on the event.

5. To quickly return to the current month, swipe up from the bottom of the screen and tap Today.

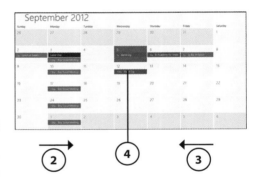

Viewing Events in Week View

Week view is helpful when you want to see an entire week of events on a single screen. In Week view, each column represents a single day and each row represents a 1-hour time slot. Therefore, Week view is a good way to get an idea of how long each event lasts at a glance.

1. Swipe up from the bottom of the screen and tap Week.

2. Drag up or down to see additional time slots.

3. Drag left and right to see additional days.

4. Swipe right to see previous weeks.

5. Swipe left to see future weeks.

6. Tap an event to see more details of the event.

7. To return to the current week, swipe up from the bottom of the screen and tap Today.

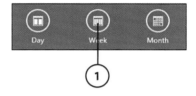

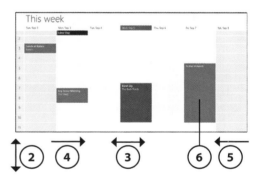

Viewing Events in Day View

Day view enables you to see two days of events side by side. Each day can be scrolled individually so that you can view the events you're most interested in.

1. Swipe up from the bottom of the screen and tap Day.

2. Drag up or down on a particular day to view more times for that day. (Each day can be vertically scrolled independently.)

3. Swipe right to see previous days.

4. Swipe left to see future days.

5. Tap an event to see more details of the event.

6. To return to the current day, swipe up from the bottom of the screen and tap Today.

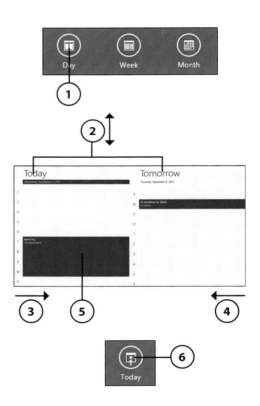

Working with Events

Events in Calendar are automatically synchronized from your online calendars. If you add or modify an event on your smartphone or another computer, Calendar reflects that change automatically. Additionally, events you create or modify in Calendar synchronize with your other devices.

Adding a Basic Event

A basic event is one without any recurrences and uses the default reminder time and other options.

1. In the Calendar app, swipe up from the bottom of the screen and tap New.

2. Tap the When drop-downs and select a month, day, and year for the event.

3. Tap the Start drop-downs and select a start time for the event.

4. Tap the How Long drop-down and select a duration for the event, or select Custom to specify your own start and end times.

5. Enter a location for the event in the Where textbox if applicable.

6. Tap the Calendar drop-down and select the calendar account in which you'd like the event created.

7. Enter a title for the event.

8. Enter a message for the event if desired.

9. Tap Save to save the event.

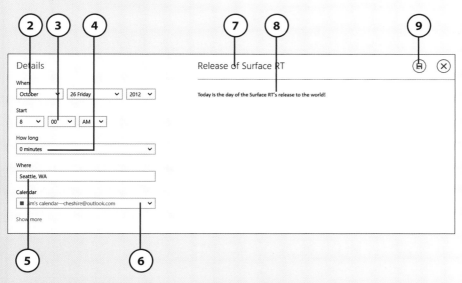

Quickly Create an Event

You can quickly create an event for a specific date and time by tapping on the desired time for the event. When you do, a new event opens with the date and time fields pre-populated based on where you tapped.

Adding a Recurring Event

You can create an event that recurs at a regular interval.

1. While creating your event, tap Show More.

2. Tap the How Often drop-down and select how often the event will occur.

3. Tap Save to save the event.

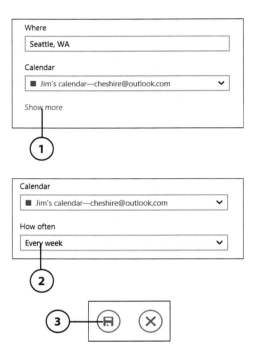

Setting Reminders

Windows RT pops up event reminders in the upper-right corner of your screen. By default, you will be reminded of events 15 minutes prior to the start time, but you can choose a different reminder time or choose not to be reminded.

1. While creating your event, tap Show More.

2. Tap the Reminder drop-down and choose a time to be reminded or None to disable the reminder.

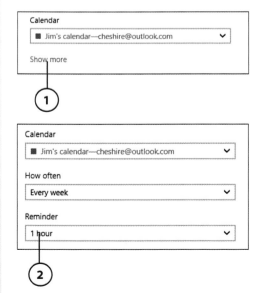

Specifying an Event Status

You can specify a status for your event of Free, Busy, Tentative, Out of Office, or Working Elsewhere. Calendar displays a unique colored left edge for the event based on the status you select. Free displays a light-colored edge, Busy displays no colored edge, Tentative displays a hashed edge of alternating colors, and Out of Office and Working Elsewhere both display a dark-colored edge.

1. While creating an event, tap Show More.

2. Tap the Status drop-down and select a status.

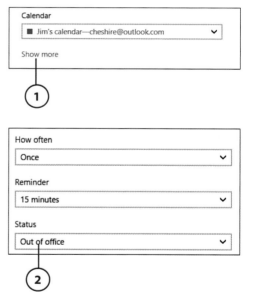

Inviting Others to an Event

You can invite others to an event. People that you invite are sent an invite as an iCalendar file. Because iCalendar is practically a universal standard, the recipient should be able to add it to his or her calendar, regardless of what calendar program or service is used.

1. While creating your event, tap Show More.

2. Scroll to the Who field and add the email address of the people whom you'd like to invite. Separate multiple email addresses with semicolons.

3. To invite someone from your contact list, tap the + button and select the contact to invite.

4. Tap Send to save and send the invite to the recipients you entered.

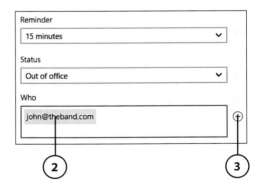

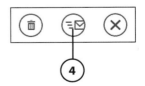

Creating a Private Event

You might want to create an event that only you can see. You can do that by marking an event as private. When you do, the event is actually created only as a local event on the device you are using. You (or others) will not be able to see the event on other devices that synchronize with your calendar.

1. While creating your event, tap Show More.

2. Tap the Private checkbox to check it.

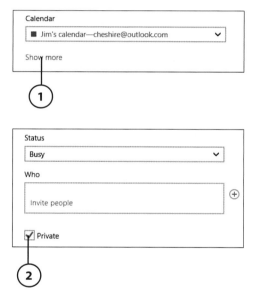

Editing an Event

If you'd like to make a change to an event, you can edit it and then resave it.

1. Tap the event you'd like to edit.

2. Make any changes you'd like to make.

3. Tap Save to save the edited event.

Save or Send

If the event you are editing includes invites to others, you will tap Send to save the edited event and send the changed event to those with whom you've shared the event.

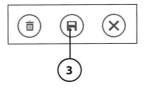

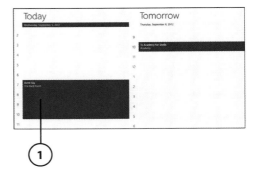

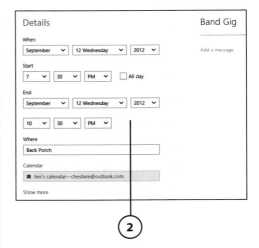

Deleting an Event

If an event has been canceled, you can
delete it from your calendar.

1. Tap the event you'd like to delete.

2. Tap Delete to delete the event.

3. If the event has invitees, tap Send
to send the cancellation or Don't
Send to cancel the event without
sending a notification to those
who were invited.

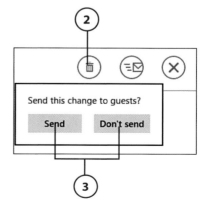

Add your own
sources based on
Internet searches.

Get news
from sources
you choose.

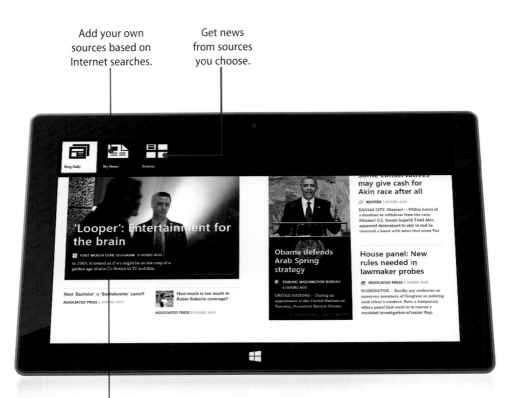

Read the latest news.

Keeping Up to Date with News

It's becoming more common for people to turn to computers instead of newspapers, radio, and television to keep up with the news. Using the News app on your Surface, you can keep track of news and read Internet articles that interest you in an attractive interface optimized for a tablet.

Reading the News

The News app keeps track of news from sources such as the Associated Press, Reuters, and various other online news sources. Articles are categorized for easy browsing and you can pin a particular category to the Start screen for instant access. When you start the News app, you'll see Bing Daily, a synopsis of news from all of these sources. However, as I show you later in this chapter, you also can add other news sources and even add your own sources.

Reading an Article

Bing Daily provides a convenient one-stop way to get up-to-date on all the latest news. You can read top news stories and you can also read stories from several different categories of news.

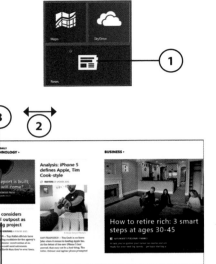

1. From the Start screen, tap the News tile to launch the News app.

2. Swipe to see more categories.

3. Tap a category name to see all news stories in that category.

4. Tap a news story to read the entire story.

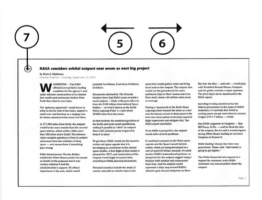

5. Swipe left to move to the next page in an article.

6. Swipe right to move to the previous page.

7. Tap Back to return to the previous screen.

8. Swipe down from the top of the screen or up from the bottom of the screen, and tap Next Article to go to the next article.

9. Tap Previous Article to go to the previous article.

10. Tap Bing Daily to return to the Bing Daily home screen.

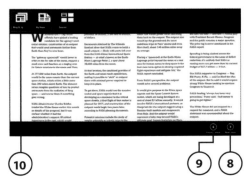

Pin a Section to the Start Screen

If you'd like a way to quickly return to a particular section in Bing Daily, you can pin it to your Start screen. You can then return to that section by tapping its tile on your Start screen.

1. While viewing Bing Daily, tap the section you want to pin to your Start screen.

2. Swipe up from the bottom of the screen.

3. Tap Pin to Start.

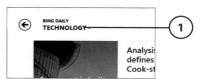

Viewing an Article in a Browser

In some cases, you might want to open an article you are reading in your web browser. You might want to do this because you want to set a bookmark in your browser. You also might want to take advantage of a feature (tabs, for example) that is only available in your browser. You can easily open an article in your browser.

1. Tap an article you are interested in reading.

2. Swipe up from the bottom of the screen and tap View in Browser.

Clearing Your Viewing History

The News app keeps track of the news sources that you use and displays your recently viewed sources in the Most Visited section of the Sources screen. You can clear this history list if you want to start fresh.

Devices

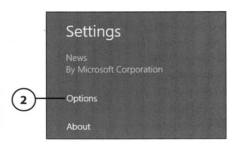

Settings

1. While in the News app, swipe in from the right edge of the screen and tap Settings.

2. Tap Options.

3. Tap Clear History to clear your history.

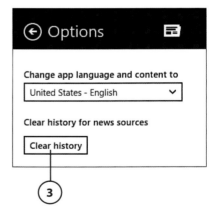

Other News Sources

Reading Bing Daily is a great way to get caught up on the latest news from the AP, Reuters, and other mainstream news organizations, but if you have an interest in reading information from other sources, you can access those as well. The News app provides news sources for entertainment, tech, science, sports, and much more.

Reading News from Other Sources

No matter what your interests are, you are sure to find something you'll want to read in the News app's news sources. Many times, articles will open directly from a source's website, but even so, the reading experience is better in the News app than it is in a web browser.

1. From the News app, swipe up from the top or bottom of the screen and tap Sources.

2. Swipe left or right to locate a news source that you'd like to read.

3. Tap a source to list articles from that source.

4. Scroll left and right to locate an article you're interested in reading.

5. Tap an article to open it.

6. Drag to position the article on the screen for easier reading.

7. Reverse-pinch to zoom in on the article.

8. Pinch to zoom out on the article.

9. Tap Back to return to the list of articles.

10. Tap Back to return to the list of news sources.

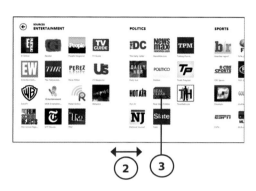

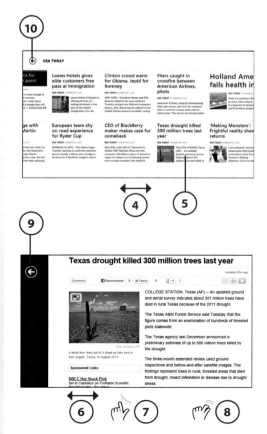

Pinning a News Source to the Start Screen

If you find that a news source is particularly interesting to you, you can pin it to the Start screen so that you can access it with a single tap.

1. While viewing the list of articles for a news source, swipe up from the bottom of the screen and tap Pin to Start.

2. Edit the name for the pinned tile if you wish.

3. Tap Pin to Start.

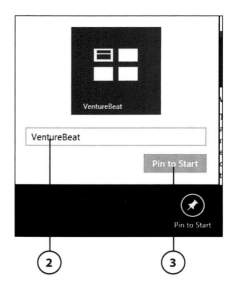

Searching for News

If you are interested in a particular news topic that might span across multiple news sources, you can easily view articles on that topic on one screen by searching for news.

1. While in the News app, swipe in from the right side of the screen and tap Search.

2. Enter a search term.

3. Tap the Search icon to search for your term.

4. Drag left and right to locate an article you'd like to read.

5. Tap an article to read the article.

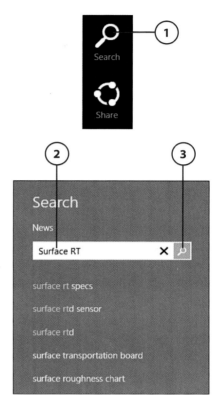

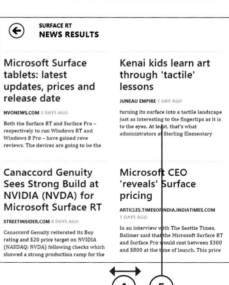

Custom News

Searching for news is a good way to find information on a topic of interest, but each time you want to see the latest news on your topic, you must conduct a search again. That's not the most convenient way to check up on a topic of interest. To make things easier, you can use My News to create a custom news source.

Adding a My News Source

News sources in My News are based on search results for the search term that you specify. For example, if you want all the latest news on Taylor guitars, you can enter **Taylor guitar** as your search term and create a custom news source that contains all the latest on Taylor guitars.

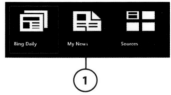

Microsoft News
Microsoft includes a My News source for Microsoft by default.

1. While in the News app, swipe down from the top of the screen and tap My News.

2. Tap the Add a Section box.

3. Enter your search term. (The News app refers to this as a section name.)

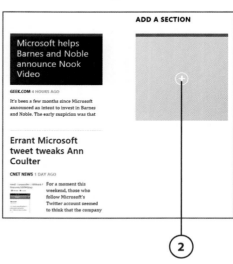

Suggested Terms
The News app displays suggested terms as you enter the name for your new section. You can tap one of those suggestions to select it if you want.

4. Tap Add.

A Faster Way
From the My News screen, you can swipe up from the bottom of the screen and tap Add Section to quickly add a My News section.

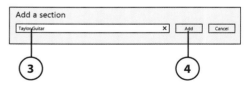

Removing a My News Source

If you decide that you're no longer interested in a particular My News source, you can remove it from the My News screen.

1. While in the My News screen, tap the source you want to remove.

2. Swipe up from the bottom of the screen and tap Remove Section.

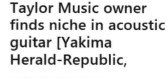

Sharing News

While reading the news, you will certainly find something that you want to share with someone. As with other apps in Windows RT, the News app enables you to use the Share charm to easily share news with others.

Emailing a News Article

You can send a thumbnail picture and synopsis text of an article to an email contact, along with a link to the full article.

1. While viewing an article that you want to share, swipe in the right edge of the screen and tap Share.

2. Tap Mail.

3. Enter the email address of the person with whom you want to share the article.

4. Enter a message if you'd like.

5. Tap Send to share the article.

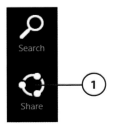

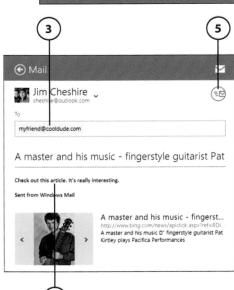

Sharing an Article on Facebook

If you want to share an article with your Facebook friends, you can easily do that without leaving the News app.

Facebook Connection

To share on Facebook, you first must configure a connection with Facebook in the People app. For more details on that, see "Working with Contacts" in Chapter 8.

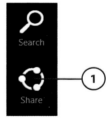

1. While viewing the article that you want to share, swipe in from the right side of the screen and tap Share.

2. Tap People.

3. Enter a message to share on Facebook.

4. Tap Send to post to Facebook.

View your files in the
cloud with SkyDrive
and networked files
with HomeGroup.

Download files from the
cloud to your local PC.

Upload your files
to the cloud.

HomeGroups and SkyDrive

As you might have realized by now, a big component of the Surface (and Windows 8 devices in general) is the capability to share files and content with friends and family. Both HomeGroups and SkyDrive make that possible, but in different ways. HomeGroups enable you to see files that others have shared on your home network. SkyDrive enables you to share files with anyone who has Internet access, and you can use SkyDrive to share files between all of your devices as well.

Using HomeGroups

Using HomeGroups is a convenient way to share files with others on your network. You can create a HomeGroup on a Windows 7 or Windows 8 PC. You then choose what you want to share on the HomeGroup. When that basic setup is complete, you can join the HomeGroup from your Surface and you'll be able to see any files that have been shared.

Creating HomeGroups

You will need Windows 7 Home Premium, Windows 7 Ultimate, or Windows 8 to create a HomeGroup. You cannot create a HomeGroup on your Surface or any other Windows RT device.

I won't go into how you create a HomeGroup in this book, but you can find that information at http://windows.microsoft.com/en-US/windows7/Create-a-homegroup.

Joining a HomeGroup

To see the files in a HomeGroup, you first must join the HomeGroup on your Surface.

1. From the Start screen, swipe in from the right side of the screen and tap Settings.

2. Tap Change PC Settings.

3. Tap HomeGroup.

4. Enter the password to join the HomeGroup.

HomeGroup Passwords

The password that's already in the text-box should be correct. However, if you need the password, the person who created a HomeGroup can find out the password from the HomeGroup settings screen on his or her PC.

5. Tap Join.

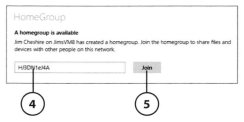

Leaving a HomeGroup

If you no longer want to be a member of a HomeGroup, you can leave it. When you do, you will no longer be able to see files shared on that HomeGroup.

1. From the PC Settings screen, tap HomeGroup.

2. Tap the Leave button.

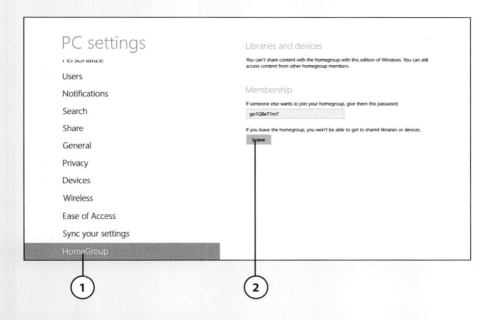

Changing Your Mind

If you change your mind, you can always rejoin a HomeGroup at any time.

Accessing Shared Files

You can access files that are shared in your HomeGroup from any app that enables you to browse for files. For example, you can open a Word document shared on your HomeGroup, or you can open a picture shared on your HomeGroup. You also can save files back to shared folders on your HomeGroup.

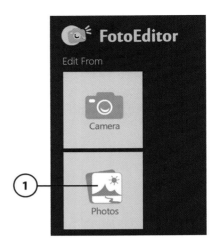

Ensuring That Files Are Available

For you to access a file on your HomeGroup, the computer where the file is saved must be powered on. If it's not, you'll be able to see the computer when browsing for files, but Windows RT won't be able to connect to it.

In this step-by-step, I use a free app called FotoEditor (available from the Windows Store) to open a picture that is shared on my HomeGroup. The steps used are essentially the same in any app.

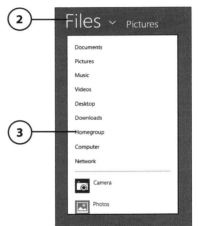

1. Within FotoEditor, tap Photos to browse for a photo to edit.

2. Tap the Files drop-down.

3. Tap Homegroup.

4. Tap the HomeGroup owner's name.

5. Tap the name of the computer where the file is located.

6. Tap the folder that contains the file.

7. Tap the file to select it.

8. Tap Open.

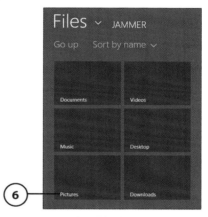

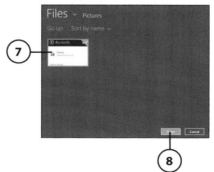

Using SkyDrive

SkyDrive is Microsoft's cloud storage service. By signing up for a Microsoft account, you get 7GB of SkyDrive storage free. You can purchase additional storage for a small fee from SkyDrive.live.com.

Microsoft Account Required

These steps require a Microsoft account to be used. For more information on using a Microsoft account, see Chapter 2, "Connecting to Networks and Your Microsoft Account."

In Chapter 9, you saw how you can send file attachments in email using SkyDrive. In this chapter, you learn how you can use SkyDrive in many more ways.

Browsing Files in SkyDrive

You can access your files in SkyDrive using the SkyDrive app included with Windows RT.

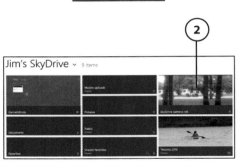

1. From the Start screen, tap the SkyDrive tile to launch the SkyDrive app.

Connect Your Microsoft Account

If you are using a local account, the first time you launch the SkyDrive app, you'll be asked to log in with a Microsoft account to access SkyDrive.

2. Tap a folder to open it.

3. Tap a file to open it.

4. Tap Back to go back to the previous view.

5. Swipe up from the bottom of the screen and tap Details to change to details view.

6. Tap Thumbnails to switch back to thumbnail view.

7. Tap Refresh to refresh the view.

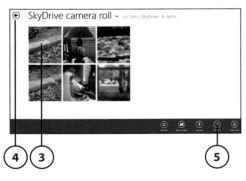

Opening Files with a Specific App

If you have more than one app installed that can open a particular file, you can, from SkyDrive, open a file using the app of your choice.

1. In SkyDrive, swipe down on a file to select it.

2. Tap Open With.

3. Check the box if you always want to open files of this type using the app you select.

4. Tap More Options to see more apps that you can use.

5. Tap an app to open the file using that app.

6. Tap Look for an App in the Store to open the Windows Store and locate an app to use to open your file.

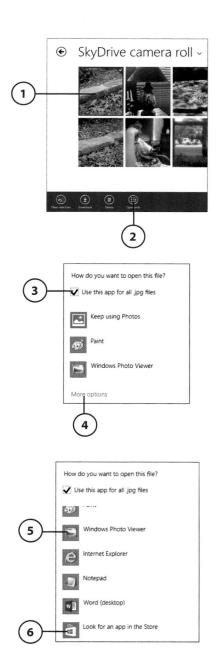

Creating a New Folder

You can create new folders in SkyDrive from the SkyDrive app. Folders enable you to better organize your SkyDrive content.

1. Navigate to the folder where you want the new folder created.
2. Swipe up from the bottom of the screen and tap New Folder.
3. Enter a name for your new folder.
4. Tap Create Folder.

Uploading Files to SkyDrive

You can upload files to SkyDrive from within the SkyDrive app, making it easy to share your files with other people or back up your files to the cloud.

1. Navigate to the folder into which you want to upload your files.
2. Swipe up from the bottom of the screen and tap Upload.
3. Navigate to the folder containing the files you want to upload.
4. Tap each file you want to upload.
5. Tap Select All to select all files in the folder.

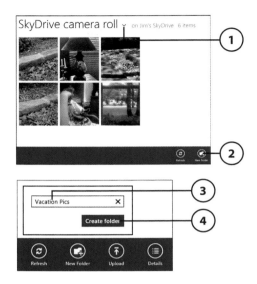

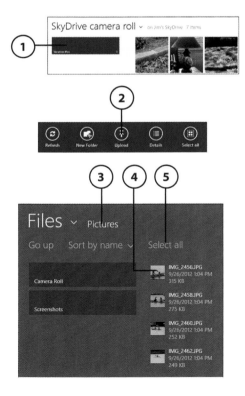

Select from Multiple Folders

You can select files in one folder and then navigate to another folder and select files in that folder without your previously selected files being deselected. This makes it easy to upload files from multiple folders at one time.

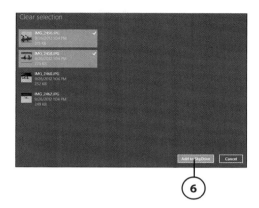

6. Tap Add to SkyDrive to upload your files.

Downloading Files from SkyDrive

If you'd like to download files from SkyDrive and save them onto your Surface, you can easily do so. This is particularly useful if you are going to be away from Internet connectivity for some reason and you need access to some of your files.

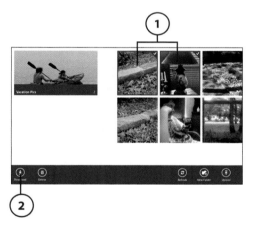

1. Swipe down on the file or files that you want to download.

2. Tap Download.

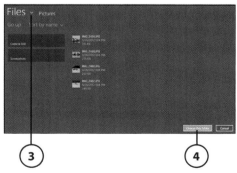

3. Navigate to the folder into which you want the files saved on your Surface.

4. Tap Choose this Folder.

5. Tap OK.

It's Not All Good

You Can Select from Only One Folder

Unlike when uploading files, when you are downloading files, you can select files from only one folder. If you select files and then move to a different folder, your selected files are automatically deselected.

Deleting Files from SkyDrive

You can delete files from your SkyDrive to free up disk space or clear up clutter from files that you no longer need. You also can delete an entire folder and the files within that folder in one step.

1. Swipe down on one or more files or folders to select them.

2. Tap Delete.

3. Tap Delete to confirm the deletion.

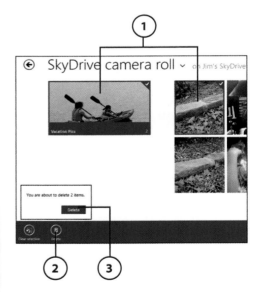

Reviewing SkyDrive Usage

As I said previously, Microsoft provides 7GB of SkyDrive storage at no charge. That's quite a lot of free storage, but if you copy a lot of pictures, music, or video into your SkyDrive folders, you might find that you need additional storage. Keeping track of your SkyDrive use is simple.

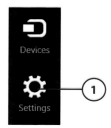

1. From the SkyDrive app, swipe in from the right side of the screen and tap Settings.

2. From the Settings pane, tap Options.

3. Here you can see how much space you have available out of your total storage allotment. If you are close to running out of storage and can't free up space by deleting files, tap Manage Storage to open the SkyDrive site in a web browser where you can buy additional storage.

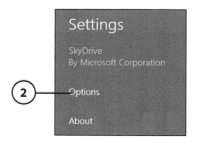

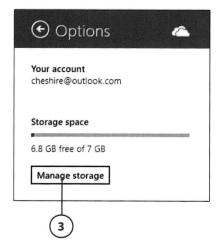

Play music in your library,
or use an Xbox Music Pass.

Explore and buy music from
the Xbox Music Store.

Use playlists to play
the music you want
to hear.

Discovering and Playing Music

Your Surface comes with Office 2013 so that you can get real work done, but it also comes with apps and features that let you play. You can discover music, listen to an astounding number of songs using Xbox Music Pass, and watch movies and TV shows, all from the comfort of your favorite relaxation place.

This chapter covers the Music app. In Chapter 14, "Watching Video," I show you how you can watch television and movies in the Video app.

Browsing Music

The Music app is your window into Xbox Music, Microsoft's online music service. When you first launch the app, you'll see several sections that enable you to explore music and find something that you might like to hear. You can buy music, download music, and explore artists.

Logging In to Xbox Music

It's a good idea to log in to Xbox Music when you first launch the Music app. This enables you to keep track of what music you've listened to, buy music, download music on your Xbox Music Pass (more on that later in this chapter), and more.

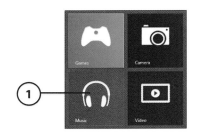

1. From the Start screen, tap the Music tile to launch the Music app.

2. Tap Sign In.

3. If necessary, accept the terms of use for Xbox Live by tapping I Accept.

Exploring an Artist

The Music app is an excellent way to explore a particular artist, listen to some of the artist's music, read about the artist, and see all the albums released by the artist.

Xbox Music Pass

These steps show you what you'll experience without an Xbox Music Pass. I show you the enhanced experience available with an Xbox Music Pass in the "Using an Xbox Music Pass" section, later in this chapter.

1. Tap an artist's tile.

Artist Tiles

Most of the tiles in the Xbox Music Store section of the Music app are actually album tiles and not artist tiles. Artist tiles show an artist's name in the Now Playing section or are labeled Artist in the Most Popular section.

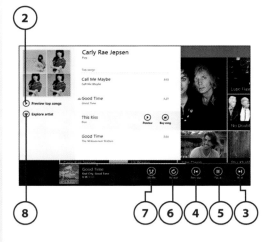

2. Tap Preview Top Songs to hear a 30-second preview of the artist's top songs.

3. Swipe up from the bottom of the screen and tap Next to hear a preview of the next top song in the list.

4. Tap Previous to hear a preview of the previous top song.

5. Tap Pause to pause playback.

6. Tap Repeat to repeat the current song preview.

7. Tap Shuffle to play the song previews in a random order.

8. Tap Explore Artist to see more information on the artist.

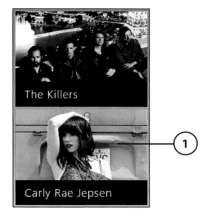

9. Tap Show Song List to see a list of the artist's top songs.

10. Tap Discography to see a list of the artist's albums.

11. Tap an album to see details of the album.

12. Tap View More to see a complete album list for the artist.

13. Tap Back to return to the Music app's home screen.

Tip

After you tap View More, you'll need to tap the X in the upper-right or tap Back before you can do anything else. The same applies if you tap View More to see an artist's bio.

Exploring the Xbox Music Store

The Xbox Music Store offers a huge assortment of music that you can explore. Exploring the Xbox Music Store is the best way to browse music that fits a particular category.

1. Tap Xbox Music Store to enter the store.

2. Featured albums are displayed by default. Tap Featured and choose New Releases or Popular to see additional items.

3. Drag up and down to see additional albums.

4. Tap an album to see details of the album.

5. Tap a track, or tap Preview to hear song previews.

6. Tap Explore Artist to explore more information about the artist.

7. Tap away from the album details to return to the list of albums.

Buying Music

I'm intentionally not showing you how to buy an album at this point. I go into details on how you can buy music in the next section, "Managing Your Music Library."

8. Tap a category of music to see a list of subcategories.

9. Tap a subcategory to see a list of albums in that category.

Searching for Music

You can search the Xbox Music Store if you're looking for a particular album, song, or artist.

1. From anywhere in the Music app, swipe in from the right side of the screen and tap Search.

2. Enter an artist, song, or album name.

3. Tap an item from the search results to go directly to that item.

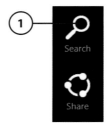

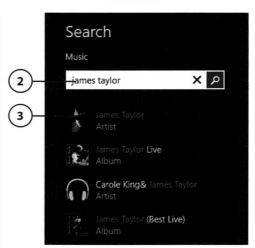

Managing Your Music Library

You probably have some digital music stored on another computer in your house or on an external hard drive or other device. You can add that music to your Music library on your Surface and it will appear in the Music app. You also can purchase music from the Xbox Music Store to add music to your library. Finally, if you have an Xbox Music Pass, you can download many songs in the Xbox Music Store to your library. (I cover using an Xbox Music Pass in the next section.)

Adding a Network Location to My Music

One way to add music to your music library is by adding a network folder to your Music library. This method has the benefit of not using any additional memory on your Surface.

1. From the Start screen, tap the Desktop tile.

2. Tap the File Explorer icon on the Windows taskbar.

3. Tap Music in the Libraries list.

4. Tap Manage to manage your Music library.

5. Tap Manage Library.

6. Tap Add to add a new location to your Music library.

7. Browse to the location where your music is located on the network or on your HomeGroup.

HomeGroups

If you'd like information on joining a HomeGroup and accessing files on a HomeGroup, see Chapter 12, "HomeGroups and SkyDrive."

8. Tap Include Folder to include the folder in your Music library.

9. Tap OK to add the folder.

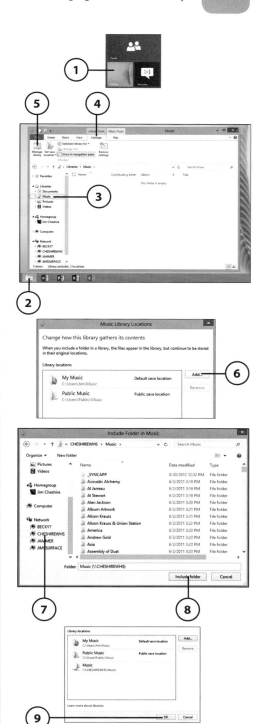

>>>Go Further

NETWORK FOLDERS

As I pointed out earlier, adding a network location to your Music library has the benefit of not using any of the memory on your Surface. However, there is a disadvantage to using this method: You must be on your network to access your music. It also requires the computer where the music files reside to be turned on for you to access the music files there.

If you have a large music collection, you might be better off using a microSD memory card for your music so that it's available no matter where you take your Surface.

Purchasing Music

There are many online purchasing options for music these days, but if you plan on listening to your music on your Surface, buying it from the Xbox Music Store is a great choice because it will be automatically added to My Music on your Surface.

Music Pass

These steps assume you do not have an Xbox Music Pass.

1. Use Search, from Xbox Music, or browse to an album.

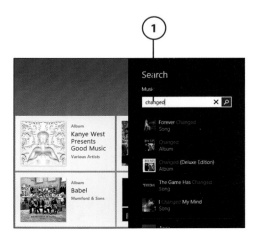

2. Tap Buy Album to purchase an album.

3. Tap a song, and tap Buy Song to purchase a song.

4. Enter the password for your Microsoft account, if prompted.

5. Tap Confirm to complete your purchase and add the purchased music to your library.

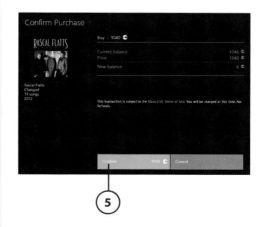

>>>Go Further

SHARING MUSIC

You can't share music that you add to My Music on your Surface. Even if you join a HomeGroup on your Surface, you cannot share your content with other members of the HomeGroup. If you want to use music from your Surface on another computer, you'll have to move the music to that computer using a USB key or a microSD memory card, or by moving it over the network using Windows Explorer.

If you want to move the files using File Explorer, you can find information on doing so using the Help system included with Windows RT.

Deleting Music from Your Library

You can delete music from your music library. Be careful when doing so because unless the music is backed up somewhere, deleting it from your Surface deletes it permanently. Music that you delete from within the Music app does not get moved to the Windows Recycle Bin.

Purchased Music

If you delete music that you originally purchased from the Xbox Music Store, you can download that music again from within the Music app.

1. From within the Music app, tap My Music.

It's Not All Good

Deleting Is Permanent

I've already said this, but it's worth repeating because I don't want you to miss it. If you delete music from the Music app, it deletes the music permanently. Make absolutely sure that you want to delete a music file before you do so.

2. Tap an album or a song to select it.

3. Swipe up from the bottom of the screen and tap Delete.

4. Tap Delete to confirm the deletion.

Requiring a Password for Purchases

By default, the Music app requires you to enter your Microsoft account password when making purchases. If you choose, you can configure the Music app so that a password isn't required.

1. From the Music app, swipe in from the right of the screen and tap Settings.

2. Tap Preferences.

3. Tap Ask Me to Sign In Before Completing Purchases or Managing My Account to change the setting to Off.

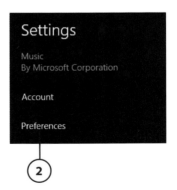

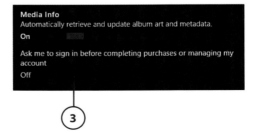

Making My Music the Default View

If you'd prefer to see your own music instead of the Xbox Music Store content when you launch the Music app, you can change the default view to My Music.

1. From the Music app Settings screen, tap Preferences.

2. Tap Open My Music When I Start the App to change the setting to On.

3. After launching the Music app, you can tap Home to see the Xbox Music Store content.

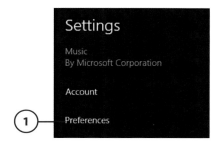

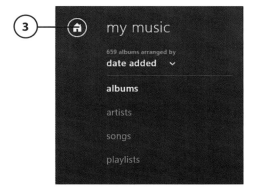

Using an Xbox Music Pass

An Xbox Music Pass is Microsoft's music subscription service. For $10 a month (or $99.90 for a year), you can stream or download a large number of songs from the Xbox Music Store. You can also play them on your Xbox 360.

In this section, I show you how to sign up for an Xbox Music Pass and how you can add Xbox Music Pass music to your library by downloading it. In the section that follows, I explain how you can play Xbox Music Pass music along with other music in your library.

It's Not All Good

No Holy Grail Here

Although it certainly is nice to have an Xbox Music Pass, it's not the Holy Grail for music lovers. There are limitations.

Not all artists and/or record labels allow their music to be played using an Xbox Music Pass; therefore, some songs and albums won't be available. Even worse, record labels can pull songs from Xbox Music Pass whenever they choose, and if they do, you will no longer be able to stream those songs. If you've downloaded a song or album and the record label pulls it, that song or album will simply disappear from your library. There one day; gone the next. This has happened to me on numerous occasions.

Finally, only Microsoft devices support Xbox Music Pass. Therefore, you can only play Xbox Music Pass music on your PC, an Xbox 360, or a Windows Phone. If you own a different phone and you want to listen to your music while on the go, you must purchase the music.

Xbox Music Pass is still a great feature, and it's one that distinguishes Microsoft's music store from anyone else's. Microsoft will allow you to use the service free for 30 days, so it's worth trying out.

Purchasing an Xbox Music Pass

You can purchase an Xbox Music Pass directly from your Surface. (You can also sign up for a trial of the Xbox Music Pass service.)

1. While using the Music app, swipe in from the right side of the screen and tap on Settings.

2. Tap Account.

3. Tap Xbox Music Pass.

4. Tap the plan you want to use.

5. Tap Next.

Billing Information

If you have not already provided your billing information for your Microsoft account, you are required to enter your billing name, address, and phone number at this point.

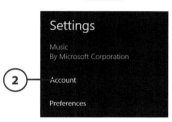

6. Select a credit card for payment, or tap Add a New Credit Card to add a credit card to your account.

7. Tap Confirm Purchase to complete your Xbox Music Pass purchase.

Automatic Renewal

Your Xbox Music Pass automatically renews, so if you signed up for the trial and you don't want to continue using the service when your trial expires, be sure you cancel your subscription before your trial ends.

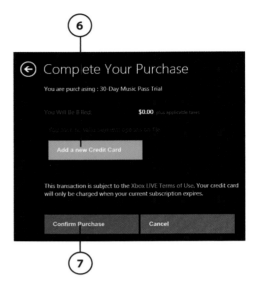

Downloading Xbox Music Pass Music

You can download Xbox Music Pass music to your Surface so that you can play it even when you're not connected to the Internet.

1. Browse or search to locate an album or song.

2. Tap Add to My Music under the album art to download the entire album.

3. Tap a song, and tap Add to My Music to download only the song.

Playing Music on Your PC and Xbox 360

You can play any of the music in your library on your Surface. If you have an Xbox Music Pass subscription, you can play Music Pass music on your Xbox 360 using what Microsoft calls PlayTo.

Playing Music

You can play music through the speakers on your Surface. You also can play music through a speaker dock, an external speaker or headphone plugged in to your Surface, or through a Bluetooth speaker system.

1. From the Music app home screen, tap a tile or tap My Music to see all of your music.

2. Tap Albums to see all albums.

3. Tap Artists to see all artists.

4. Tap Songs to see all songs.

5. Tap Playlists to see all playlists.

Playlists

For information on using playlists, see "Music Playlists," later in this chapter.

6. Tap the sort drop-down to choose how albums, songs, or playlists are sorted.

7. Tap Play All Music to play all your music.

8. To play an album, tap the album and tap Play Album.

9. To play a song, tap the song, and then tap Play.

10. To pause playback, swipe up from the bottom of the screen and tap Pause.

11. To resume playback, tap Play.

12. To move to the next song, tap Next.

13. To move to the previous song, tap Previous.

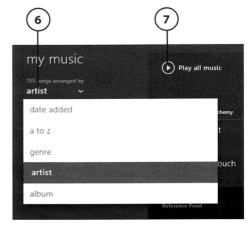

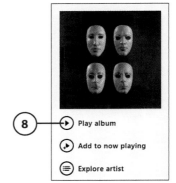

14. To see the properties of a song (such as the release year, the length, track number, and so forth), swipe up after tapping the song and tap Properties.

Shortcut to Playback Controls

If you press the volume control on your Surface, you can access the playback controls from within any app. You can even access them from the Desktop while using a desktop app.

Playing Music on an Xbox 360

You can play Xbox Music Pass music on your Xbox 360 and use your Surface as a remote for the music. This is a cool way to control your music from a portable device while enjoying the high-fidelity sound quality of your entertainment system.

SmartGlass Is Required

Before you go through these steps, you'll need to install Xbox SmartGlass from the Windows Store. It's a free app that enables you to play music from your Surface on your Xbox 360. It also provides other interactivity between your tablet and your Xbox.

Keep in mind that even though it might look like you're in the Music app while you are playing music on your Xbox 360, you're actually in the SmartGlass app.

1. In the Music app, tap a song or an album to select it. (You can either do this from your music library or from within the Xbox Music Store.)

2. Swipe up from the bottom of the screen and tap Play on Xbox 360.

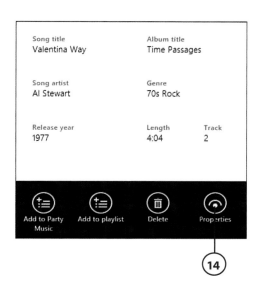

3. Tap Get Started in the SmartGlass dialog.

4. Follow the steps displayed on your screen, and tap Next.

5. While your music is playing, swipe up from the bottom of the screen to access the playback controls.

Xbox Controls

If you tap the Xbox Controls button after swiping up from the bottom of the screen, you can control your Xbox from your Surface.

Music Playlists

Music playlists are a great way to play through a series of songs that you choose. For example, if you're having a party, you might want to play a certain type of music for your guests. A playlist makes it possible to do so easily.

Adding Songs to the Now Playing Playlist

The Music app auto-creates a playlist called Now Playing when you start playing any music. Think of the Now Playing playlist as a queue of songs to which you can add songs.

1. Tap a song, an artist, or an album to select it.

2. Tap Add to Now Playing to add the item and start playing.

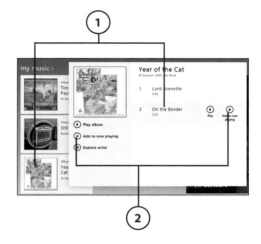

Creating a Playlist

You can create your own playlists using songs from your library and from Xbox Music Pass.

1. After selecting the song, album, or artist that you want to add to the new playlist, swipe up from the bottom of the screen and tap Add to Playlist.

2. Tap New Playlist from the menu.

3. Enter a name for your playlist.

4. Tap Save.

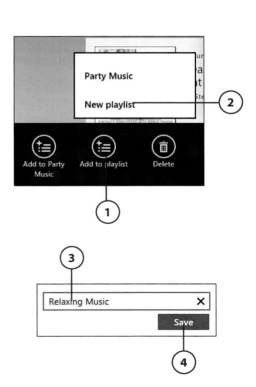

Adding Songs to a Playlist

You can add songs to a playlist you've already created. As you've already seen, you can add a single song, an entire album, or all songs by a particular artist.

1. While viewing an album, artist, or song that you want to add to your playlist, swipe up from the bottom of the screen and tap Add to Playlist.

2. Tap the name of the playlist to which you'd like to add your songs.

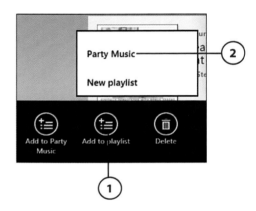

Editing a Playlist

You can edit a playlist by removing songs from it or by changing the order of songs. Note that deleting a song from a playlist only removes the song from the list. It doesn't actually delete the song from your library.

1. From My Music, tap Playlists.

2. Tap the playlist you would like to edit.

3. To remove a song, tap the song and tap Remove from Playlist.

4. To move a song up in the play order, tap the up arrow.

5. To move a song down in the play order, tap the down arrow.

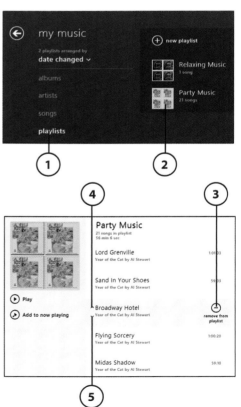

Deleting a Playlist

If you want to delete a playlist entirely, you can do so. Keep in mind that there isn't a way to restore a playlist once you do that. Note that deleting a playlist does not delete the songs in your library.

1. From My Music, tap Playlists.

2. Tap the playlist that you would like to delete.

3. Swipe up from the bottom of the screen and tap Delete.

4. Tap the Delete button to confirm.

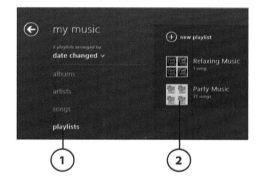

Seeing What's Playing

While you are playing songs on a playlist, you can see the songs that have already played, the song that's currently playing, and what's coming up.

1. From the home screen of the Music app, tap Now Playing while your playlist is playing. (The Now Playing link isn't active if playback is paused.)

2. Tap the View More button. (The button is unlabeled in this view.)

View More Button

If you wait too long, the View More button will disappear. Just tap on the name of the song currently playing to make it reappear.

---

3. Tap the Close button to close the list and return to the Now Playing screen.

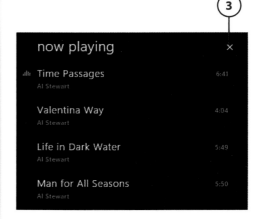

Shuffling or Repeating Songs in a Playlist

If you want to mix things up, you can shuffle the playback order of songs in your playlist. (This also applies to the Now Playing playlist.) You can also turn on Repeat mode so that playback will repeat until you explicitly stop it.

1. While your playlist is playing, swipe up from the bottom of the screen and tap Shuffle to enable shuffle mode.

2. Tap Repeat to turn on repeat mode.

Toggle

Both the Repeat and the Shuffle buttons are toggle buttons. In other words, if the feature is turned on and you tap the button, the feature turns off. The buttons will have a white background when the feature is enabled and a dark background when the feature is disabled.

Watch your personal videos
on your Surface.

Rent and purchase movies
and TV shows.

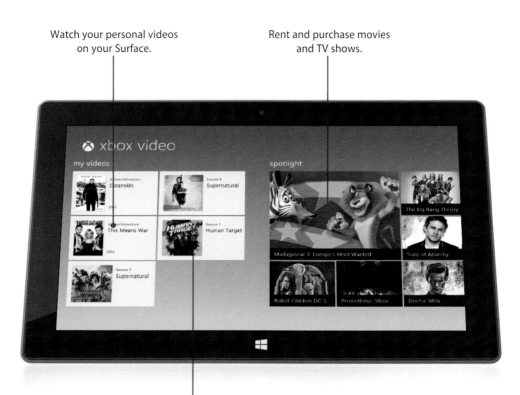

Watch purchased videos
on your Xbox 360.

Watching Video

Managing My Videos

The My Videos section of the Video app contains videos that are in your video library. You can add videos to your video library to add them to My Videos. To remove a video from My Videos, delete the video from your video library.

Adding Videos to My Videos

Videos are added to My Videos from Windows Explorer on the Windows RT Desktop. The easiest way to add videos to your video library is to add the folder containing your videos to your video library.

1. From the Start screen, tap the Desktop tile.

2. Tap the Windows Explorer icon on the taskbar.

3. In the Libraries list, tap Videos.

4. Tap Manage under Library Tools.

5. Tap Manage Library.

6. Tap Add.

7. Browse to the folder containing your videos, and tap it to select it.

8. Tap Include Folder.

9. Tap OK to add the folder.

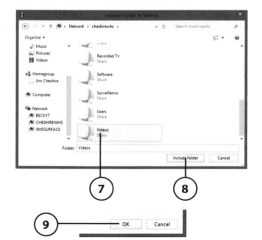

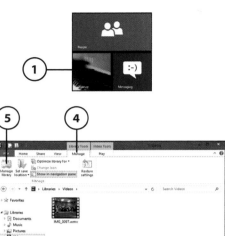

It's Not All Good

Video Over Networks

If the folder you add to your video library is a network folder on another computer, you might experience choppy performance when playing videos from that folder. If you want to use a network folder for video, make sure that you test playback. If playback isn't as good as you'd like, you can copy the video files to a local drive for better performance.

Deleting Videos from My Videos

You can remove videos from My Videos by deleting them from your video library.

1. While viewing your video library in Windows Explorer, tap the video you want to remove from My Videos.

2. Tap Delete.

3. Tap Yes to confirm the deletion of the video.

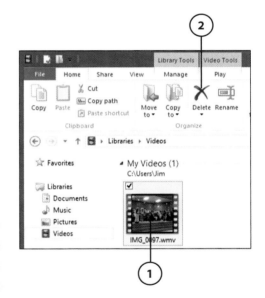

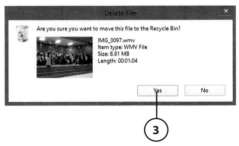

It's Not All Good

Deleting from Network Locations

If you are deleting a video from a local drive, the video file is moved to the Recycle Bin and you can restore it later if you want, assuming you haven't emptied the Recycle Bin. However, if you delete a movie from a network drive, the file is permanently deleted and there is no way to restore it unless you have a backup of the file in another location.

Making My Videos the Default View

When you launch the Video app, it displays your recently accessed videos from My Videos and links to the Xbox Video Store. If you'd prefer, you can configure the Video app so that it opens in the My Videos view. This is convenient if you aren't interested in often renting or purchasing videos.

1. From the Video app, swipe in from the right side of the screen and tap Settings.

2. Tap Preferences.

3. Tap Open My Videos When I Start the App to change the setting to On.

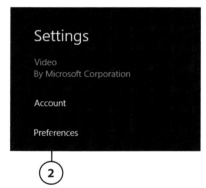

Exploring, Buying, and Renting Videos

In addition to watching your own videos, you can watch movies and television shows from the Xbox Video Store. You can purchase or rent videos.

Browsing the Movies Store

Finding something to watch is sometimes a challenge, not because of a limitation on content in the store, but simply because there is so much good content available. There are some features of the Xbox Video Store that make it easier to find a video to fit your current mood.

This section describes how to browse the Xbox Video Store for movies. In a later section, I show you how to browse for TV shows.

1.   From the Start screen, tap Video to launch the Video app.

2.   Tap a tile in the Spotlight or Movie Store section to see more details on that item.

3.   Tap Movies Store to enter the Movies section of the Xbox Video Store.

4.   Tap a category to see more movies.

5.   Swipe left or right to see more movies.

6.   Tap a movie's tile to see details on the movie.

7.   Tap Play Trailer to watch the movie trailer for the movie.

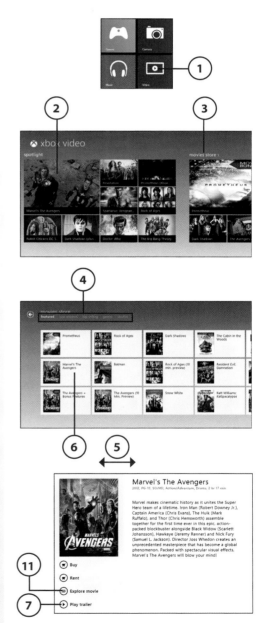

8. While the trailer is playing, tap the video for playback controls.

9. Tap Fullscreen to see the video in full-screen mode.

10. Tap Back to go back to the movie details.

11. Tap Explore Movie to see more information on the movie.

12. Swipe left and right to see more information about the movie.

13. Tap Play Trailer to view the movie's trailer.

14. Tap View More to see more information about the movie.

15. Tap the Close button to return to the movie's information screen.

Search

You can search the Xbox Video Store. Use the technique you learned earlier and search for a movie or television show title.

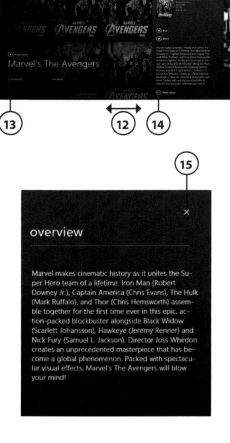

overview

Marvel makes cinematic history as it unites the Super Hero team of a lifetime. Iron Man (Robert Downey Jr.), Captain America (Chris Evans), The Hulk (Mark Ruffalo), and Thor (Chris Hemsworth) assemble together for the first time ever in this epic, action-packed blockbuster alongside Black Widow (Scarlett Johansson), Hawkeye (Jeremy Renner) and Nick Fury (Samuel L. Jackson). Director Joss Whedon creates an unprecedented masterpiece that has become a global phenomenon. Packed with spectacular visual effects, Marvel's The Avengers will blow your mind!

Renting Movies

You can rent movies for 14 days or 24 hours from the time you start watching your rental. Options are available for both streaming and downloading, and many movies enable you to choose between standard and high-definition versions.

1. After selecting a movie, tap Rent to rent the movie.

2. Select the rental option you'd like.

Rental Options

Not all rental options are available for all movies.

3. Tap Next.

4. Select your payment option.

Payment Options

If you've previously selected a payment option when renting or buying movies or TV shows, this step will be skipped.

5. Tap Next.

6. Tap Confirm to rent your movie.

Renting Movies

Movies that you rent and choose to download are added to My Movies once you download them. You are given the opportunity to download the movie once your rental is complete.

It's Not All Good

Streaming and Downloading

Many movies require you to choose between streaming and downloading when you rent them. For those movies that require you to choose, you will only be able to play the movie using the option you select. If you choose to stream the movie, you won't be able to download it, and vice versa. This is important to keep in mind because if you select the streaming option, you must be connected to the Internet the entire time you are watching the movie.

Buying Movies

If you'd like to add a movie to your music library without any time limits on watching it, you can purchase the movie. You can then watch it on your PC, Xbox 360, or Windows Phone.

1. After tapping a movie you'd like to purchase, tap Buy.

2. Tap a purchase option.

3. Tap Next.

4. Tap Confirm to complete your purchase.

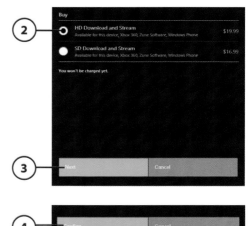

It's Not All Good

Copy Protection

When you buy a movie, you are actually just buying a license to play it whenever you want on the devices I listed. (You can play rented videos only on the device on which you rented them.) You don't have the right to burn it to a DVD or watch it on another device because copy protection will prevent it. This may surprise you because most music you buy can be freely used on any device and can also be burned onto a CD for listening in your car or on your stereo. Unfortunately, the movie companies and television studios haven't yet been persuaded to drop the copy protection from videos, so there are still some stiff restrictions in place even after you buy a video.

Browsing the Television Store

In addition to movies, the Xbox Video Store provides access to a large number of television shows that you can buy. You can buy single episodes, an entire season that has already aired, or a season pass for a current season so you can keep up with the show as it airs.

1. From the home screen in the Xbox Video Store, navigate to and tap Television Store.

2. Tap a category to filter your view.

3. Some categories will also have subcategories. Tap the subcategory drop-down, and tap a subcategory to see all shows in a particular subcategory.

4. Tap the Arrange By drop-down to change the order of shows.

5. Tap a show's tile to see more about the show.

6. Tap Explore Series to see details on the show.

7. Tap Seasons to see the show's seasons that are available.

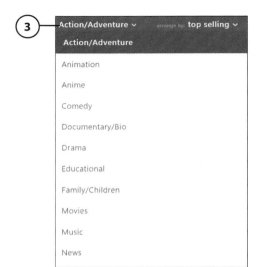

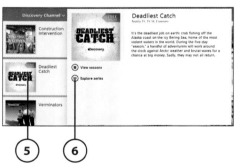

8. Tap View More to see a full list of seasons.

9. Tap a season to see the available episodes in that season.

10. Swipe up to see more episodes.

11. Tap away from the season to select another season.

12. Tap Back to return to the show details, and tap Back again to return to the list of shows in the Television Store.

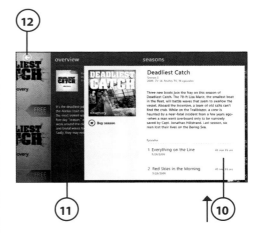

Buying TV Shows

Television shows cannot be rented, but you can purchase an entire series of a television show or one or more single episodes.

1. Tap the tile for a show you would like to purchase.

2. Tap View Seasons.

3. Tap a season.

4. To purchase the entire season, tap Buy Season.

5. Tap an episode you're interested in purchasing. (You can swipe up to see additional episodes.)

6. To purchase an episode, tap Buy Episode.

7. Select the viewing option you'd like to purchase.

8. Tap Next.

9. Tap Confirm to complete your purchase.

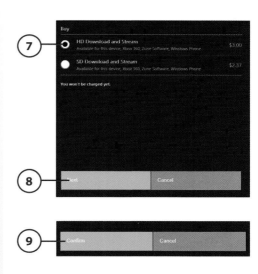

It's Not All Good

It's All or Nothing

When you buy a season pass, you must pay for the entire season (typically about $15 for SD and $25 for HD) up front. Many video stores enable you to pay for episodes as they are made available and cancel a season pass to stop being billed for episodes. The Xbox Television Store doesn't offer this option.

I'll often buy season passes when I want to get caught up on a show that I've just started watching because it allows me to easily buy all episodes up to the current episode in one step. If you want to do this with Xbox Television Store purchases, you'll need to purchase each episode individually instead. The end result is the same, but it's a bit of a hassle.

Require a Password for Purchases

By default, the Video app does not require a password when you purchase or rent videos. You can change this behavior to add a level of security to your account.

1. From within the Video app, swipe in from the right side of the screen and choose Settings.

2. Tap Preferences.

3. Tap Ask Me to Sign In Before Completing Purchases to change the setting to On.

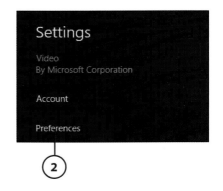

Sharing Videos with Email

You can share movies and television shows in email messages. This is a great way to recommend a movie to a friend.

1. While exploring the television show or movie that you want to share, swipe in from the right side of the screen and tap Share.

2. Tap Mail.

3. Enter the email address of the person with whom you want to share the video.

4. Enter a message for your email message.

5. Tap Send to send the email.

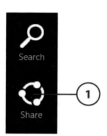

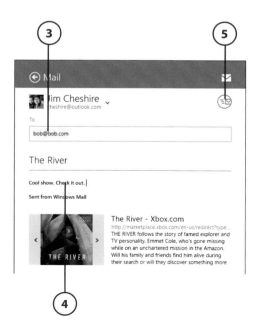

Sharing Videos on Facebook

You can also share videos on Facebook so that all of your Facebook friends can see the movies and television shows that you recommend.

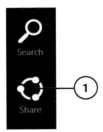

1. While exploring the television show or movie that you want to share, swipe in from the right side of the screen and tap Share.

2. Tap People.

3. Enter a message to post on Facebook.

4. Tap Send to post your message.

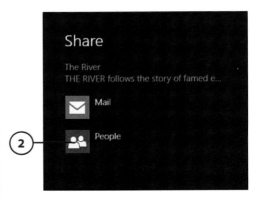

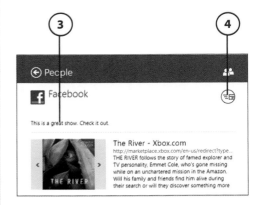

Playing Videos

Your Surface has a high-resolution screen that is excellent for watching video. However, you can also play videos on your Xbox 360 so that you can watch them on your home entertainment system.

Playing Videos on Your Surface

Videos can be streamed or downloaded to your Surface. If you're going to stream videos, you'll need to be connected to the Internet throughout the playback of the video.

Stream and Download

It's up to the rights owner of a video as to whether you can download a video. The Xbox Video Store lets you know what rights are available to you when you buy or rent a video.

Notice that the images you see in this walkthrough show a video that allows for both streaming and downloading; therefore, I can tap Download to download a video for offline watching.

1. From the Video app, tap on the video you'd like to play.

2. Tap Play. (If you tapped a television series in step 1, you'll need to tap an episode first.)

3. While a video is playing, tap the video to access playback controls.

4. Drag the scrubber handle to quickly move to a particular part of the video.

5. Tap Back to return to the Video app home screen.

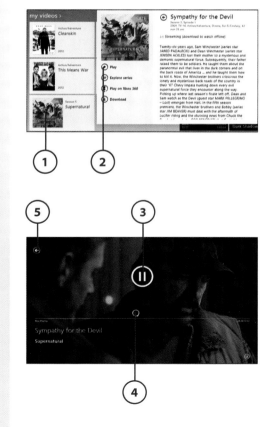

Playing Videos on Your Xbox 360

You can use your Xbox 360 to watch videos that you've purchased using your Surface tablet. Note that this applies only to Xbox Video Store purchases. If you copy your own videos into My Videos, you cannot play those on your Xbox 360 using this method.

1. After purchasing your movie or television episode, select it from My Videos.

2. Tap Play on Xbox 360.

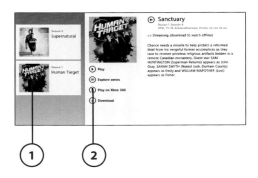

Xbox SmartGlass Required

Playing a video from your Surface on your Xbox 360 requires the free Xbox SmartGlass app available from the Windows Store. If you don't have Xbox SmartGlass, you'll be prompted to download it when you attempt these steps.

3. When the video start playing, swipe up from the bottom of the screen to access playback controls.

4. Tap Xbox Controls to access Xbox controls from your Surface.

5. Tap Play Here to transfer playback to your Surface.

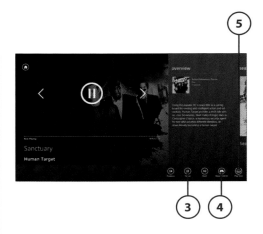

It's Not All Good

If you rent a movie or television show on your Surface and you later decide that you want to watch that video on your Xbox 360, you'll have to repurchase the video to watch on your Xbox 360. Unfortunately, there isn't an option to switch devices for rented movies at this time.

View pictures saved on your Surface, and take pictures and video with the built-in camera.

Use your favorite pictures as backgrounds in Windows RT and share them with others.

View pictures on Facebook and other cloud services.

15

Pictures

Adding Pictures to the Photos App

The Photos app is the repository for pictures on your Surface device, in the cloud, and on other computers on your network. Before you can view pictures in the Photos app, you'll need to add pictures to the Pictures library on your device, add one or more cloud services, or add a connection to other computers on your network.

Populating the Pictures Library

Like other libraries in Windows RT, the Pictures library contains a collection of files on your Surface, and you can also add additional locations such as network locations or external hard drives.

1. From the Desktop, tap the File Explorer icon on the taskbar.

2. Tap Pictures in the Libraries section of the navigation pane.

3. Tap Manage to add other locations to your Pictures library.

Adding Locations to Pictures Library

For information on how to add other locations to a library, see "Managing Your Music Library" in Chapter 13. All libraries are managed the same way in Windows RT.

Connecting to the Cloud

You can connect the Photos app to SkyDrive, Facebook, or Flickr so that you can view any pictures from those cloud services.

1. From the Start screen, tap the Photos tile to launch the Photos app.

2. Tap the cloud service you want to connect to the Photos app.

3. Tap Connect to connect to the cloud service.

4. Enter your username and password.

5. Tap Log In.

Facebook Connections

If you've already connected to Facebook using the People app, you will already see your Facebook pictures in Photos.

6. Tap Done to complete the connection.

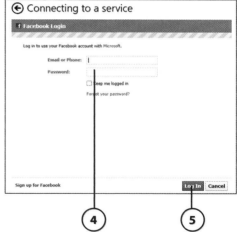

Importing Pictures

If you have files on a removable drive, a microSD memory card, or a digital camera that can be connected to your Surface using USB, you can import pictures from the device into your Surface.

1. From the Start screen, tap Photos to start the Photos app.

2. With your device connected to your Surface, swipe up from the bottom of the screen and tap Import.

3. Tap the device that contains the pictures you want to import.

4. Swipe down to deselect any pictures you don't want to import.

5. To deselect all pictures, tap Clear Selection. You can then swipe down on those pictures that you want to import to select them.

6. Enter a name for the folder into which the pictures will be imported.

7. Tap Import to import the pictures.

8. Tap Open Folder to open the folder into which the pictures were imported on your Surface.

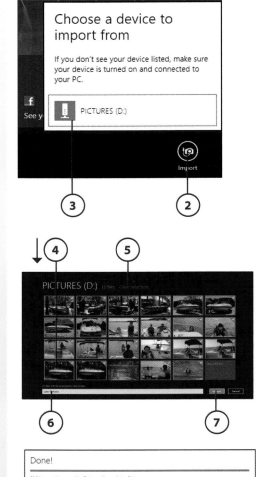

Choosing Which Pictures Show in the Photos App

You can choose which services and computers you see in the Photos app. This is convenient if you want to hide the tiles for services that you haven't connected to the Photos app. It's also a way that you can hide pictures from one or more sources if you'd prefer not to see them in the Photos app.

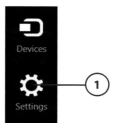

Devices

Settings — ①

1. From the Photos app, swipe in from the right side of the screen and tap the Settings charm.

2. Tap Options.

3. Tap a checked source to uncheck it and hide it in the Photos app.

4. Tap an unchecked source to check it and show it in the Photos app.

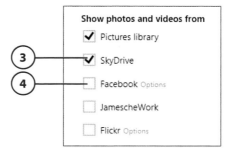

Settings

Photos
By Microsoft Corporation

② — Options

About

Help

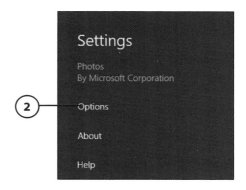

Show photos and videos from

- ☑ Pictures library
- ③ — ☑ SkyDrive
- ④ — ☐ Facebook Options
- ☐ JamescheWork
- ☐ Flickr Options

Viewing Pictures and Video

Once you've added some pictures to your Pictures library, you can view them in the Photos app. You also can watch a slide show of images, view a video montage, set a picture as your lock screen image, and more.

Browsing Pictures

You can browse through all the pictures in your Pictures library and pictures from any cloud services you've added.

1. From the Photos app, tap the Pictures Library tab or the tab for the cloud service or computer that contains the pictures you want to see.

2. Swipe left or right to see additional folders if necessary.

3. Pinch to zoom out to semantic zoom so that you can see more folders on one screen.

Semantic Zoom

Semantic zoom is available whenever you are viewing a list of folders or pictures. Pinch to zoom out and reverse pinch to zoom back in again.

Here's another great tip: When you reverse pinch to zoom back in, you'll zoom in so that the folder or pictures you reverse pinched on will be visible when you zoom in. This is a convenient way to quickly navigate to a particular point in a group of pictures or folders.

4. Tap a folder to open the folder and see the pictures within it.

5. Swipe left and right to see additional pictures.

6. Tap a picture to see the picture full screen.

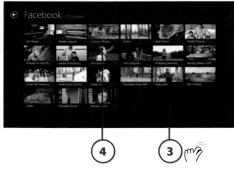

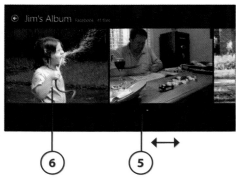

7. Reverse pinch to zoom in on a picture.

8. Drag to move the picture while zoomed in.

9. Pinch to zoom out on a picture.

10. Tap the screen and tap Back to go back to the previous screen.

Going Back

You can continue to tap Back to go all the way back to the home screen of the Photos app.

Browsing Pictures by Date

If you have a lot of pictures in a lot of folders, it might be easier to browse them by date rather than view them in their folders. When browsing by date, instead of seeing the folder name, you'll see the month and year when pictures were taken. Tapping on a month displays all pictures taken during that month.

1. While viewing folders, swipe up from the bottom of the screen and tap Browse by Date.

2. Tap a month to view all pictures taken during that month.

3. Swipe up from the bottom of the screen and tap Browse by Folder to return to folder view.

4. Tap Back to return to the previous screen.

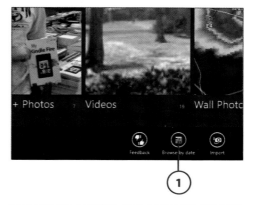

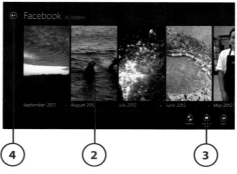

Watching a Slide Show

You can view a slide show of pictures. When you are viewing a slide show, the Photos app transitions through all the pictures in the folders that are visible when you start the slide show. Each picture is displayed for four seconds.

1. In the Photos app, tap a folder that contains the pictures you want to view in your slide show.

2. To view all pictures in the folder in your slide show, swipe up from the bottom of the screen and tap Slide Show.

3. To view only some of the pictures in your slide show, swipe down on the pictures you want to view in your slide show to select them, and then tap Slide Show to view them in a slide show.

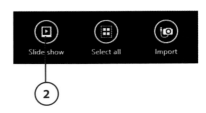

Stopping a Slide Show

You can stop a slide show simply by tapping the screen or switching away from the Photos app.

Selecting Pictures

You can select pictures from only one source at a time. For example, if you select one or more pictures from your Facebook pictures and then switch over to your Pictures library and attempt to select a picture there, you'll be notified that you already have pictures selected from Facebook and you'll be asked to deselect them first. You can do that by tapping Clear Selection.

It's Not All Good

No Slide Show Settings

When viewing a slide show, you cannot control the transition or the length of time that pictures are displayed. Your pictures will always fade from one to the next, and each picture will always be displayed for four seconds.

Deleting Pictures

You can delete pictures from the Photos app, but only those pictures that are in your Pictures library.

1. Browse to the folder that contains the picture or pictures that you want to delete.

2. Swipe down on one or more pictures to select them. (You can also tap Select All to select all pictures.)

3. Tap Delete.

4. Tap Delete to confirm the deletion.

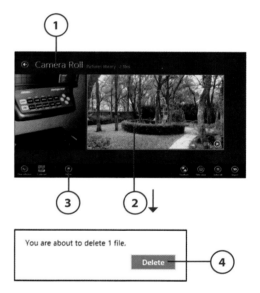

You are about to delete 1 file.

Delete

Using a Picture in Your Lock Screen

You can change the background image for your lock screen so that it displays one of your favorite pictures.

1. While viewing the picture you want to use as your lock screen background image, swipe up from the bottom of the screen and tap Set As.

2. Tap Lock Screen.

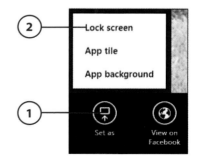

Lock screen

App tile

App background

Set as   View on Facebook

No Cropping

Windows RT uses the full picture as your lock screen background. There is no option to crop the image or reposition it. If you want to use a cropped image for your background, you'll need to crop the image first and then set it as your lock screen picture.

Setting the Pictures App Tile Image

By default, the Photos app's tile shuffles through pictures from the Photos app. However, you can choose to have it display one picture on the tile.

1. While viewing the picture that you want to use as the tile's background, swipe up from the bottom of the screen and tap Set As.

2. Tap App Tile.

Shuffling Pictures on the App Tile

If you've set a picture as the background picture for the Photos app's tile and you want to switch back to the default setting where pictures are shuffled, you can do that from the Options pane.

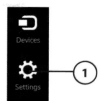

1. While in the Photos app, swipe in from the right side of the screen and tap the Settings charm.

2. Tap Options.

3. Tap the Shuffle Photos on the App Tile to turn on photo shuffling.

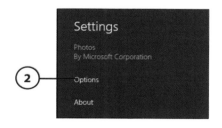

Setting the Pictures App Background

When you first enter the Photos app, you'll see a background image of the London Eye, the famous Ferris wheel in London. If you wish, you can change this background picture to one of your own.

1. While viewing the picture that you want to set as the app's background, swipe up from the bottom of the screen and tap Set As.

2. Tap App Background.

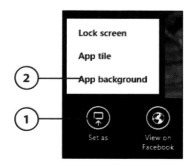

Sharing Pictures

One way that you'll undoubtedly share pictures on your Surface is by handing the device to someone else so that he or she can look at the pictures on the screen. However, if you want to share pictures from someone who's not nearby, you can use the Share charm to share pictures through email, SkyDrive, or the People app.

Sharing a Picture with Email

You can share pictures using email with the option to either send the picture as an attachment or using SkyDrive. When a picture is sent using SkyDrive, a link to the picture is sent and the recipient of the email can download the picture from SkyDrive.

1. Select one or more pictures that you want to share.

2. Swipe in from the right side of the screen and tap the Share charm.

3. Tap Mail.

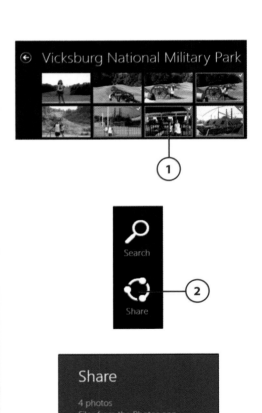

4. Files are attached to your mail message by default. To send a link to the files in SkyDrive instead, tap Send Using SkyDrive Instead.

5. Enter one or more email addresses.

6. Enter a subject for your email.

7. Enter a message for your email if you'd like to.

8. Tap Send to send the email.

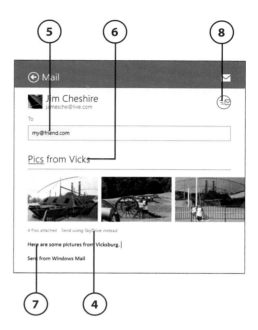

SEND USING SKYDRIVE

When you send pictures using SkyDrive, the pictures will be automatically uploaded to the Pictures folder in SkyDrive. A folder is created inside Pictures and named using the subject line of your email. The recipients of your mail can then view the pictures by clicking the link in the email, or they can download the picture using a Download link in the email.

For more information on sending email attachments using SkyDrive, see "Composing and Sending Email" in Chapter 9.

>>>Go Further

Uploading Pictures to SkyDrive

You can upload pictures to SkyDrive using the Share charm. You can choose the folder on your SkyDrive where you want the pictures uploaded.

1. Select one or more pictures that you want to share.

2. Swipe in from the right side of the screen and tap the Share charm.

3. Tap SkyDrive.

4. Tap a folder into which you'd like to upload your pictures.

5. Tap Upload.

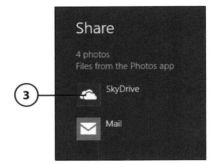

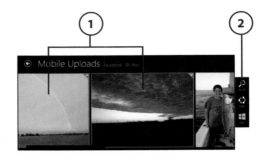

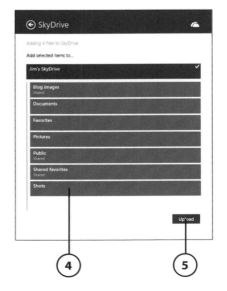

>>>Go Further

USING SKYDRIVE TO SHARE BETWEEN COMPUTERS

While I was writing this book, I took a lot of screenshots on my Surface that I needed to copy over to my laptop where I was doing my writing. I used the Share charm to upload the screenshots to SkyDrive, and then I used the SkyDrive app in Windows 8 to access those pictures on my laptop. It was extremely convenient to be able to share pictures between two PCs using SkyDrive in this way.

Sharing a Picture with People

You can share pictures with your Facebook friends or your Twitter followers. However, you can only do so with pictures that are in your SkyDrive.

1. Select one picture in your SkyDrive. If you select more than one picture, you cannot share with the People app.

2. Swipe in from the right side of the screen and tap the Share charm.

3. Tap People.

4. Tap the drop-down to select either Facebook or Twitter.

5. Enter a message to be shared along with your picture.

6. Tap Send.

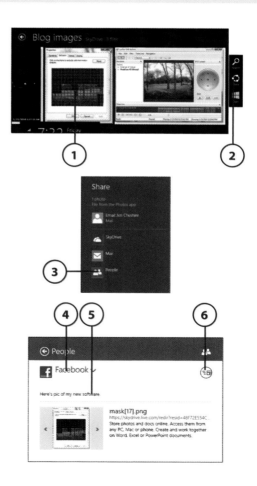

Using the Camera App

Your Surface has two cameras that you can use to take pictures and video. Pictures and video taken with the Camera app are added to your Pictures library in the Photos app.

Taking Pictures

You can take pictures with either the front-facing camera or the rear-facing camera. The front-facing camera is typically used for videoconferencing. The rear-facing camera is better suited for taking pictures that you might normally take with a point-and-shoot camera.

1. From the Start screen, tap the Camera tile to launch the Camera app.

2. Tap Change Camera to toggle between the front-facing and rear-facing camera.

3. Tap Timer to enable a 3-second timer that will count down prior to a photo being taken.

4. Tap anywhere on the screen to take a picture.

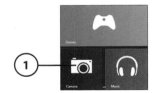

Taking Screenshots

Screenshots are saved into a Screenshots folder in your Pictures library.

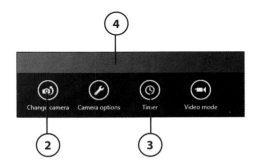

Changing Photo Resolution

By default, your Surface takes pictures at a resolution of 0.9 megapixels. You can change the resolution if you'd like to take pictures at a lower resolution. Doing so enables you to take pictures that use less space on your Surface.

1. In the Camera app, tap Change Camera to select the desired camera.

2. Tap Camera Options.

3. Tap the Photo Resolution drop-down.

4. Tap the desired resolution for the selected camera.

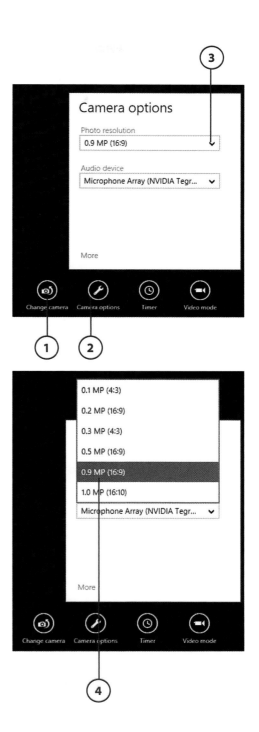

Changing Picture Appearance

You can change the brightness, contrast, and exposure for pictures that you take with your Surface. Brightness and contrast affect not only the appearance of the image on the screen, but also the resulting picture.

1. While viewing an image in the desired camera, tap Camera Options.

2. Tap More.

3. Drag the Brightness slider to the left to decrease the brightness or to the right to increase brightness.

4. Drag the Contrast slider to the left to decrease contrast or to the right to increase contrast.

Resetting Brightness and Contrast

Brightness and contrast settings are reset to the default settings when you switch away from the Camera app.

5. To change exposure, tap the Exposure slider to set it to Manual, and drag the slider to adjust exposure.

Exposure Settings

When you change exposure, it doesn't affect the way the camera's image looks on the screen. Results are only visible after you take the picture.

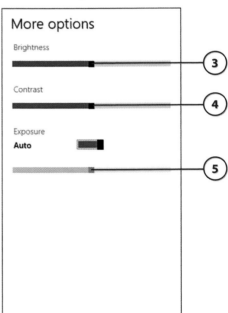

Taking Video

In addition to taking still pictures, you can shoot video with your Surface. Videos are also saved to your Pictures library.

1. Tap Video Mode to turn on the video camera. The background of the Video Mode button turns white.

2. Tap the screen to start recording video. A video timer displays in the lower-right corner of the screen.

3. Tap the screen again to stop recording and save the video to your Pictures library.

Get directions to addresses
and places.

See color-coded
traffic speeds.

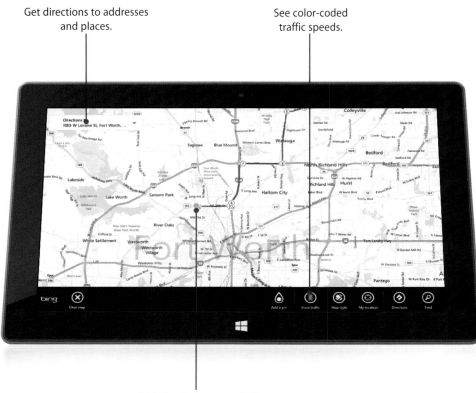

Add pins for easy recall of
landmarks and addresses.

Using Maps

The Maps app enables you to use the Bing Maps service to explore maps, search for places and addresses, and find directions. You can view road maps with minimal clutter as well as aerial maps that provide a satellite view of an area. In many cases, you can also view an angled aerial view that provides a 3-dimensional perspective of the map.

Exploring Maps

The Maps app provides maps of practically the entire world, and satellite imagery is available for many areas. There are many tools that enable you to easily explore any area you wish.

Viewing and Zooming

While you are viewing the map, you can easily move around and zoom in and out using touch.

1. From the Start screen, tap Maps to launch the Maps app.

2. If prompted, tap Allow to let the Maps app use your location or Block to prevent the Maps app from using your location.

3. Tap and slide to move around on the map.

4. Reverse-pinch to zoom in on the map.

5. Pinch to zoom out on the map.

6. Double-tap to zoom in and center the map on the point where you double-tapped.

Map Scale

There is a map scale displayed in the lower-right corner of the map. Use this to determine distances while viewing the map.

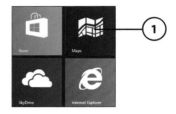

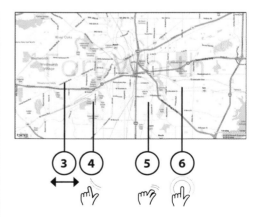

LOCATION SERVICES

Many apps you use might use location services to provide you with a better experience. The Maps app uses location services so that it can show you your current location on the map, and so it can provide a better experience when you are getting directions.

Every Wi-Fi access point transmits a unique identifier called a MAC address. There are companies that drive around the country collecting these MAC addresses and the approximate GPS coordinates of each one. Your Surface uses services provided by these companies to get your approximate location based on the MAC addresses that your tablet picks up.

Using Zoom Controls

For more precise control over zooming, you can use zoom controls in the Maps app. Zoom controls are off by default, so before you can use them, you'll need to turn them on.

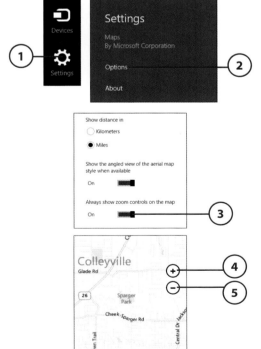

1. While viewing a map, swipe in from the right side of the screen and tap the Settings charm.

2. Tap Options.

3. Tap Always Show Zoom Controls on the Map to turn on the setting.

4. Tap the + sign to zoom in on the map.

5. Tap the – sign to zoom out on the map.

Viewing Your Location

If you've allowed the Maps app to use your location, when you launch the app, it will center the map on your current location. When you drag to move the map elsewhere, you can return the map to your current location.

1. While viewing the map, swipe up from the bottom of the screen.

2. Tap My Location to center your current location on the map.

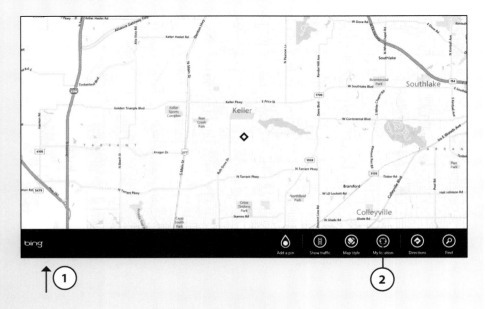

Changing the Units of Measurement

By default, the Maps app shows distances using miles as the unit. If you'd prefer, you can switch the Maps app to use kilometers instead.

1. While in the Maps app, swipe in from the right side of the screen and tap the Settings charm.

2. Tap Options.

3. Tap Kilometers to switch to using kilometers for distance measurement.

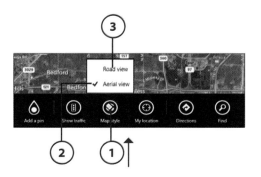

Changing the Map Style

The Maps app shows maps using the Road style by default. This style of map is similar to paper maps and uses a solid-colored background and displays roads using different colors based on the size of the road. You can switch to Aerial style, which uses a satellite image for the map with colored roads drawn on top of the image.

1. While viewing the map, swipe up from the bottom of the screen and tap Map Style.

2. Tap Aerial View to switch to Aerial view.

3. To switch back to Road view, tap Road View.

Using Angled View

Many larger metropolitan areas offer an angled, 3-D perspective view when the map is in Aerial view, provided the feature is enabled. (It's enabled by default.)

No Angled View in Road View

Angled view is available only when the Aerial View map style is enabled.

1. From the Options pane, tap Show the Angled View of the Aerial Map Style When Available if necessary to turn on the feature.

2. Reverse-pinch to zoom in. Angled view activates automatically when you reach a zoom level where 1 inch is equal to 200 yards.

3. Tap the compass rose to change your view. Each press of the button rotates the map 90 degrees.

4. The fourth press of the compass rose button turns off angled view. Tap the square button to reenable angled view.

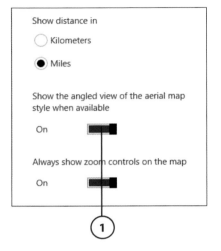

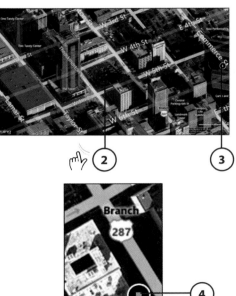

Showing Traffic

The Maps app can show you traffic congestion from Microsoft's Bing service. Maps uses colors overlaid on roads to indicate the speed of traffic. Areas where traffic is very slow are shown in red, slow traffic is orange, somewhat slow traffic is yellow, and fast traffic is green. If a road doesn't show any of these colors, traffic data for that road isn't available.

No Cause for Congestion

When accessed using your web browser, the Bing traffic data enables you to easily see why traffic is slow in a certain area. That information is not available in the Maps app on Windows RT.

1. While viewing a map, swipe up from the bottom of the screen and tap Show Traffic.

2. To turn off the display of traffic, tap Show Traffic again.

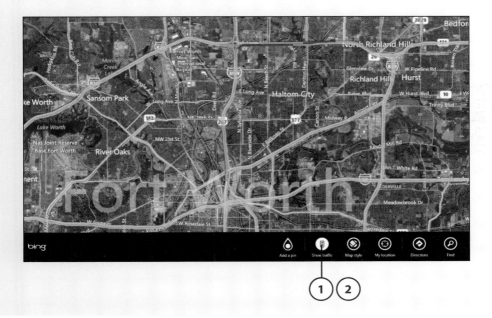

Searching Maps

In addition to browsing through a map, you can search the Maps app for an address or a place of interest.

Searching for a Place

You can search for a business or a place using the Maps app. For example, you can use the Maps app to find museums by searching for "museum."

1. Swipe up from the bottom of the screen and tap Find.

2. Enter a place name or a search term and press Enter.

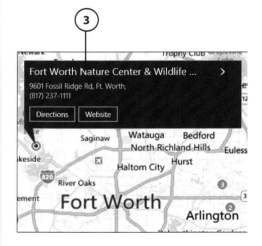

Use Search History

You can easily find a place or address you've previously searched for by tapping the search term in the search history that is listed directly under the search box.

3. To view more information about a search result, tap the name of the place that was found.

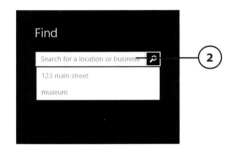

4. Tap Back to return to a list of search results.

5. Tap another search result to see details on that search result.

6. To clear your search results from the map, swipe up from the bottom of the screen and tap Clear Map.

Finding an Address

You can use this same technique to find an address on the map.

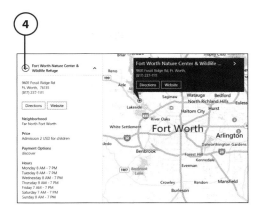

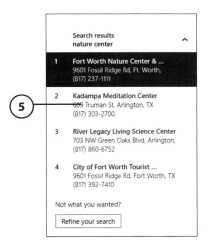

Adding Pins

You can drop a pin on a visible place on the map. Pins are used to save a location on the map for future reference. As you'll see later, you can also use pins to get directions to a visible location on the map.

1. While viewing the map, swipe up from the bottom of the screen.

2. Tap and hold on Add a Pin and drag it to the map, releasing it when it is on the location where you want the pin added.

3. To remove all pins from the map, tap Clear Map.

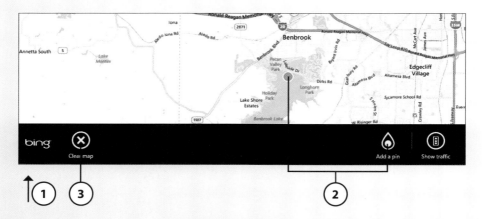

Clearing or Disabling Search History

As you search for places and addresses, the Maps app stores each search in history so that you can easily search for the same place or address by simply tapping it in the search history.

You can clear the search history list. You also can turn off search history so that the Maps app no longer stores a list of places and addresses for which you've searched.

1. Swipe in from the right side of the screen and tap the Settings charm.

2. Tap Options.

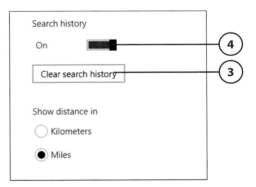

3. Tap Clear Search History to clear the search history.

4. Tap the slider to disable search history.

Getting Directions

The Maps app can generate directions so that you can easily find an address or a place on the map. This feature works best when you've allowed the Maps app to use your current location.

Allowing Maps to Use Your Location

You can control whether the Maps app can use your current location. If you chose to block access to your current location when you first launched the Maps app, you can also use these steps to turn on location services in the Maps app.

1. From the Settings panel, tap Permissions.

2. Tap the Location slider to change the setting to On to allow the Maps app to use your current location.

Getting Directions to a Pinned Address

Once you add a pin to the map, you can easily get directions to the pinned location.

Adding Pins

For information on how you can add pins to the map, see "Adding Pins," earlier in this chapter.

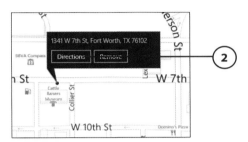

1. Tap a pin that you've added to the map.

2. Tap Directions.

3. Tap the arrow to map directions from your current location, or enter a different location and then tap Search.

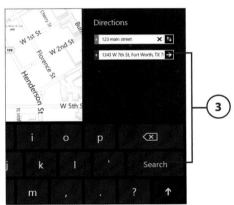

4. Tap one of the waypoints in the directions list to highlight that waypoint on the map.

5. Tap a numbered waypoint on the map to highlight that waypoint in the directions list.

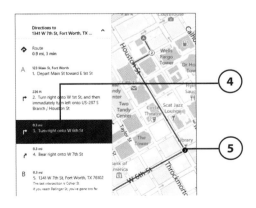

Getting Directions by Searching

You can find directions to unpinned locations by searching. In some cases, the Maps app will locate more than one result that matches your search term. In such cases, you'll have an option to choose which result you want to use for your directions.

1. Swipe up from the bottom of the screen and tap Directions.

2. By default, the starting point is your current location. Tap inside the A box and enter a new address to use a different starting location.

3. Enter a destination place name or address in the B box. You can also tap the crosshairs to use your current location for a destination. If you do, you'll need to enter a starting point in the A box.

4. Tap the arrow, or tap Search on the keyboard to generate the directions.

5. To choose a different result for your search, swipe up and tap Directions again and choose a new result from the list.

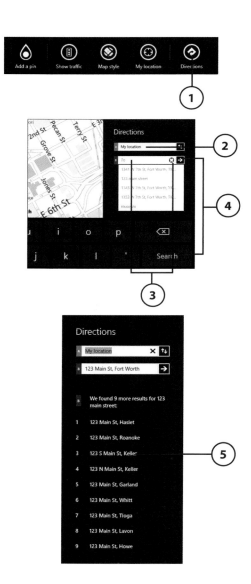

Sharing Maps

You can share maps with others using email. Sharing a map provides others with an image of the map you are sharing, and if you are viewing directions when you share a map, you can share the directions along with screenshots of the map.

Sharing with Other Windows 8 Users

When you share a map or directions, users of Windows 8 who receive your shared map will be able to open the shared map inside the Maps app.

Sharing Maps with Email

Sharing maps with email is a great way to send someone directions to a particular location. Recipients of the email can open the shared map in Bing Maps in a browser or in the Maps app (if they are using Windows 8), or see details in the email message that you send.

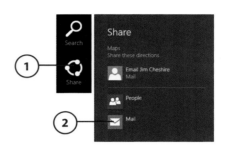

1. While viewing the map you want to share, swipe in from the right side of the screen and tap the Share charm.

2. Tap Mail.

3. Enter a recipient email address.

4. Enter a message.

5. Tap Send to send the message.

It's Not All Good

No People Sharing

Notice that the People app shows up when you tap the Share charm; however, you cannot share maps with the People app. If you try, you're told to try another app, such as Mail.

Enter and format text, including using styles for advanced formatting.

Add pictures for a more engaging document.

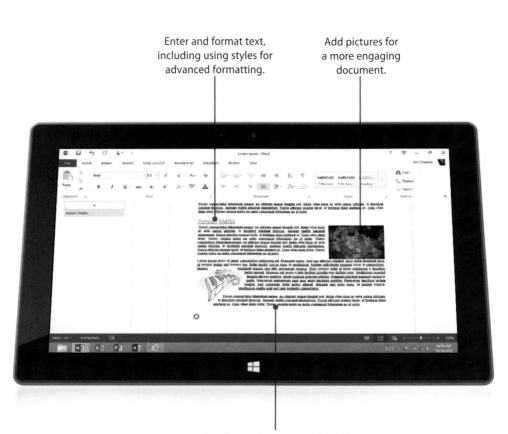

Proof your document with spell check, a thesaurus, and more.

Creating Documents with Microsoft Word 2013

Windows RT includes Microsoft Word 2013, a powerful word processor with all the features necessary to create complex documents. Complete coverage of Microsoft Word would require an entire book, but this chapter provides you with the skills you need to start creating and editing documents. I end this chapter with a few tips and tricks that will make using Microsoft Word more enjoyable and productive.

Creating, Opening, and Saving Documents

Like other Microsoft Office 2013 applications, Word is cloud-enabled by default, which means that not only can you save your documents to your SkyDrive, but you can also create documents using templates that Microsoft makes available in the cloud.

Creating a New Blank Document

A blank document is based off of Word's default template. The default template contains a collection of basic styles that you can use to format your document.

Styles

For more information on using styles to format your document, see "Formatting Text," later in this chapter.

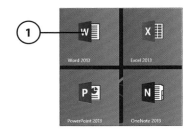

---

1. From the Start screen, tap Word 2013 to launch Word.

Desktop Apps

Office 2013 apps are desktop apps. When you launch one of them, it launches in the Windows RT desktop.

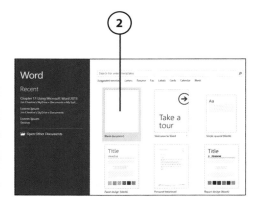

---

2. Tap the Blank Document template to create a new document. Notice that there are several other template styles you can select. You learn more about them in the next section.

Creating a Document from a Template

When you create a blank document, you start with a clean slate. In some cases, you might want to create a document based on a template instead. Document templates can supply boilerplate content, styles, and other tools to make it easier to create documents.

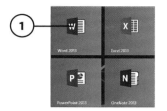

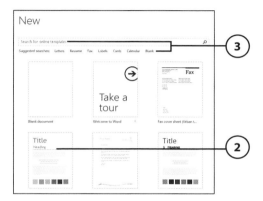

1. From the Start screen, tap Word 2013 to launch Word.

2. Tap a template to create a new document based on the template.

3. To see more templates, tap a suggested search, or enter a search term and tap the Search button.

4. To filter your search results, tap a category from the list.

5. Tap a template.

6. Tap Create to create a document based on the template you selected.

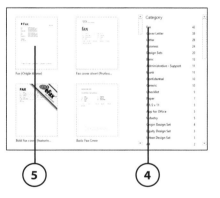

Saving Documents to Your Tablet

You can save a document to your tablet so that you can access it even when you don't have Internet access.

1. When ready to save your document, tap File.

2. Tap Save As.

3. Tap Computer.

4. Tap Browse.

5. Navigate to the folder where you want to save the document.

6. Enter a name for the document.

7. Tap Save.

Quick Save

After you save a document for the first time, you can quickly save revisions to that document by tapping Save instead of Save As. You also can tap the blue diskette icon on the Quick Access toolbar at the top of the Word window.

For more information on the Quick Access toolbar, see "Tips and Tricks," later in this chapter.

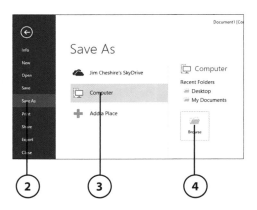

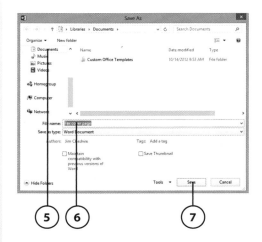

Saving Documents to SkyDrive

Saving a document to SkyDrive is a convenient way to ensure that the document will be available to you on any PC that you use.

1. Tap File.

2. Tap Save As.

3. Tap your SkyDrive account.

4. Tap Browse.

5. Navigate to the folder where you want to save the file.

6. Tap Save.

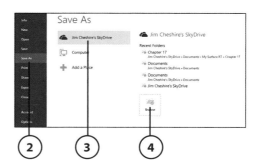

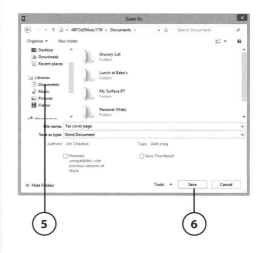

Opening Documents on Your Tablet

When you're ready to continue working on a document you previously saved to your tablet, you will first need to open the document in Word.

1. Tap File.

2. If your document appears in Recent Documents, tap it to open it; otherwise, tap Computer.

3. Tap Browse.

4. Browse to the folder containing your document, and tap your document.

5. Tap Open.

Open Documents When Starting Word

When you start Word, you are automatically taken to the Open screen so that you can open a new document.

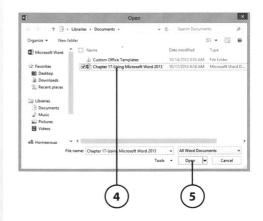

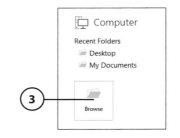

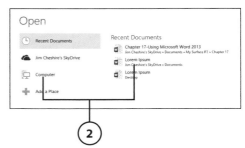

Opening Documents on SkyDrive

If you're connected to the Internet, you can open documents directly from your SkyDrive.

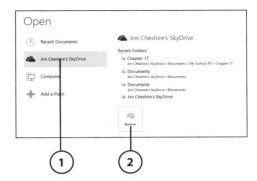

1. From the Open screen, tap your SkyDrive account.

2. Tap Browse.

3. Navigate to the folder containing your document, and tap the document.

4. Tap Open.

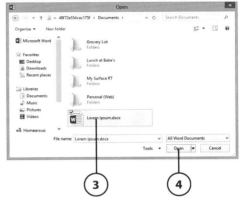

Managing Recent Documents

Word maintains a list of recent documents so that you can quickly open a document that you've worked on previously. You can remove documents from this list or clear the list if you want. You also can pin documents to the list so that they remain on the list even after you've cleared it.

1. From the Open screen, tap Recent Documents.

2. Tap and hold on a document.

3. Tap Remove from List to remove the document from the list.

4. Tap Pin to List to pin the document so that it remains on the list even after the list is cleared.

5. Tap Clear Unpinned Documents to remove all unpinned documents from the list.

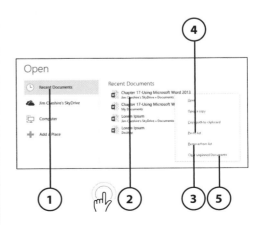

Switching Microsoft Accounts

Word's connection to SkyDrive is tied to your Microsoft account. If you'd like to connect to the SkyDrive of a different Microsoft account, you'll need to switch the Microsoft account used in Word.

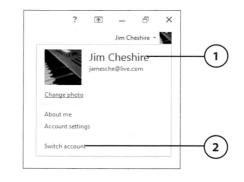

1. In Word, tap the current Microsoft account in the top-right corner.

2. Tap Switch Account.

3. Tap Microsoft Account.

4. Enter your Microsoft account email address.

5. Enter your password.

6. Tap Sign In.

Quickly Switching Accounts

If you've previously switched to a different Microsoft account, when you tap Switch Account, you'll see a list of the Microsoft accounts you've used previously. You can switch to one of the other accounts by tapping the account.

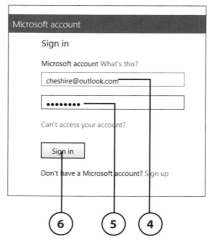

Formatting Text

Adding text to a document is simple and intuitive, but to create the kind of compelling documents you likely want, you must know how to format your text. In this section, I show you how you can format text directly and using styles.

Formatting Existing Text

You can change the formatting of anything from a single letter up to an entire document by selecting it and then applying the desired formatting.

1. Tap to place the insertion point at the beginning of the text you want to format.

2. Drag the selection indicator to select the text you want to format.

Use Zoom for Easier Selection

You will find it easier to select text using touch if you reverse-pinch on your document to zoom in.

3. Tap the selected text.

4. Tap a formatting option on the pop-up toolbar to format your text.

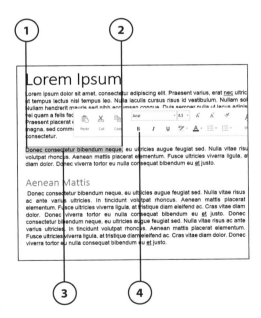

Formatting New Text

If you enable a particular style of formatting, any text you enter will take on that formatting until you explicitly change the formatting settings. For example, if you enable bold formatting, any text you enter will be bolded until you explicitly disable bold formatting.

1. With no text selected, tap Home to display the Home ribbon.

2. Tap to select the desired formatting from the formatting options on the Home ribbon.

3. Add text to your document and it will use the formatting you've selected.

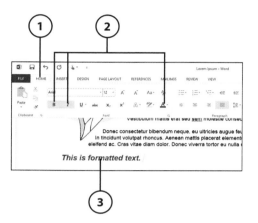

Formatting Text Using Styles

I've shown you how you can directly format text; however, you also can indirectly format text using styles. The benefit of using styles is that you can easily reformat an entire document by editing the style. When a style is edited, any text formatted using that style is automatically reformatted.

1. Select the text you want to format.

2. Tap Home to open the Home ribbon.

3. Tap the Styles drop-down.

4. Tap a style to apply the style.

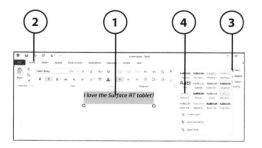

STYLES

There are two types of styles in Word: character styles and paragraph styles. Character styles can be applied to only parts of a paragraph. Paragraph styles, which show a small paragraph character next to the name in the Styles drop-down, apply to an entire paragraph. Therefore, a paragraph can contain several different character styles, but only one paragraph style can be applied to a paragraph.

It's important to realize that even if a paragraph is formatted with a paragraph style, character formatting remains intact. For example, if a word in a paragraph is formatted in the color red and you then apply the No Spacing paragraph style to the paragraph, the word will still be red because the color applied to it is character formatting and not part of the paragraph style.

Using styles is an advanced feature of Word, and I don't cover the feature in its entirety in this book. For a full explanation of using styles and other advanced Word features, read *Office 2013 In Depth* from Que Publishing.

Editing Styles

As I said earlier, you can reformat parts of your document that are formatted with a style by editing the style. When you edit your style, any content that is formatted with that style updates automatically.

1. Tap the Home tab to display the Home ribbon.

2. Tap the Styles button to display the Styles panel.

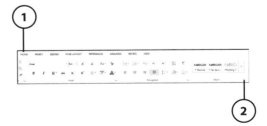

3. Tap and hold on the style you want to edit.

4. Tap Modify.

5. Make any desired modifications to the style.

6. To modify other style properties, tap Format and select a property.

7. Tap OK to apply your change.

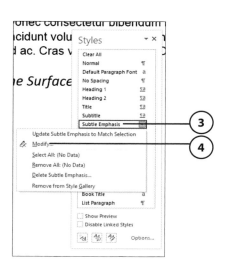

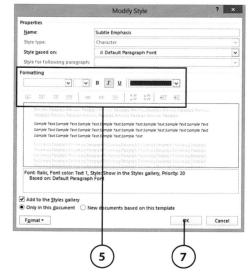

Creating a New Style

If you can't find a style that fits your needs, you can create your own style. Your new style can be made available only in the current document or to any document you use from now on.

1. Format text the way that you want your new style to look.

2. Tap the Home tab to display the Home ribbon.

3. Tap the Styles drop-down.

4. Tap Create a Style.

5. Enter a name for your new style.

6. Tap Modify if you'd like to change any properties of the style.

7. Tap OK to create the style.

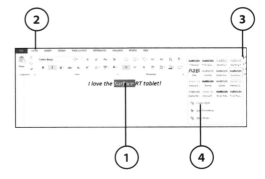
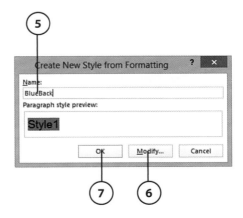

Style Preview

The style preview might not show exactly what the style will look like. For example, in the figure shown here, the preview doesn't show the white text for my new style because the white text is direct character formatting. Even so, when you apply the style, the white text will be applied.

Adding Pictures

Nothing drives a point home in a document better than pictures. (Just think of what this book would be like without the figures!) Word 2013 makes it easy to add pictures to your documents. You can also format pictures and change the way that they are laid out and how text flows around them.

Adding Pictures from Your Tablet or Removable Media

If you have pictures on your tablet that you'd like to add to your Word document, you can do so. If you have pictures on a removable drive or on a memory card (such as pictures on your digital camera), you can add those directly from the removable media. It's not necessary to copy them to your tablet first.

1. Tap to place the insertion point where you want your picture to be added.

2. Tap Insert to display the Insert ribbon.

3. Tap Pictures.

4. Browse to the folder where your picture is located, and tap the picture to select it.

5. Tap Insert.

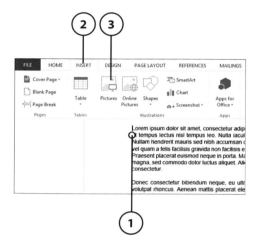

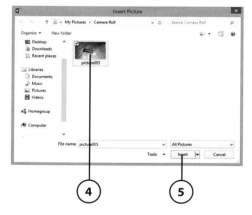

Formatting Pictures

Your picture probably doesn't look exactly the way you want it to look at this stage. I show you how to format and position the picture later in this section.

Adding Pictures from the Cloud

You can add pictures from Office.com, Bing, your SkyDrive, or Flickr. After you insert the picture, you don't need to be connected to the Internet to view it in your Word document. Word will actually save the image as part of the document.

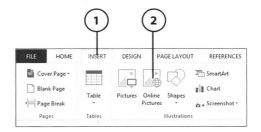

1. With the insertion point at the place where you want the picture inserted, tap Insert to show the Insert ribbon.

2. Tap Online Pictures.

3. To add a picture from Office.com or from Bing, enter a search term and tap Search.

4. To add a picture from Flickr, tap See More.

5. To add a picture from your SkyDrive, tap Browse.

6. Tap a picture to select it.

7. To see a larger preview, tap the magnifying glass.

8. Tap Insert to insert the picture into your document.

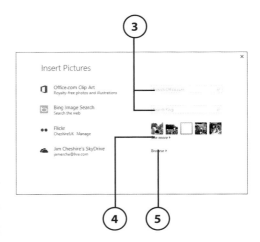

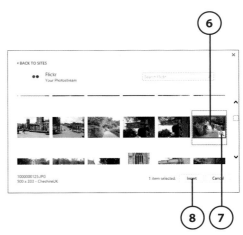

Formatting Pictures

It's likely that your picture is large and not formatted exactly the way you might want it to be. You can resize your picture and format it right within Word.

1. Tap the picture to select it.

2. Drag a sizing circle to resize the picture. Dragging a corner will resize the picture while keeping proportions.

3. Drag the rotation handle to rotate the picture.

4. Tap Format to show the Format ribbon where you can perform additional formatting, such as adding a border, applying a style, or positioning it on the page.

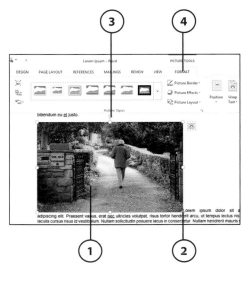

Changing Picture Layout

By default, your picture will be inserted inline with text. This might not be what you want because it can cause a large amount of white space surrounding your picture. You can easily change a picture's layout so that it flows better with your document.

1. Tap the picture.

2. Tap the Layout Options button.

3. Tap a layout option. When you select an option, the picture's layout is changed automatically.

4. If you selected a text wrapping layout, tap and drag the picture to position it where you want it to be.

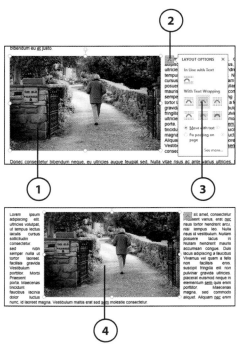

Proofing Documents

Word checks your spelling while you type, but its proofing tools don't stop there. You also have access to a dictionary and a thesaurus right within Word.

Correcting Misspelled Words

As you type, Word checks your spelling. Any word that it believes you've misspelled is underlined in red. You can correct a misspelled word quickly and easily.

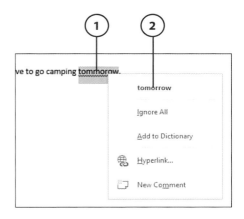

1. Tap and hold on a word that Word has underlined with a red, squiggly line.

2. Tap the correctly spelled word from the context menu to replace the misspelled word with the correctly spelled word.

Adding Words to the Dictionary

Some words that Word marks as misspelled may be spelled correctly. This happens often with names and other proper nouns. In these cases, you may choose to add the word to the dictionary so that it's no longer marked as misspelled.

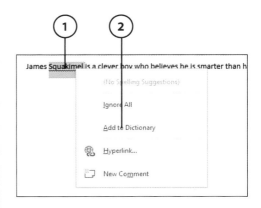

1. Tap and hold on a word that you want to add to the dictionary.

2. Tap Add to Dictionary.

Using the Dictionary

So far, you've seen how to use the spelling dictionary, but that doesn't help you if you want to look up a particular word in the dictionary. Word provides several dictionaries in the Office Store that you can download and use in Word.

1. Tap Review to display the Review ribbon.

2. Tap the Dictionaries button.

3. Tap Download to download a dictionary. (If you've already downloaded a dictionary, this step is skipped.)

4. Enter a word that you'd like to look up in the dictionary.

5. Tap Search.

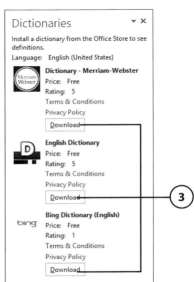

Easier Lookups

If you select a word before tapping the Dictionary button, a search for that word is automatically entered for you.

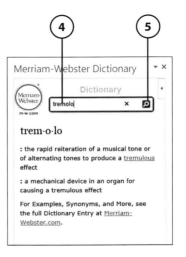

Using the Thesaurus

Word can also help you find synonyms and antonyms for words in your document. (You must download a dictionary using the steps in "Using the Dictionary" before you can use a thesaurus.)

1. Select the word you want to look up in the thesaurus.

2. Tap Review to display the Review ribbon.

3. Tap the Thesaurus button.

4. Tap a word in the thesaurus to replace the selected word.

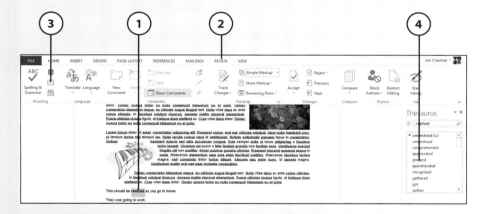

Searching the Thesaurus
Just as with the dictionary, you can search for words in the thesaurus by entering the word in the search box and tapping Search.

Sharing Documents

Sharing documents isn't a new concept, but Word 2013 makes it easier than ever to share not only through email, but also using Facebook or Twitter. Word documents are shared using the Word Web App, a cloud-based version of Microsoft Word.

Sharing from the Desktop
Because Word runs from the desktop, you can't use the Share charm to share a Word document. Instead, Word provides its own interface for sharing.

Sharing Documents Using Email

When you share a document using email, you can choose whether to require that those viewing your document log in using a Microsoft account before accessing the document. You also can choose whether others can view or edit the document.

1. Tap File.

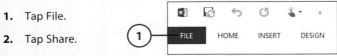

2. Tap Share.

3. Tap Invite People.

4. Enter an email address or the name of one of your contacts.

5. Tap Address Book to select a contact from your contact list.

6. Tap Can Edit, and select Can View in the drop-down if you don't want the person with whom you're sharing the document to be able to edit it.

7. Enter a message.

8. Tap Require a User to Sign In Before Accessing Document if you want to require that users sign in using a Microsoft account before accessing the document. This is especially useful when allowing editing so that you can see who last saved the document.

9. Tap Share.

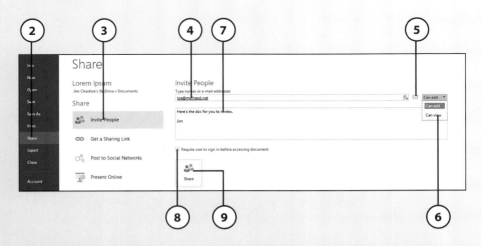

What Happens on the Other End?

When someone receives an email sharing a document, she can click the link to the document and open the document in Word Web App. Word Web App doesn't require that the user have Microsoft Word installed on her computer.

Sharing Using Social Networking

You can share a document using Facebook or Twitter. Sharing over social networks also uses the Word Web App.

1. From the Share screen in Word, tap Post to Social Networks.
2. Check Facebook to share the document on Facebook.
3. Check Twitter to share the document on Twitter.
4. Tap Can View, and change it to Can Edit if you want the document to be editable.
5. Enter a message.
6. Tap Post.

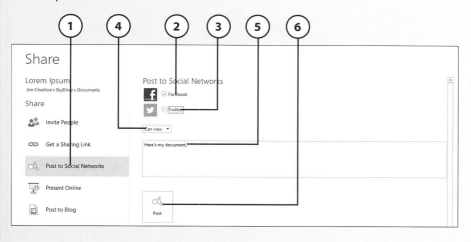

It's Not All Good

Unsharing

Although Word does enable you to unshare documents, doing so doesn't seem to have any effect on other users accessing the document. Even after unsharing a document and waiting for more than an hour, I was still able to open a shared document and make edits to it.

Printing Documents

Word provides many options for printing your documents. You can print an entire document or specific pages of a document.

Printing an Entire Document

You can print an entire document to any installed printer, but you also can print to the Microsoft XPS Document Writer to create a portable document that users who don't have Word can read.

Reading XPS Documents on a Mac

If you have a Mac and you want to read an XPS document, download NiXPS View from www.nixps.com.

1. Tap File.

2. Tap Print.

3. Enter the number of copies to print.

4. Select a printer.

5. Tap Page, and select Print All Pages.

6. Tap the Print button.

Printing Specific Pages

You can print specific pages or combinations of pages.

1. From the Print screen, enter the number of copies to print.

2. Select a printer.

3. In the Pages box, enter the pages to print. Multiple pages should be separated by commas, and regions of pages should use a dash.

4. Tap the Print button.

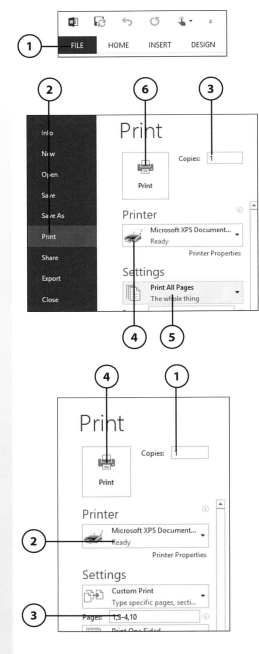

Tips and Tricks

I've just scratched the surface of what you can do in Word 2013. Here are some other features that will make your use of Word more enjoyable.

Using the Quick Access Toolbar

The Quick Access toolbar appears above the ribbon in the upper left of the Word window. By default, the Quick Access toolbar contains a Save button, an Undo button, a Redo button, and the Input Mode button. However, you can customize the Quick Access toolbar so that it contains the buttons you use often.

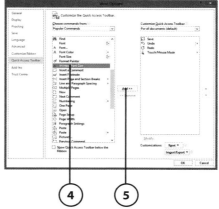

1. Tap the Customize Quick Access Toolbar button.

2. Tap a command to add it to the Quick Access toolbar.

3. To see more commands, tap More Commands.

4. Tap a command from the list.

5. Tap Add to add the command to the Quick Access toolbar.

Locating Commands

You can filter the list of commands by tapping the Choose Commands From drop-down and selecting a tab name where the command is located.

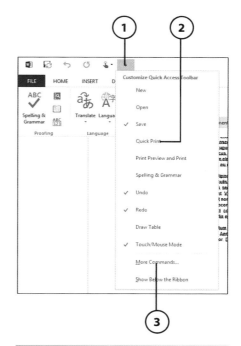

Adjusting Input Mode

Word provides two different input modes: Touch mode (the default in Windows RT) and Mouse mode. Touch mode provides increased spacing between menu commands and larger buttons so that you can easily use touch in Word. Mouse mode is better suited to using a mouse. You can choose the input mode that best fits how you use Word.

1. Tap the Input Mode button on Word's Quick Access Toolbar.

2. Tap Mouse to switch to Mouse input mode.

3. Tap Touch to switch to Touch input mode.

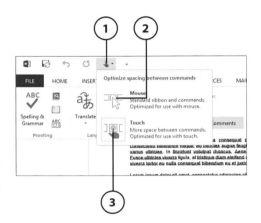

It's Not All Good

Fat Fingers

Even if you turn on Touch input mode, you'll likely encounter frustration with the size of some user interface elements. For example, if you want to dismiss a pane that appears on the left or right side of the Word interface, you simply have to tap the X in the upper-right corner of the panel. However, the X is so small that it's almost impossible to activate using touch. One way to resolve this is to purchase a stylus for use with your tablet.

Using the Format Painter

The Format Painter is a powerful tool that makes it easy to copy formatting from one part of your document to another.

1. Select a word that contains the formatting you want to copy.

2. Tap Home to display the Home ribbon.

3. Tap Format Painter.

4. Tap or select one or more words that you'd like to be formatted like the original word.

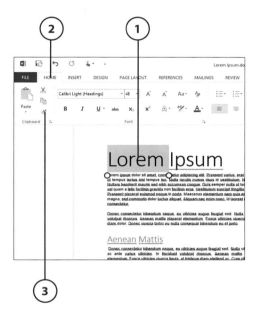

Keep track of important information.

Use formulas to do math for you.

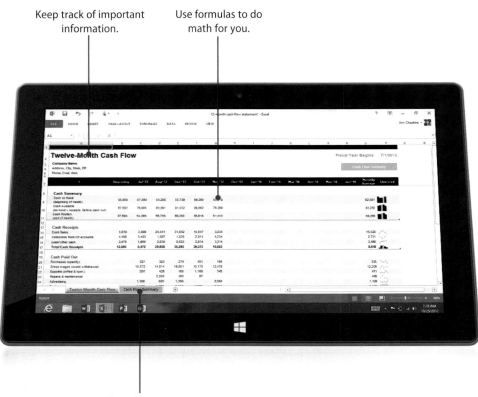

Organize your data in sheets.

18

Crunching Numbers with Microsoft Excel 2013

Computers are great at math, and Microsoft Excel 2013 makes it easy for you to take advantage of that. Excel can track your personal budget and expenses, compute your expense reports, and even track your weight loss. It's a versatile application that many PC users have never used because they find it intimidating. As you'll see in this chapter, there's no need to fear Excel.

Creating, Opening, and Saving Workbooks

Excel files are called *workbooks*. When you first launch Excel, you'll have an opportunity to create a new workbook. Like Microsoft Word, Excel uses templates so that you can have rich functionality without having to create a workbook from scratch.

Creating a Workbook

When you create a new workbook, you have the option of choosing a template or creating a blank workbook that you can customize however you want.

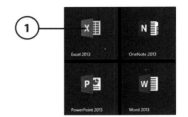

1. From the Start screen, tap Excel 2013 to launch Excel.

Desktop App

Excel is a desktop app, so when you launch it, you'll automatically be taken to the desktop.

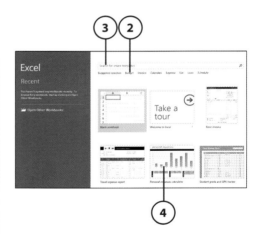

2. Tap a suggested search to find other templates.

First Launch

When you first start Excel, you're taken to the New screen. You can return to the New screen by tapping File and then tapping New.

3. Enter a search term to search for online templates.

4. Tap a template to create a workbook based on that template.

5. Tap Create to create your workbook. (You won't see this prompt if you choose the Blank Workbook template.)

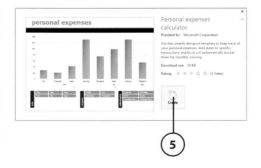

Opening a Workbook

You can open workbooks from your PC or from the cloud. Excel also provides a list of recently opened workbooks so that you can reopen a workbook.

1. From within Excel, tap File.

2. Tap Open.

3. Tap a recent workbook to reopen that workbook.

4. Tap your SkyDrive account to open a workbook saved on your SkyDrive.

5. Tap Computer to open a workbook that is on your PC.

6. Browse to the workbook you want to open, and tap to select it.

7. Tap Open.

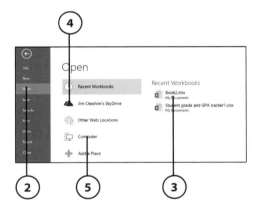

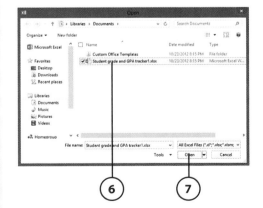

Saving a Workbook

You can save your workbook to your local PC, or you can save it to your SkyDrive account. By saving it to your SkyDrive account, you can access it from other PCs and devices.

1. From within Excel, tap File.

2. Tap Save As.

Quickly Saving

If you've already saved your workbook at least once, you can easily save it to the same location and filename by tapping Save instead of Save As.

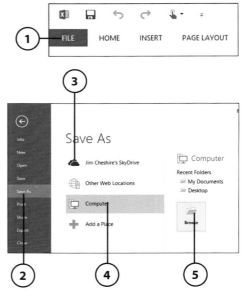

3. Tap your SkyDrive account to save the workbook to SkyDrive.

4. Tap Computer to save your workbook to your local PC.

5. Tap a recent folder, or tap Browse.

6. Browse to the location where you want to save your workbook.

7. Enter a filename for the workbook.

8. Tap Save to save the workbook.

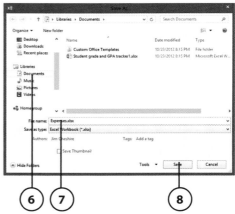

Entering Data

Excel data is typically a mixture of text and numbers. Text typically is used to describe the numerical data. For example, a grid of numbers will usually have column and/or row labels that use text.

Excel enables you to format data as needed and also contains some nice features for quickly adding data.

Adding Data

Data in Excel is entered into a cell located on a grid made up of rows and columns. Rows are identified using a number beginning with row 1, and columns are identified using a letter starting from the letter A. Therefore, the cell in the upper-left corner of your workbook is cell A1. The cell immediately to the right of that cell is cell B1. The cell immediately below cell A1 is cell A2.

1. Tap the cell where you want to add your data.

2. Enter your data using the keyboard.

3. Tap Enter.

4. Press your keyboard's arrow keys, or tap a cell to move to a new cell and enter additional data.

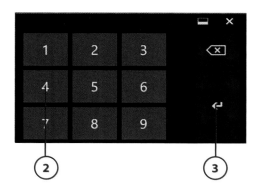

Resizing a Column

By default, columns in your workbook are all the same width. As you enter data into your workbook, you might find that you want to adjust the width of a column to accommodate more data or to make your workbook more legible.

1. Tap the column header for the column you want to resize.

2. Drag the slider to the right to increase the column's width or to the left to decrease the column's width.

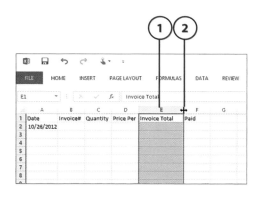

Changing Data Formatting

Excel uses a general format for all workbook data by default. You can change the format of one or more cells to be more appropriate for the type of data that is used in the cell. For example, if you are displaying dollar amounts, you might want a dollar sign to be added, and you might want negative values to show in red. This is easily accomplished by changing the data formatting.

1. Tap on the cell that contains the value you want to format.

Formatting Multiple Cells

You can format multiple cells by dragging the selection handles to enclose all the cells you want to format. You also can tap a header to select an entire column or row and format all data in that column or row.

2. Tap Home to display the Home ribbon.

3. Tap the format drop-down and select a format for the data.

4. For more formats, tap More Number Formats.

5. Tap a category.

6. Tap a format.

7. Tap OK to apply the formatting.

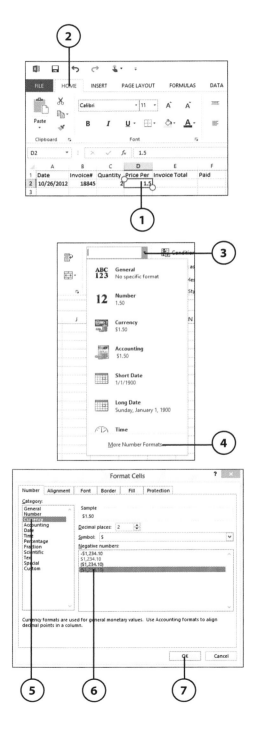

Adding Data with AutoFill

Some data that you enter will follow a predictable pattern. For example, if you are entering invoices into a spreadsheet, the invoice number might be an incremented number. If you are entering a weight loss journal, you might have a column with days of the week. In such cases, you can use Excel's AutoFill feature to automatically enter data for you.

1. Enter one or more values to define a pattern.

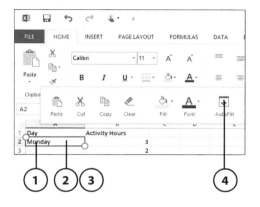

Defining Patterns

The amount of data you must enter to establish a pattern depends on many factors. If you want to use AutoFill with dates or days of the week, for example, you often only need to enter one value before you use AutoFill. If you want to use AutoFill for a more obscure pattern, you might need to enter three or more values for Excel to figure out the pattern in your data.

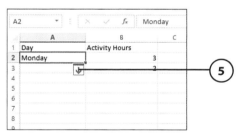

2. Tap the first value to select it.

3. Tap the value again to display the context menu.

4. Tap AufoFill.

5. Tap and drag the AutoFill icon down or across, depending on which direction you want AutoFill to populate your cells.

6. Release your finger, and AutoFill will fill the selection based on your pattern.

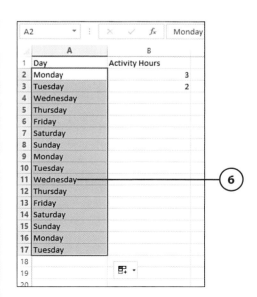

Creating Formulas and Functions

The true power of Excel lies in formulas and functions. Excel can do rudimentary mathematics, such as adding numbers and so on, but it can also perform complex mathematics.

Directly Entering a Formula

You can enter formulas directly into the formula bar. Formulas you enter always start with an equal sign.

1. Tap a cell where you want the result of the formula to be displayed.

2. Tap inside the formula bar.

3. Enter **=3.14/9.24**. (This is an example formula that divides 3.14 by 9.24.)

4. Tap Enter to insert the result of the formula into the selected cell.

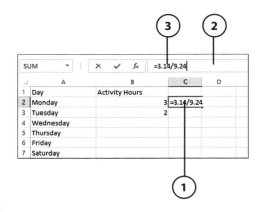

Cell Selections

When you tap Enter, Excel automatically moves to the next cell so that you can continue entering data into your workbook.

Using the Insert Function Dialog

Complex formulas are called *functions*. Functions take two or more values and return a result based on a calculation. Excel makes using functions easy using the Insert Function dialog.

1. Tap the cell where you want to insert the result of your function.

2. Tap the Insert Function button.

3. Tap the desired function. If you aren't sure which function to use, enter a description of what you want to do and tap Go to search.

4. Tap OK.

5. Enter any arguments the function requires. (Your options will differ based on which function you selected.)

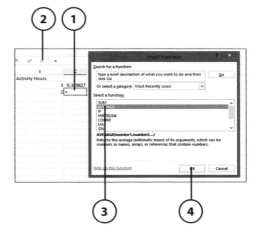

Use Cell Values

If you want your function to use values in a particular cell in your workbook, you can enter the cell location (for example, C2 as shown in the figure) and your function will use the value contained in that cell. If you use this method, changing the value in the cell you use in your function automatically changes the value in the cell displaying the function's result.

Note that Excel displays the function result in the dialog as you are entering your arguments.

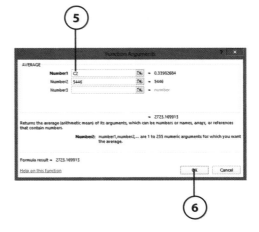

6. Tap OK to insert the function's result into the selected cell.

Creating Formulas from Selections

In many cases, you might want to add a formula that uses a selection of cells to calculate a result. For example, you might want to display the sum of a list of numbers in a column.

1. Select the cells you want to use in your formula.

2. Tap the Quick Analysis button.

3. Tap the type of analysis you want your formula to perform.

4. Tap a function to perform and the result of the formula is entered automatically next to the selection.

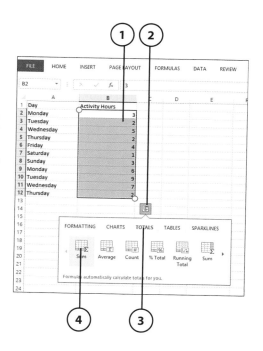

More Excel

Formulas in Excel are extremely powerful, and I've only touched the surface of what they can do. For more information on using formulas in Excel, read *Microsoft Excel 2013 In Depth* from Que Publishing.

Tips and Tricks

In addition to what you've already learned, there are some other features of Excel that can make using it more productive.

Freezing Panes

If you are working with a workbook that is wider or taller than your screen, you might find it convenient to freeze panes. When you freeze panes, part of the workbook (such as header columns or row labels) remains frozen while you scroll.

1. Tap on the cell where you want to freeze panes. Any rows above or columns to the left of the selected cell will be frozen.

2. Tap View to display the View ribbon.

3. Tap Freeze Panes.

4. Tap Freeze Panes.

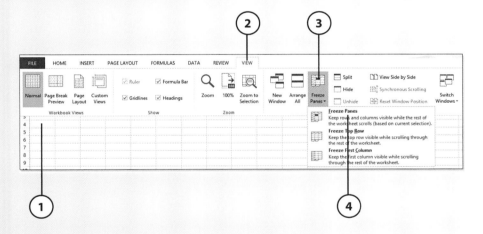

Freezing Without Selecting

You can tap Freeze Top Row to freeze the top row of your workbook or Freeze First Column to freeze the first column of your workbook, regardless of what is currently selected.

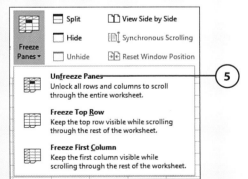

5. To unfreeze previously frozen panes, tap Unfreeze Panes.

Creating Sheets

Workbooks are made up of sheets. Each sheet is represented by a tab at the bottom of the screen. If you have multiple sets of data you want to keep track of in your workbook, you can create a new sheet.

1. Tap + to add a new sheet.

2. Tap and hold the new sheet to display the context menu.

3. Tap Rename.

4. Enter a descriptive name for your new sheet.

Switching Sheets

You can switch between the sheets in your workbook by tapping on a sheet's tab.

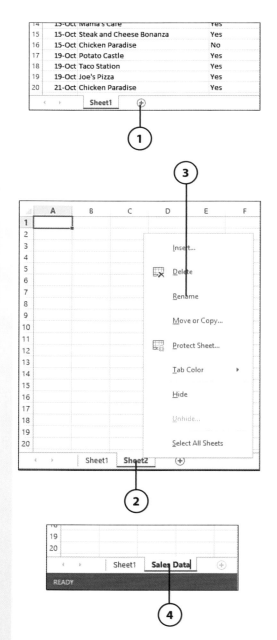

Presenting with Microsoft PowerPoint 2013

Microsoft PowerPoint 2013 enables you to create engaging and informative onscreen presentations. Just as with the other Office applications you've seen up to this point, PowerPoint uses templates to give you a head start in being creative. It also shares the capability to save to and open from the cloud as well as your tablet.

Creating, Opening, and Saving Presentations

When you launch PowerPoint for the first time, you have the option of starting with a blank presentation or choosing a template that applies certain styles and colors. When you've finished working on a presentation, you can save it to your tablet or your SkyDrive so that you can access it on your other devices.

Creating a Presentation

Just as with the other Office applications you've seen, PowerPoint provides access to thousands of templates for jump-starting your presentation.

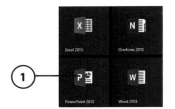

1. From the Start screen, tap PowerPoint 2013 to launch PowerPoint.

2. Tap a suggested search to locate a particular type of template.

3. Enter a search term, and tap Search if you don't see a template that suits you.

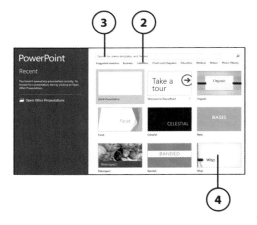

4. Tap a template to choose it.

5. Tap the arrow to see more images of other slide types with the selected template applied.

6. Tap a variation of the template to choose a different color scheme.

7. Tap Create to create your presentation.

Change Your Mind

You're not locked into the template or variation that you choose now. You can easily change it at any time. I'll show you how later in this chapter.

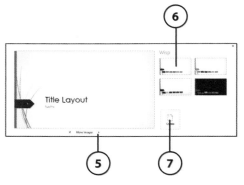

Saving a Presentation

When you are ready to stop working on a presentation, you can save it to your tablet or your SkyDrive.

1. From within PowerPoint, tap File.

2. Tap Save As.

3. Tap your SkyDrive account to save to your SkyDrive.

4. Tap Computer to save to your tablet.

5. Tap a recent folder, or tap Browse.

6. Browse to the location where you want to save your presentation.

7. Enter a name for your presentation.

8. Tap Save to save the presentation.

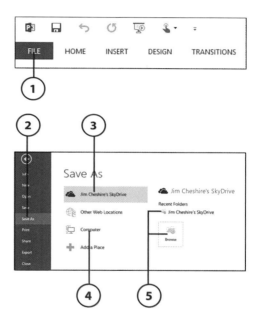

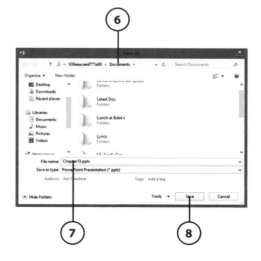

Opening a Presentation

You can open presentations stored on your tablet or your SkyDrive.

1. After launching PowerPoint, tap a recent file from the list to open that file.

2. Tap Open Other Presentations to browse for a presentation.

3. Tap your SkyDrive account to open a presentation from your SkyDrive.

4. Tap Computer to open a presentation from your tablet.

5. Tap a recent folder, or tap Browse to browse to a folder.

6. Browse to the folder containing your presentation.

7. Tap your presentation to select it.

8. Tap Open to open the presentation.

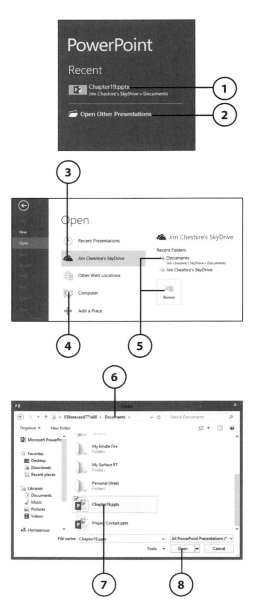

Creating Slides and Content

PowerPoint presentations consist of a series of slides. Slides can contain text, graphics, and other elements used to illustrate a particular point. PowerPoint has specialized tools for creating and laying out slides.

Creating a New Slide

When you create a new slide, it takes on the appearance and attributes applied by the theme you are using. There are numerous types of slides based upon what type of content you want the slide to convey. For example, there are slide layouts appropriate for title slides, slides that provide general content, slides that are great for a side-by-side comparison, and so forth.

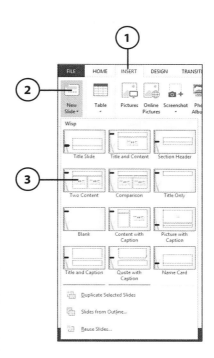

1. After creating or opening your presentation, tap Insert to display the Insert ribbon.

2. Tap New Slide.

3. Tap the slide type you want to insert. A thumbnail of each is provided to make it easier to decide.

Deleting a Slide

If you want to delete a slide you've added, you do so from the thumbnails pane.

1. Tap and hold on the slide you want to delete.

2. Release to display the context menu, and tap Delete to delete the slide.

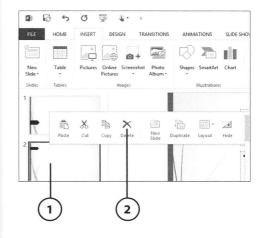

Changing Slide Layout

When you create a new slide, you choose an appropriate layout. If you decide to change the layout, you can. Any text or other content you have already added to the slide will be preserved.

1. Tap the slide for which you want to modify the layout.

2. Tap Home to display the Home ribbon.

3. Tap Layout.

4. Tap the desired layout to change the slide's layout.

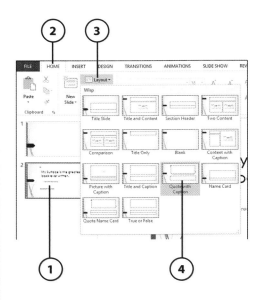

Adding Text to a Slide

Text is added to PowerPoint slides in text boxes that are outlined with a dotted line. Each layout of a slide has different text boxes for entering text.

1. Tap the area where you want to add your text.

2. Enter the desired text.

3. Format the text using the formatting options available on the Home ribbon.

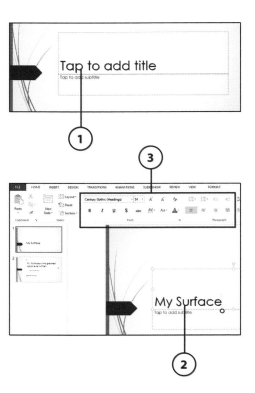

Adding Shapes to a Slide

Shapes are often used in PowerPoint slides because they offer more visual appeal than plain text. Shapes can also contain text overlaid on top of the shape.

1. Tap the slide onto which you want to insert your shape.

2. Tap Insert to display the Insert ribbon.

3. Tap Shapes.

4. Tap the Shape you want to insert.

5. To add text to the shape, tap and hold on the shape.

6. Release to reveal the context menu, and tap Edit Text.

7. Type the text you want to appear in the shape.

Quickly Add Text

You can start typing immediately after adding a shape to add text to the shape. However, you'll need to use the steps provided here if you want to edit the text after adding it.

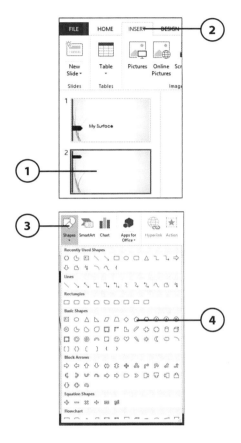

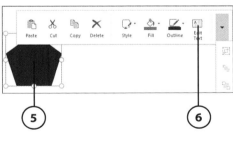

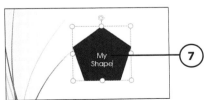

Aligning Objects

If you add two or more shapes or other objects to a slide, you'll likely want to align the objects so that they are more visually appealing. For example, you might want the tops of all of your shapes to line up on your slide.

1. Tap the first shape you want to align.

2. Tap the shape again and hold your finger on it.

3. Tap any additional shapes you want to align to select them.

4. Tap Format to display the format ribbon.

5. Tap Align.

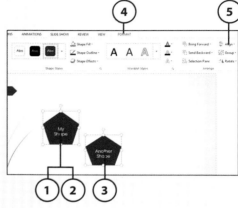

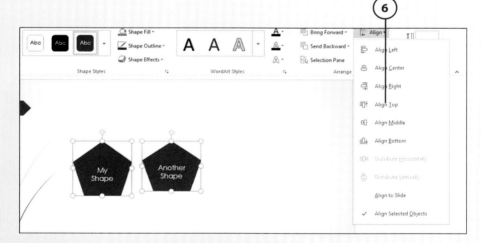

6. Tap an alignment option to align the objects.

Drag to Align

If you are trying to align one object with another one, you can drag the object until you see a dotted line drawn along the point where you want to align the objects. This is a convenient way to align two objects, but if you have more than two objects to align, the Format ribbon is the best choice.

Using Themes

Themes in PowerPoint not only provide an attractive (usually) color scheme for your slides, but they also provide other visual elements that can make your presentation more effective.

Applying a Theme

If you created your presentation using any template other than the blank presentation template, you already have a theme in place. However, you can apply a different theme at any time to change the appearance of your slides.

1. Tap Design to display the Design ribbon.

2. Tap a theme to apply the theme to your presentation.

3. Tap the drop-down to see additional themes.

4. Tap a theme from the dialog to apply the theme.

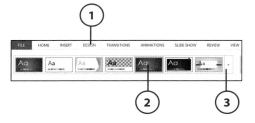

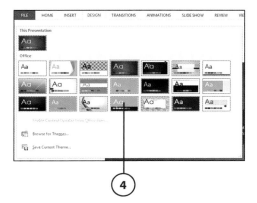

Modifying a Theme

You can change the variation of a theme
to change the color scheme. You also
can modify other parts of a theme to
make it suit your needs.

1. Tap Design to display the Design
   ribbon.

2. Tap a theme variant to change
   the color scheme.

3. Tap the drop-down to display
   other properties that you can
   change.

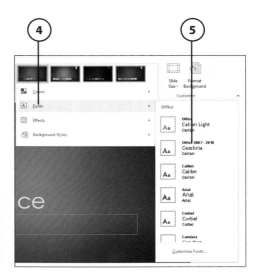

4. Tap a category from the drop-
   down.

5. Tap an option for the category to
   modify the template.

Using Animations and Transitions

Animations and transitions can make a presentation more interesting.
Transitions are applied when a presentation changes from one slide to
another. Animations are used to control how objects on a slide appear and
disappear.

Applying a Transition

You can apply different transitions to different slides. It's not required that a slide have a transition applied to it. If you don't apply a transition, the slide will instantly appear onscreen when you switch to it during a presentation.

1. Tap the slide for which you want to apply the transition.

2. Tap Transitions to display the Transitions ribbon.

3. Tap a transition to select it.

4. Tap the Transitions drop-down to see more transitions.

5. Tap a transition from the dialog to apply the transition.

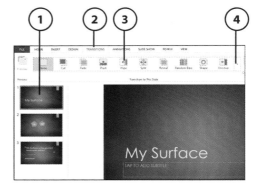

What Does It Look Like?

After you apply a transition, you'll see it played for you in the main PowerPoint window. (You can tap the Preview button on the Transitions ribbon to replay the preview.) If you don't like the transition, you can choose others until you are satisfied.

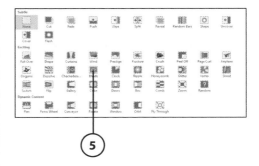

Customizing a Transition

PowerPoint provides several options
for customizing a transition. Transition-
specific options are available, and you
can also add a sound to your transition
and control the duration of it.

1. Tap to select the slide to which
   the transition has been applied.

2. Tap Transitions to display the
   Transitions ribbon.

3. Tap Effect Options to display
   options for the transition.

4. Tap an effect option to apply it.
   (Options vary based on the effect
   you've chosen.)

5. Tap Sound and select a sound
   to associate a sound with the
   transition.

6. Tap Duration and enter a new
   value to change the duration of
   the transition.

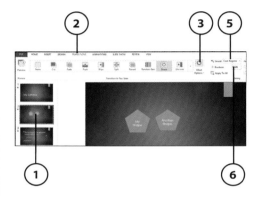

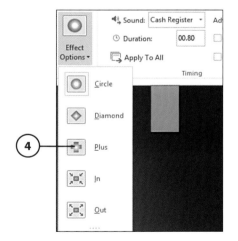

Adding an Animation

Animations are used to control how objects appear and disappear from a slide. By default, objects appear as soon as the slide appears, but you can alter that behavior using animations.

More Than One

You can apply as many animations as you want to an object. PowerPoint plays back all the animations that you apply in the order you applied them.

1. Tap the object to which you want to apply the animation.

2. Tap Animations to display the Animations ribbon.

3. Tap Add Animation.

4. Tap an animation from the dialog.

Choosing Animations

Some animations are well suited for playing when an object appears (an object's entrance), and others are better for playing when an object disappears (the object's exit). To find the appropriate animation, tap on More Entrance Effects or More Exit Effects to see more effects.

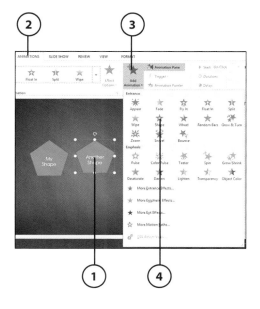

Configuring an Animation Trigger

By default, animations play when you click on a slide. You can change an animation's trigger so that it plays automatically at a certain point.

1. Tap the object to which the animation is applied.

2. Tap the Start drop-down.

3. Tap With Previous to automatically play the animation simultaneously with the animation immediately preceding it.

4. Tap After Previous to automatically play the animation after the preceding animation finishes playing.

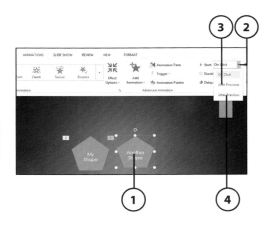

More Information

I've obviously just touched on the functionality available in PowerPoint 2013 here. If you want additional information, read *PowerPoint 2013 Absolute Beginner's Guide* by Que Publishing.

Presenting with PowerPoint

When you've finished creating your PowerPoint presentation, you can present it to others. When you are presenting a presentation, slides are presented in the order in which they appear in the thumbnail panel.

Changing Slide Order

If the slides in the thumbnail panel aren't in the desired order, you can rearrange them before presenting your presentation.

1. Tap View to display the View ribbon.

2. Tap Slide Sorter.

3. Tap and drag slides to the desired location.

4. Tap Normal to switch back to Normal view.

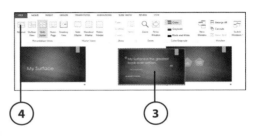

Entering Slide Show Mode

To present your presentation, you must enter Slide Show mode. If you have another monitor connected to your tablet, you can choose which monitor to use for your slide show.

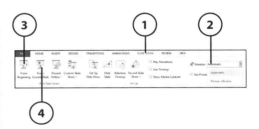

1. Tap Slide Show to display the Slide Show ribbon.

2. If you have another monitor connected, tap Monitor and select the monitor to use for your slide show.

3. Tap From Beginning to start your slide show from the first slide.

4. Tap From Current Slide to start the slide show from the currently selected slide.

5. While in Slide Show mode, tap the screen, and tap Next to move to the next slide or play the next animation.

6. Tap End Slide Show to end the slide show and return to Normal view.

Advancing Slides

While in Slide Show mode, you can advance slides and animations using a mouse button as well.

Tips and Tricks

There are a couple of other features of PowerPoint that you'll find convenient to use in your presentations.

Using Sections

If you have a lot of slides in your presentation, using sections that place slides into groups is a great way to organize your slides.

1. Tap the slide you want to be the first slide in a new section.

2. Tap Home to display the Home ribbon.

3. Tap Section.

4. Tap Add Section.

5. Tap Section again.

6. Tap Rename Section.

7. Enter a name for your new section.

8. Tap Rename.

Section Names

Section names are displayed in the thumbnail panel and in the Slide Sorter.

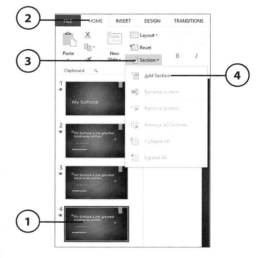

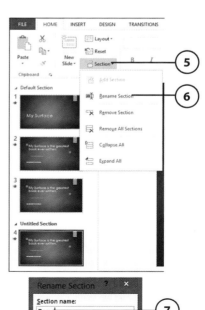

Using Headers and Footers

If you have information you want to display at the top or bottom of every slide, you can set a header or a footer. This feature is commonly used to display copyright or other such information.

1. Tap Insert to display the Insert ribbon.

2. Tap Header & Footer.

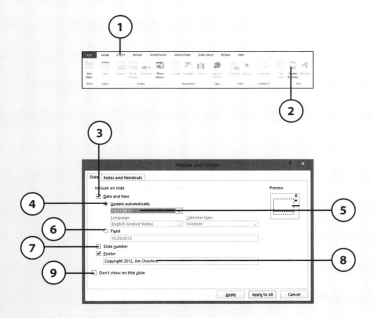

3. Check Date and Time to display the date and time at the top of each slide.

4. Tap Update Automatically if you want the date to automatically be updated based on the current date.

5. Tap the drop-down and choose a display format for the date and time.

6. Tap Fixed and enter a value to display a fixed value on each slide.

7. Check Slide Number to display the slide number on each slide.

8. Check Footer and enter a value to display at the bottom of each slide.

9. Check Don't Show on Title Slide if you don't want the header and footer displayed on the title slide.

Create multiple notebooks
for organizing notes.

Organize notebooks with
sections and pages.

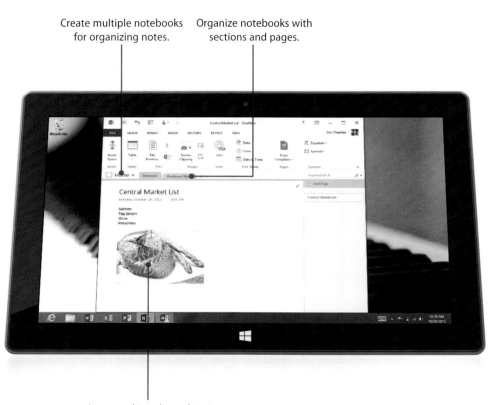

Insert multimedia and text
into notes.

Organizing Notes with Microsoft OneNote 2013

OneNote 2013 is Microsoft's app for taking notes on your Surface. Note-taking apps are nothing new, but OneNote adds some significant features that make it a great choice.

Notes in OneNote are kept in notebooks. Each notebook can have one or more sections, and each section can have one or more pages. Your notebooks are synchronized across your devices using your Microsoft account.

More on OneNote 2013
This chapter covers the basics of OneNote 2013. For full coverage of OneNote 2013, read *My OneNote 2013* from Que Publishing.

Creating and Organizing Sections

Notebooks in OneNote are organized into sections. Sections are displayed as tabs along the top of the OneNote app, and you can move among sections by tapping its tab.

Auto-Save

As you move through this section of the book, you might wonder how to save a OneNote notebook. In fact, your OneNote notebooks are saved automatically, so you never have to worry about manually saving your work.

Creating a Section

You can create as many sections as you need in any particular notebook.

1. From the Start screen, tap OneNote 2013 to launch OneNote.

2. Tap the + tab to create a new section.

3. Enter a name for the new section, and press Enter on your keyboard.

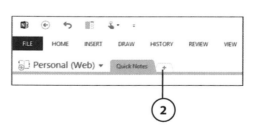

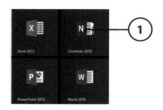

Adding Notes

In the next section, "Creating and Editing Pages," I discuss pages and how you can add notes and content to your notebook sections.

Changing a Section's Color

Sections are color coded. When you create a new section, OneNote assigns a random color for it. You can change the color to something that suits you.

1. Tap and hold on the section's tab, and then release to display the context menu.

2. Tap Section Color.

3. Tap a color from the list.

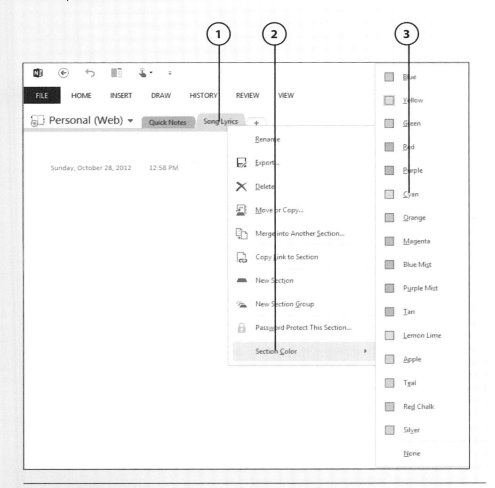

No Color

One of the options in the color menu is None. If you select None, your section will be colored light gray.

Renaming a Section

You might want to rename a section to reflect a more appropriate name. You can rename a section at any time.

1. Tap and hold on the section's tab, and release to display the context menu.

2. Tap Rename.

3. Enter the new name and press Enter to commit it.

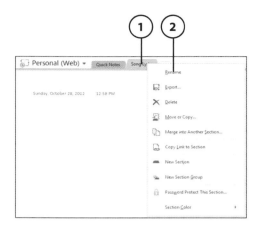

Merging Sections

You might find that you have notes in multiple sections that should be combined into a single section. You can easily merge content from two or more sections into a single section.

1. Tap and hold on a section that you want to merge into another section, and release to display the context menu.

2. Tap Merge into Another Section.

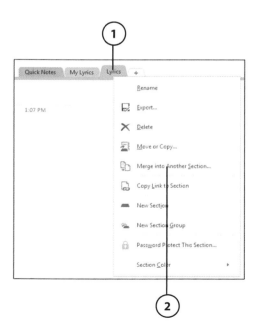

3. Tap the section into which you want to merge the section. If necessary, you can search for a section by entering text that appears in the section's title.

4. Tap Merge to merge the section into the selected section.

5. Tap Merge Sections in the dialog.

6. Tap Delete if you want to delete the original section.

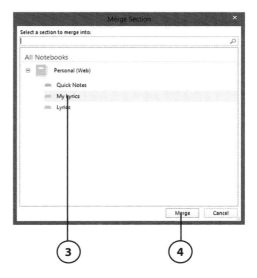

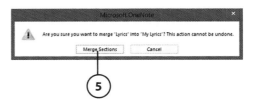

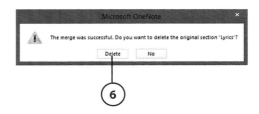

Moving or Copying a Section

Section tabs appear in the order in which the sections were created. If you want to better organize your sections, you can move or copy one or more sections. When you copy a section, a new section is created and the original section remains.

1. Tab and hold on the section you want to move, and release to display the context menu.

2. Tap Move or Copy.

3. Tap the section name after which you want your section to appear.

4. Tap Move to move the section, or Copy to copy the section to the location you selected.

Moving with Mouse or Track Pad

If you're using a mouse or a track pad with your Surface, you can also drag and drop section tabs to move sections.

Moving Between Notebooks

If you've created more than one notebook, you'll have the option to also move a section to another notebook.

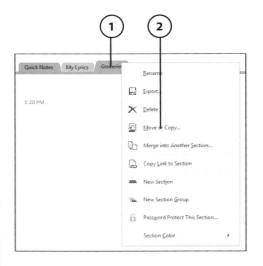

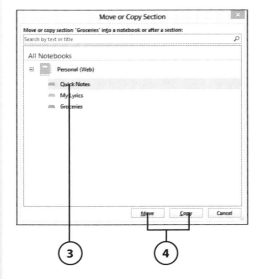

Deleting a Section

If you no longer need a section, you can delete it.

1. Tap and hold on the section you want to delete. Release to display the context menu.

2. Tap Delete.

3. Tap Yes to delete the section.

Deleting Isn't Permanent

When you delete a section, the section is moved into the notebook's Recycle Bin. Later in this chapter, I show you how to use the Recycle Bin to recover deleted items.

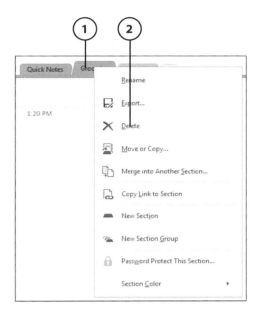

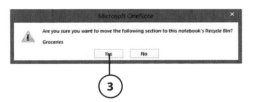

Creating and Editing Pages

Notes in a section are contained in one or more pages. Pages appear as tabs within a section along the right edge of the OneNote app. In the previous section, I created a notebook section called Lyrics that can be used to store lyrics to songs. In this scenario, each song can be stored into its own page.

Creating a Page

When you create a new section, a blank page called Untitled Page is created for you. However, you can add additional pages as you need them.

1. Tap the section to which you want to add a new page.

2. Tap Add Page to create a new page.

3. Enter a title on the page to name the page.

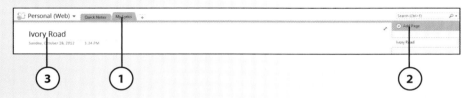

Adding Text to a Page

You can add text to a page and then move that text freely so that it's positioned exactly where you want it.

1. Tap the desired section.

2. Tap a page, or create a new page for your note.

3. Tap anywhere on the page to place the cursor at that point.

4. Enter text for your note.

5. Tap and hold on the bar above your text, and drag it to position it elsewhere on the page.

6. To add additional text, tap within the box and enter additional text.

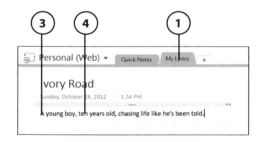

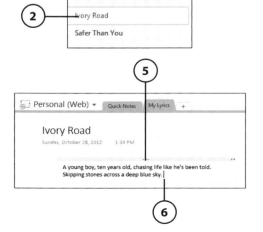

Adding Pictures on Your Tablet to a Page

In addition to text, your notes can contain pictures that are stored on your tablet.

1. Tap on a page where you want to insert a picture.

2. Tap Insert to display the Insert ribbon.

3. Tap Pictures.

4. Browse to the picture you want to insert, and tap it to select it.

5. Tap Insert.

6. Drag the sizing handles to resize the picture if necessary.

7. Drag the directional arrows to position the picture on your page.

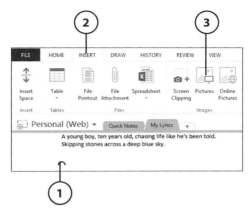

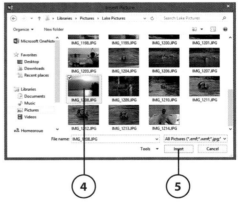

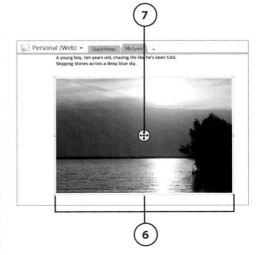

Adding Pictures from the Cloud to a Page

In addition to adding pictures from your tablet, you can add pictures from the cloud to your page.

1. Tap on your page where you want the picture inserted.

2. Tap Insert to display the Insert ribbon.

3. Tap Online Pictures.

4. Tap Office.com Clip Art or Bing Image Search and enter a search term to search for a picture.

5. Tap Flickr or your SkyDrive to insert a picture from either of these cloud services.

6. Tap a picture to select it.

7. Tap Insert to add the picture to your page.

8. Drag the sizing handles if necessary to resize your picture.

9. Drag the directional arrows to reposition the picture.

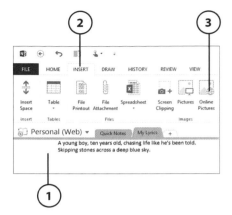

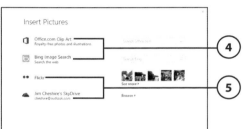

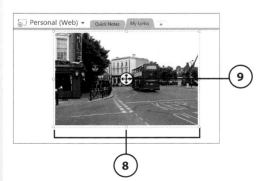

Renaming a Page

You can change the name of a page. Doing so changes the name that you see on the tab and the name on the page itself. In fact, when you choose to rename a page, you do it by changing the header on the page.

1. Tap and hold on the page you want to rename, and then release to display the context menu.

2. Tap Rename.

3. Enter a new name for your page.

Another Way to Rename

You can also rename a page by simply navigating to the page and changing the text that appears on the page's header.

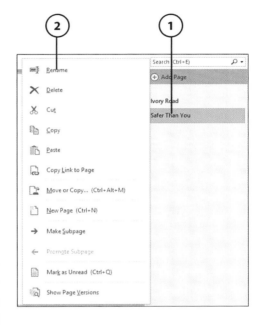

Moving or Copying a Page

You might want to move or copy a page to another section in the current notebook or to another notebook altogether. When you move a page, the page is removed from its original location and added to the new location. When you copy a page, the page is added to the new location and the original copy remains.

1. Tap and hold on the page you want to move, and release to display the context menu.

2. Tap Move or Copy.

3. Tap the location where you want to move or copy the page.

4. Tap Move to move the page or Copy to copy the page.

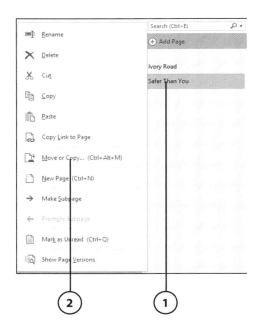

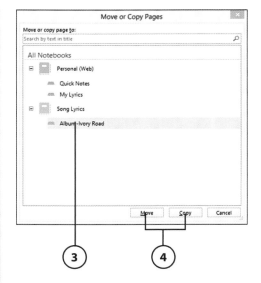

Deleting a Page

If you no longer need the information on a page, you can delete the page.

1. Tap and hold on the page you want to delete, and release to display the context menu.

2. Tap Delete.

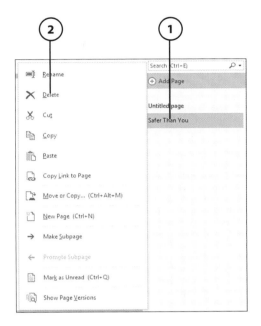

Deleting Isn't Permanent

When you delete a page, it actually gets moved to the notebook's Recycle Bin. I show you how to use the recycle bin later in this chapter.

Creating and Organizing Notebooks

So far you've been using the Personal notebook that OneNote creates for you automatically. You can create additional notebooks so that you can better organize your notes. Notebooks can be stored on your tablet or in your SkyDrive so that you can access them from any Internet-connected computer.

Not Limited to Windows

OneNote isn't just available on Windows devices. You can get OneNote on your iPhone, iPad, Mac, and Android devices. Notebooks on your SkyDrive are available on any of these devices.

Creating a Notebook

Notebooks are a great way to keep your notes organized. I keep one notebook for work notes, one notebook for home notes (for things like shopping lists and so forth), and numerous other notebooks for various hobbies. You can create as many notebooks as you need to keep your notes organized.

1. From within OneNote, tap File.

2. Tap New.

3. Tap your SkyDrive account to create the notebook in your SkyDrive.

4. Tap Computer to create the notebook on your tablet.

5. Enter a notebook name.

6. Tap Create Notebook.

7. Tap Not Now when asked if you want to share the notebook. I show you how to share a notebook a little later in this chapter.

More Places for Notebooks

You can also create notebooks on Office 365 SharePoint locations, but I don't cover that in this book. For details on using OneNote and Office 365, read *My OneNote 2013* from Que Publishing.

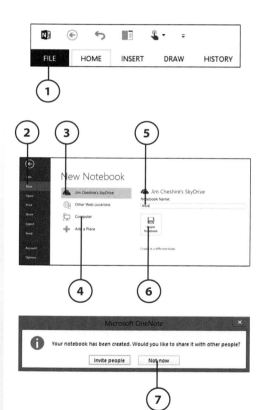

Switching and Opening Notebooks

You can switch between your open notebooks and open other notebooks stored on your tablet or your SkyDrive.

1. Tap the name of the currently open notebook.

2. Tap another open notebook to switch to that notebook.

3. Tap Open Other Notebooks to access other notebooks you might have but aren't currently listed.

4. Tap a notebook on your SkyDrive to open it.

5. Tap a recently opened notebook to open it.

6. Tap Computer to see notebooks stored on your tablet.

7. Tap a folder on your tablet to browse notebooks in that folder.

8. Tap Browse to browse for a notebook in a different folder.

9. Browse to the location of your notebook, and tap it to select it.

10. Tap Open.

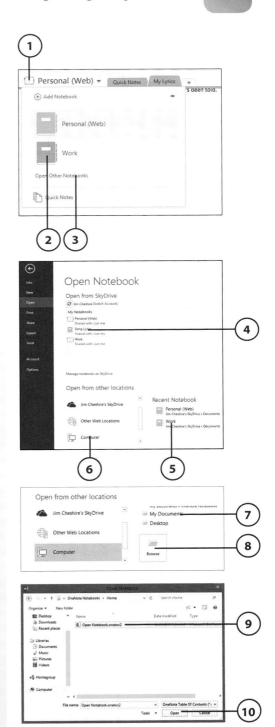

Moving and Sharing a Notebook

You can move a notebook from your tablet to your SkyDrive. When a notebook is on your SkyDrive, you can share it with other people.

1. Open a notebook that's stored on your tablet, and then tap File.

2. Tap the Settings button for the notebook you want to share.

3. Tap Share or Move.

Another Way to Share

You can also share a notebook by tapping the Share on Web or Network link.

4. If you want to use a different name for your notebook when it's moved to SkyDrive, enter a new name.

5. Tap Move Notebook.

6. Tap OK.

7. Enter the email address for one or more people with whom you want to share the Notebook.

8. Tap the Can Edit drop-down and select Can View if you don't want others to be able to edit your notebook.

9. Enter a message.

10. Tap Require User to Sign In Before Accessing Document if you want users to sign in with a Microsoft account before accessing the notebook. This is useful if you want to keep track of who is accessing the notebook.

11. Tap Share to share the notebook.

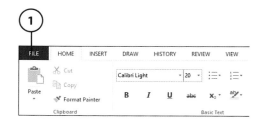

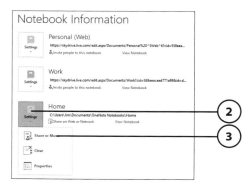

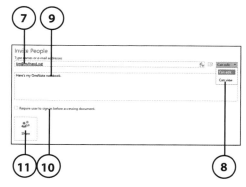

Using the Recycle Bin

When you delete pages or sections from a notebook, they aren't permanently deleted—they are moved to the notebook's Recycle Bin. You can then choose to restore them.

1. Delete a section or page from a notebook.

2. Tap History to display the History ribbon.

3. Tap Notebook Recycle Bin.

4. Tap and hold on a section or page you want to restore, and release to display the context menu.

5. Tap Move or Copy.

6. Tap the location where you want to restore the item.

7. Tap Move.

8. Tap Notebook Recycle Bin again to see your restored item.

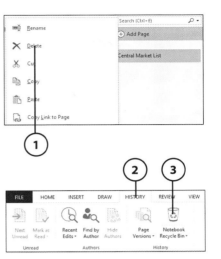

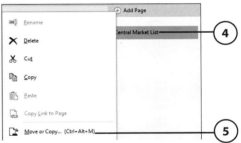

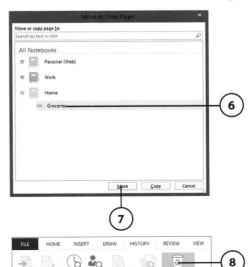

It's Not All Good

Items Deleted After 60 Days

Items in a notebook's Recycle Bin are automatically deleted after 60 days. When they are automatically deleted, there is no way you can recover them.

Using Send to OneNote

OneNote is designed to enable you to add almost anything to a note, and Send to OneNote makes it easy to add screen clippings or content from other apps, or jot down a quick note as you're using your tablet.

Send to OneNote Launched Automatically
Send to OneNote is launched automatically when you start OneNote.

Capturing a Screen Clipping

If you need to add a screen shot of what you are viewing on your tablet to a note, you can do so using Send to OneNote.

1. While viewing something that you want to add to a note, tap the Send to OneNote tool on the taskbar.

2. Tap Screen Clipping.

3. Drag across the screen to select the region that you want to add to your note. Release your finger when the desired region is selected.

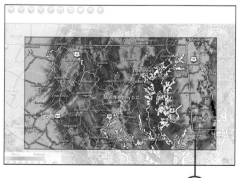

4. Tap the section or page where you want the item to be added.

5. Tap Send to Selected Location.

Manipulating Screen Clippings

After you add a screen clipping to a page, you can manipulate it just as you would any other picture.

Copying to the Clipboard

You can tap Copy to Clipboard to copy the selected screen region to the Windows Clipboard instead of moving it directly into a notebook. You can then paste the image wherever you like.

It's Not All Good

Limited Use in Windows RT

Send to OneNote's screen clipping feature works only in desktop apps, so on Windows RT, you can only use it with Office documents, File Explorer, Windows desktop utilities such as Control Panel, and desktop Internet Explorer.

Sending Content to OneNote

You can send content from other Office apps or desktop Internet Explorer to OneNote using Send to OneNote.

1. Open an Office document or browse to a website in desktop Internet Explorer.

2. Tap Send to OneNote on the taskbar.

3. Tap Send to OneNote.

4. Tap the section or page where you want to add the content.

Same as Printing

When you send content to OneNote using Send to OneNote, what you see in your OneNote notebook is the same as what you would see if you were to print the content to a printer.

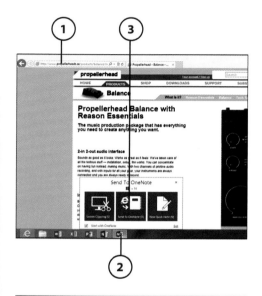

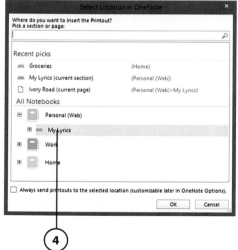

Adding a QuickNote

If you want to jot down a quick note while using your tablet, the New Quick Note feature of Send to OneNote is convenient.

1. Tap Send to OneNote on the taskbar.

2. Tap New Quick Note.

3. Enter your note.

4. Tap the X to close the Quick Note dialog.

Location of Quick Notes
Quick Notes are added to the Quick Notes section of the Personal notebook.

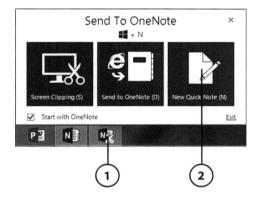

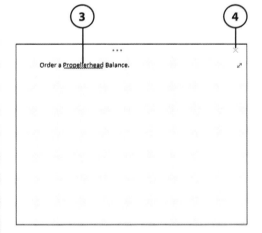

Enhance your Surface tablet with apps from the Windows Store.

Find and install the latest apps.

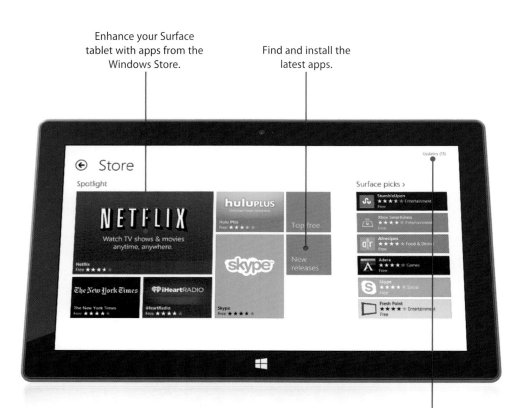

Update your apps to fix bugs and add features.

Enhancing Windows with Apps

The Surface tablet is a powerful tablet with enormous capabilities straight out of the box, but by adding additional apps from the Windows Store, you can make it even more powerful. Thousands of apps are available in the app store, and more apps are being added all the time.

Browsing the Windows Store

The Windows Store is the source of apps for your Surface. Apps are categorized for easier browsing, but you can also search for apps using the Search charm.

Browsing Categories

Apps in the Windows Store are categorized for easier browsing. You can browse apps by category when you're looking for a particular type of app.

1. From the Start screen, tap the Store tile.

2. Swipe left and right to view highlighted apps from each category.

3. Tap Top Free to see the top free apps from a category.

4. Tap New Releases to see new apps in a category.

5. Tap a category name to view all apps in a category.

6. Tap the Subcategories drop-down to filter on subcategories.

7. Tap the Prices drop-down to filter apps by price.

8. Tap the Sort drop-down to change the sort order of apps.

9. Swipe left to see additional apps in the category.

10. Tap an app to see additional details on the app.

11. Tap Back to return to the previous screen.

12. Swipe down from the top of the screen, and tap Home to return to the Windows Store home screen.

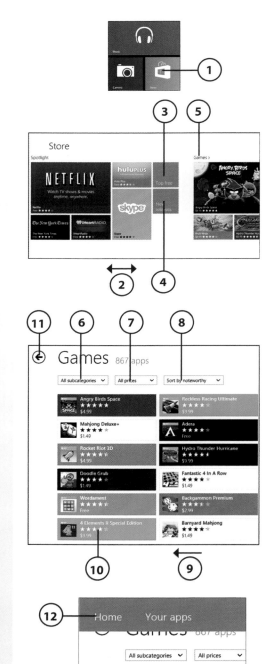

Exploring Apps

Plenty of information is available to help you decide whether you want to purchase an app. You can view screenshots, reviews of the app from other users, and more.

1. Tap an app in the Windows Store that you're interested in.

2. Swipe up and down in the Overview section to see more information.

3. Swipe left on the screenshot to see additional screenshots.

4. Tap Details to see additional details on the app.

5. Tap Reviews to see app reviews.

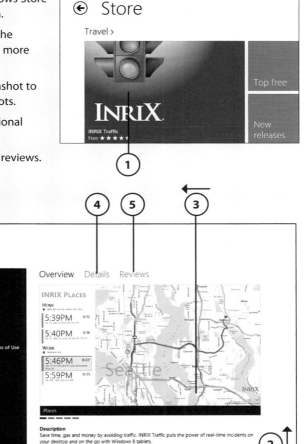

6. Swipe up to see additional reviews.

7. Tap Yes or No to vote on whether a review is helpful.

8. Tap Report this Review to report an inappropriate review.

9. Tap Sort By to change the sort order for reviews.

10. Tap Back to return to the list of apps.

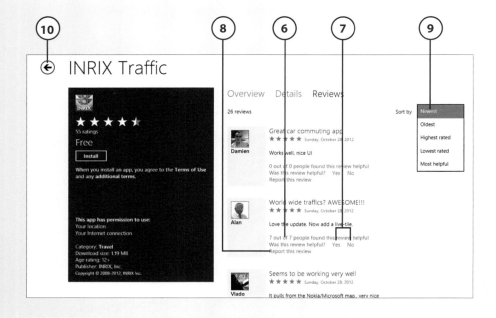

Searching for Apps

When you need to find a specific app or a specific type of app, searching for apps is often your best choice.

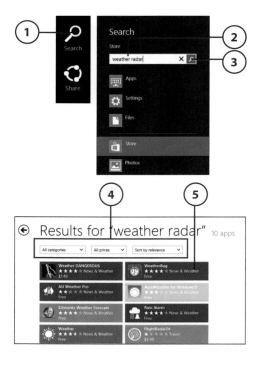

1. In the Windows Store, swipe in from the right side of the screen and tap the Search charm.

2. Enter a search term. You can search for keywords or specific app names.

3. Tap Search.

4. Use the drop-downs to filter and sort the search results.

5. Tap an app to view more details on the app or to install it.

Installing and Uninstalling Apps

When you have found an app that you want to use, you'll need to install it on your Surface. If you later decide you don't want the app, you can remove it from your Surface by uninstalling it. Finally, you can easily locate apps that you've purchased and reinstall them on your Surface.

Installing Apps

Many apps are free, while other apps require you to pay for them. However, many of these paid apps offer trial versions so that you can try the app and decide whether it's worth purchasing. You can install any of these apps onto your Surface tablet immediately via the Windows Store.

Computer Limit

To install an app onto your tablet, it must be associated with your Microsoft account. You can associate up to five devices with your Microsoft account. For details on how to do that, see "Changing from a Local Account to a Microsoft Account" in Chapter 4, "Security and Windows RT."

1. Locate an app that you want to install, and tap it to view the details on the app.

2. Tap Buy to purchase the app. You'll be able to confirm your choice before the purchase is finalized.

3. Tap Try to install a trial version of the app.

Free Apps

Free apps have an Install button instead of a Buy button. Tapping the Install button installs a free app.

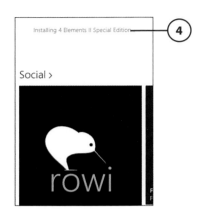

4. Tap the notification to see the install status.

5. Tap an app, and then tap Pause Download to pause the download of the app.

6. Tap Cancel Install to cancel the app's installation.

7. When a notification that the app has been installed appears, tap the app's tile on the Start screen to launch the app.

Canceling Install of a Purchased App

If you cancel the installation of an app that you purchased, you can install the app later without paying for it again. I show you how in the "Reinstalling Purchased Apps" section of this chapter.

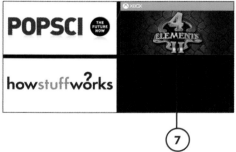

Uninstalling Apps

If you want to free up space on your Surface, you can uninstall apps that you no longer want. You can always reinstall the app later without having to pay for it again, and I show you how in the next section.

1. Locate the app's tile on the Start screen, and swipe down on it to select it.

2. Tap Uninstall to uninstall the app.

3. Tap Uninstall to confirm the uninstall of the app.

Reinstalling Purchased Apps

Microsoft keeps track of the apps that you purchase, and you can reinstall any apps you've purchased under your Microsoft account.

1. From the Windows Store, swipe down from the top of the screen and tap Your Apps.

2. By default, apps not installed on your tablet are displayed. Tap the drop-down and select a different option to see all apps you own or apps that are installed on another PC you own.

3. Tap the Sort drop-down to change the sort order of apps.

4. Tap one or more apps that you want to install, or tap Select All to select all apps.

5. Tap Install to install the selected apps.

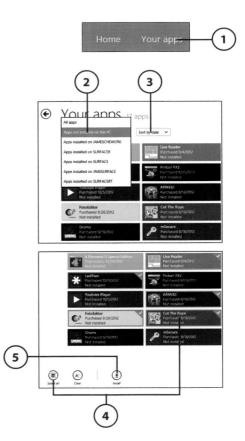

Updating Apps

The Windows Store displays a numeric indicator in the upper-right corner of the screen whenever one or more apps have an update available. Updates for apps are free, and you should install them when they're available because they often fix bugs and provide added stability.

Manually Checking for Updates

Windows RT automatically checks for updates for your apps, but you can also manually check for updates.

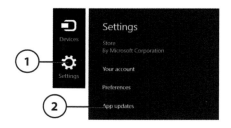

1. From the Windows Store, swipe in from the right side of the screen and tap Settings.

2. Tap App Updates.

3. Tap Check for Update to check for app updates. (I show you how you can install updates for your apps in the next section.)

Sync Licenses

If you're not seeing updates for apps you own, you can tap Sync Licenses and Windows RT will ensure that it has up-to-date information for all of your app licenses.

Installing App Updates

There are a few ways you can be notified of app updates. When updates are available, the Windows Store tile displays the number of available updates in the lower-right corner of the tile. The Windows Store app also displays the number of available updates in the upper-right corner of the app interface. Finally, you can manually check for updates. When an update is available, you can install it quickly and easily.

1. From the Windows Store, tap the Updates link in the upper-right corner of the app.

2. Tap Install to install all updates.

3. If you want to install updates only for specific apps, tap to deselect any apps that you do not want to update.

4. The status of update installs is displayed as the updates are downloaded and installed.

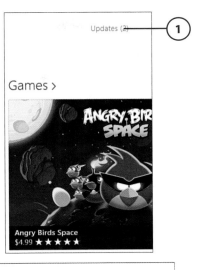

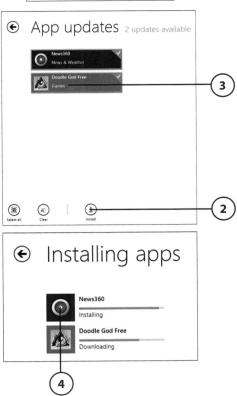

Great Apps for Your Surface

Thousands of apps are available in the Windows Store. Here are a few that I find particularly nice for enhancing your Surface.

Netflix

If you're a Netflix subscriber, the Netflix app will almost certainly become one of your favorite apps. You can browse the Netflix library, manage your instant queue, and watch TV shows and movies on your Surface.

1. Tap a recently watched title to continue watching it.

2. Tap an item from your instant queue to watch it.

3. Tap Top 10 for You to see recommendations from Netflix.

4. Tap New Releases to see all new releases.

5. Tap Genres to browse the Netflix library by genre.

6.   Tap a title to see more details.

7.   Tap Add to Queue to add the item to your instant queue.

8.   Tap a star to rate the title.

9.   Tap a name to see other titles for that actor or director.

10.   Tap Play to play the title.

Skype

Skype turns your Surface into a videoconferencing device. You can make both video and audio calls to other Skype users using the camera and microphone on your Surface.

1. Tap the phone icon to make phone calls (for a fee) with Skype.

2. Tap one of your contacts to initiate a call with that person. If the person is not a Skype user, you'll have the option of sending a message using the Windows Messenger service.

3. Tap the status icon to change your status when you don't want to show as available for calls.

4. Tap the plus sign to add favorite contacts.

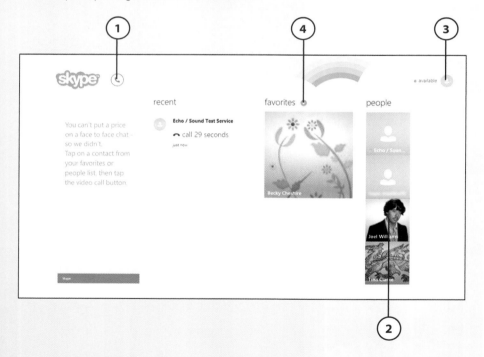

Angry Birds Space

Angry Birds Space is the latest release in the Angry Birds family of games. Angry Birds Space is a physics-based game where you shoot animated birds from a slingshot at pigs in all sorts of challenging structures. It sounds silly, but it's fun and a great game for the whole family.

1. Tap and drag to load a bird in the slingshot.

2. Release your finger to launch the bird at the pig.

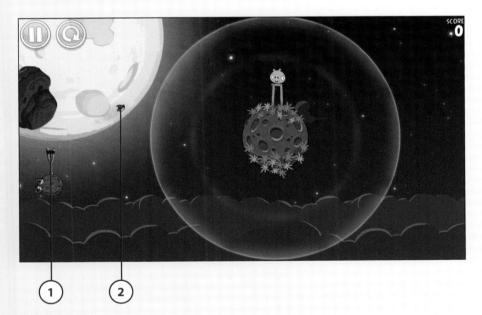

Rowi

Rowi is a Twitter client for Windows RT. If you're a Twitter user, Rowi is a good choice because it's free and feature-rich.

1. Tap New Tweet to tweet something.

2. Tap a tweet to select it.

3. Tap the hash tag to see a list of trending hash tags on Twitter.

4. Tap Quote to quote the selected tweet and add your own message.

5. Tap Retweet to retweet the selected tweet.

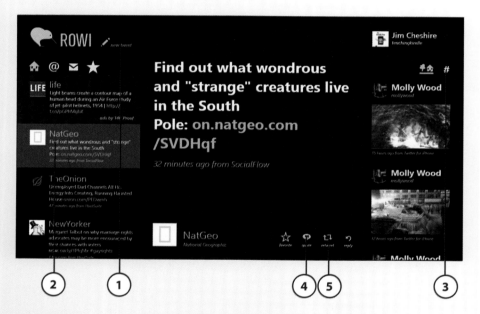

YouTube+

There are several YouTube apps in the Windows Store, but YouTube+ is my favorite. There is a paid version, but the ad-supported trial version contains full functionality and doesn't time out.

1. Tap a popular video to see more details.

2. Enter a search phrase to search for a video.

3. Tap the Quality drop-down to see available video quality settings.

4. Tap the video, and tap Pause to pause playback.

5. Tap the video, and tap Full Screen to watch the video in full screen.

6. Tap Comments to see comments on the current video.

7. Tap Author to see information on the video's author and subscribe to his feed.

8. Tap Related to see related videos.

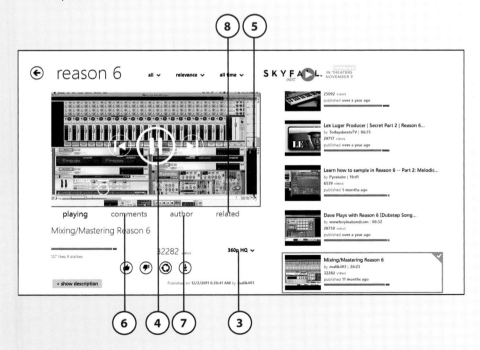

iHeartRadio

iHeartRadio is a streaming music app that makes your favorite music available to you on your Surface. You can listen to radio stations all over the country, but you can also create your own station by entering an artist and letting iHeartRadio find music that you might enjoy.

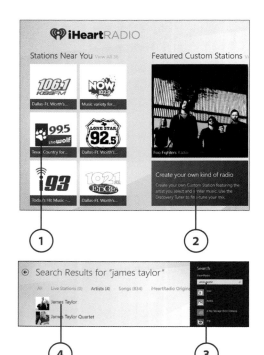

1. Tap a station or artist to listen to music.

2. Tap Create Your Own Kind of Radio to create your own station.

3. Enter an artist, a song name, or another search term.

4. Tap a search result to create your own station.

Kindle

The Kindle app makes your Amazon Kindle eBook library available on your Surface.

1. Tap Cloud to see books in your library that are stored on Amazon's servers.

2. Tap Device to see books that are stored on your tablet.

3. Tap Kindle Store to open Internet Explorer and browse the Kindle Store.

4. Tap a book to open it for reading.

5. While reading, tap the page to display a menu of options.

6. Tap Library to return to your library.

7. Tap Go To to navigate sections of the book or to a particular location number.

8. Tap View to change view options such as typeface, size, and background color.

9. Tap Bookmark to add or remove a bookmark at the current position.

10. Tap Notes/Marks to display notes and bookmarks you've added to the book.

11. Tap Sync to manually sync to the furthest page read across your devices.

12. Tap Pin to Start to pin the current book to the Start screen.

13. Drag the slider to quickly move to a part of the book.

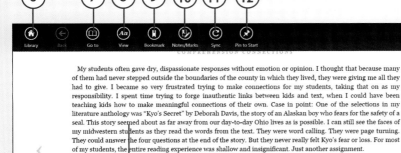

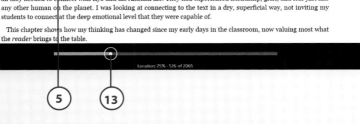

My students often gave dry, dispassionate responses without emotion or opinion. I thought that because many of them had never stepped outside the boundaries of the county in which they lived, they were giving me all they had to give. I became so very frustrated trying to make connections for my students, taking that on as my responsibility. I spent time trying to forge inauthentic links between kids and text, when I could have been teaching kids how to make meaningful connections of their own. Case in point: One of the selections in my literature anthology was "Kyo's Secret" by Deborah Davis, the story of an Alaskan boy who fears for the safety of a seal. This story seemed about as far away from our day-to-day Ohio lives as is possible. I can still see the faces of my midwestern students as they read the words from the text. They were word calling. They were page turning. They could answer the four questions at the end of the story. But they never really felt Kyo's fear or loss. For most of my students, the entire reading experience was shallow and insignificant. Just another assignment.

I've learned that whenever my students are just going through the motions, I should look for an error in *my* belief system or in *my* approach. When it came to prior knowledge, I was trying to forge connections that were not authentic, believing that because my students were not well traveled, they couldn't do it on their own. Wrong. How shallow to think that geographic location is the only way to connect to a text! Truth be told, my students had all they needed to connect with Kyo and his Alaskan life. They had experienced friendship, grief, and fear just like any other human on the planet. I was looking at connecting to the text in a dry, superficial way, not inviting my students to connect at the deep emotional level that they were capable of.

This chapter shows how my thinking has changed since my early days in the classroom, now valuing most what the *reader* brings to the table.

Location: 25% - 526 of 2065

WeatherBug

Windows RT comes with a weather app, but WeatherBug is a much better app for weather. You can see weather for your current location and add additional locations.

1. Tap Current to see detailed weather information about current conditions.

2. Tap Today to see an hour-by-hour forecast for today.

3. Tap Forecast for a six-day forecast.

4. Tap Notifications to set up notifications for different types of weather. Notifications appear on your tablet.

5. Tap Alerts to see any active weather bulletins, such as storm warnings.

6. Tap Maps to see weather maps.

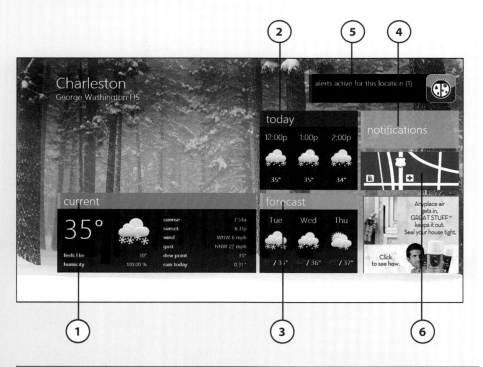

Adding Locations

If you want to add more locations to WeatherBug, swipe down from the top of the screen and tap Locations. You can search by city name or ZIP code.

News360

News360 is a highly customizable news app for your tablet. You can browse news stories using an attractive and functional app that makes the most of the Windows RT interface.

1. When you first launch News360, choose the types of news that you want to see.

2. Tap Assemble News360 to continue.

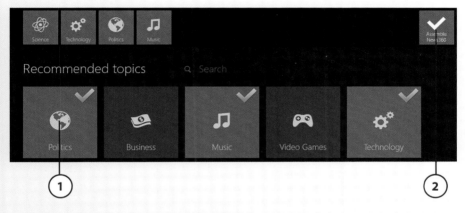

3. Swipe left and right to see additional stories.

4. Tap a tile to see the entire story.

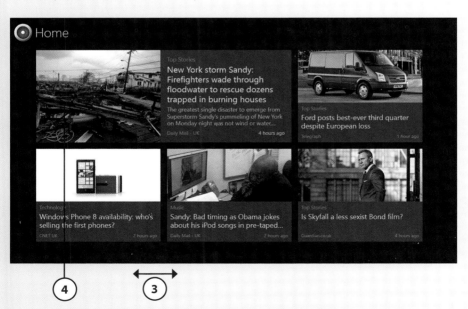

5. Swipe left and right on images to see pictures from various sources.

6. Tap a news source to read more from that source.

7. Swipe up and down to read more of the current article.

8. Tap the browser window to read the article from the original source in Internet Explorer.

9. Tap Back to return to the previous screen.

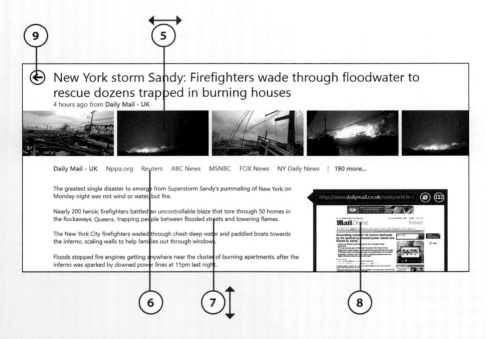

Custom News Sources

If you swipe down from the top of the screen in News360 and tap Add/Edit, you can add other news sources, including custom news sources based on search terms.

eBay

The eBay app makes browsing and buying items on eBay a pleasure. Touch is a great way to peruse eBay, and the eBay app is well-designed and simple to use.

1. Tap a tile to see items or search for items.

2. Tap a daily deal to see details on specials.

3. Tap Sort to sort items.

4. Tap Condition to filter on condition of items.

5. Tap Price to filter by price.

6. Tap Format to filter on auctions and Buy It Now items.

7. Tap a category to see items in that category.

8. Swipe left and right to see additional items.

9. Tap an item for more details.

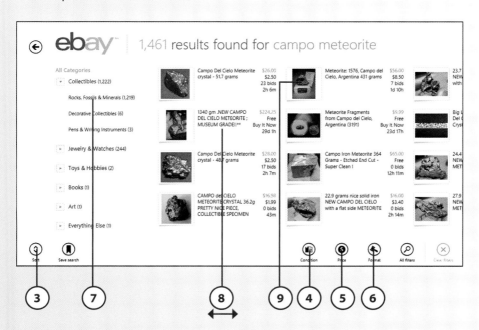

10. Tap the arrow to see additional pictures.

11. Tap a picture to see a larger image.

12. Tap Place Bid to bid on an item.

13. Tap Watch to watch an item.

14. Swipe left to see additional details, such as a description and information on the seller.

15. Tap Back to return to the previous screen.

Refresh your Surface while
keeping personal files.

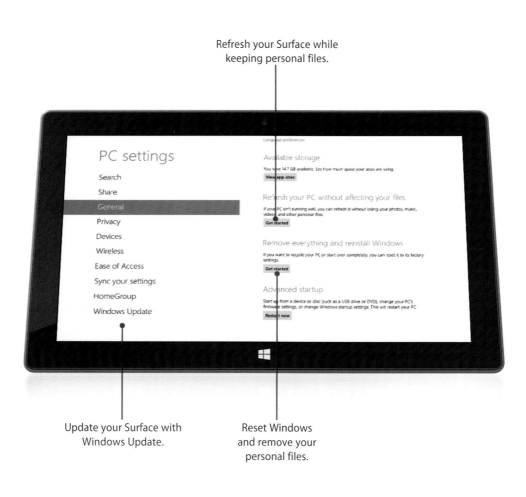

PC settings

Search

Share

General

Privacy

Devices

Wireless

Ease of Access

Sync your settings

HomeGroup

Windows Update

Language preferences

Available storage

You have 14.7 GB available. See how much space your apps are using.

View app sizes

Refresh your PC without affecting your files

If your PC isn't running well, you can refresh it without losing your photos, music, videos and other personal files.

Get started

Remove everything and reinstall Windows

If you want to recycle your PC or start over completely, you can reset it to its factory settings.

Get started

Advanced startup

Start up from a device or disc (such as a USB drive or DVD), change your PC's firmware settings, or change Windows startup settings. This will restart your PC.

Restart now

Update your Surface with
Windows Update.

Reset Windows
and remove your
personal files.

22

Updating and Troubleshooting Windows RT

Updating with Windows Update

Windows Update automatically keeps your Surface up to date. By default, updates are downloaded automatically, and many updates install automatically behind the scenes without you even knowing about it. However, if a restart is required to install an update, you'll be notified.

What's in a Name?

Windows Update's name isn't by fluke. Windows Update downloads and installs updates for Windows (and Office 2013) only. Updates for Windows Store apps, including those that came with your Surface, are installed through the Windows Store app and not Windows Update. I cover this in Chapter 21, "Enhancing Windows with Apps."

Checking for and Installing Updates Manually

Your Surface checks for updates to Windows every day. However, you can force a manual check for updates if you want to and then choose to manually install any updates that are available.

1. From the Start screen, swipe in from the right and tap the Settings charm.

2. Tap Change PC Settings.

3. Tap Windows Update.

4. Tap Check for Updates Now.

5. Tap the link to see what updates are available.

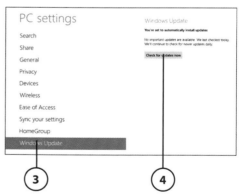

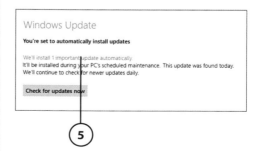

6. Tap Install to install updates that are available.

7. Tap Cancel while updates are installing to cancel the updates; otherwise, wait until the updates are complete.

8. If prompted, tap Restart Now to complete the installation of updates. Your computer will be updated and then restarted.

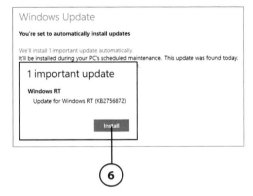

Windows Update

You're set to automatically install updates

We'll install 1 important update automatically.
It'll be installed during your PC's scheduled maintenance. This update was found today.

1 important update

Windows RT
Update for Windows RT (KB2756872)

Install

6

Windows Update

Installing updates

Cancel

7

Windows Update

Restart your PC to finish installing updates

Your PC will automatically restart in 2 days if you don't restart now.

All users will be signed out and could lose any unsaved work when you restart your PC.

Restart now

8

Installing Optional Updates

Windows Update automatically installs important updates. However, some updates (including updates to your Office apps) are optional updates and you'll need to install them manually.

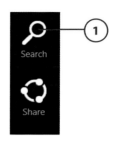

1. From the Start screen, swipe in from the right and tap the Search charm.

2. Enter **optional**.

3. Tap Settings.

4. Tap Install Optional Updates, which takes you to the Windows desktop.

5. Tap Check for Updates to check for optional updates.

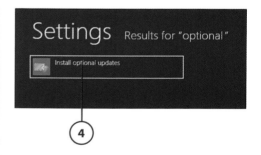

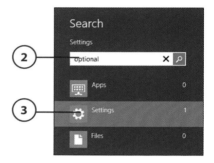

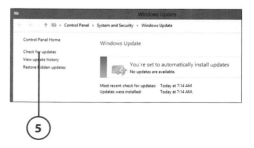

6. Tap the link to see details on available updates.

7. Check the updates that you want to install, and tap Install.

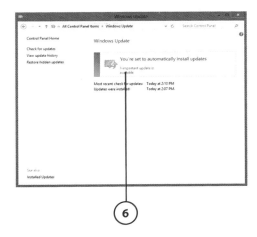

6

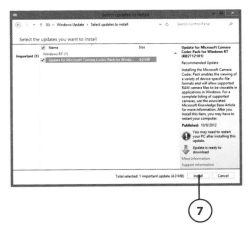

7

Troubleshooting Windows RT

If you are having trouble with Windows RT on your Surface, you have a couple of options for troubleshooting. You can refresh and repair your PC, a process that restores all Windows settings while keeping all your personal files. You can also reset your PC, a process whereby Windows RT is reinstalled and all your personal files are removed.

Refreshing and Repairing Your PC

If you find that your Surface is having problems and not operating correctly, you often can fix it by refreshing and repairing your PC. When you do so, your personal files are not impacted and remain on the device.

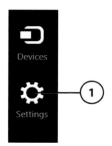

What About Apps?

When you refresh or repair your Surface, any apps you've installed remain on the device.

Before you start this process, plug in your Surface so that it's running on AC power and not the battery.

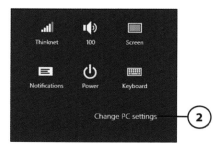

1. From the Start screen, swipe in from the right side of the screen and tap the Settings charm.

2. Tap Change PC Settings.

3. Tap General.

4. Swipe up to scroll to the bottom of the screen.

5. Tap Get Started under Refresh Your PC Without Affecting Your Files.

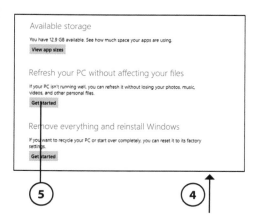

6. Tap Next.

7. Tap Refresh to refresh your PC. Your PC will restart and refresh back to its original settings without affecting your pictures, music, or other personal files.

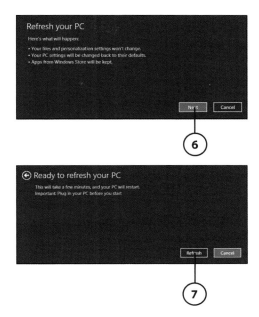

Refreshing to Defaults

After you run a refresh on your PC, your PC reverts to the settings that existed when you powered it on for the first time. After you refresh, it's a good idea to check for updates and install any that are available from Windows Update and the Windows Store.

WHEN TO REFRESH

Your Surface is a reliable PC, and there's a good chance that you will never have to refresh it. However, when it comes to technology, there's always the possibility that things can go wrong. How will you know when you need to refresh? There aren't any specific rules for when to refresh, but if you notice that you are seeing numerous errors, if your Surface restarts on its own, or if you are experiencing slowness when using your Surface, refreshing your PC is a good first step. There's a good chance that it will fix any problems you're having.

>> Go Further

Resetting Windows

You can reset Windows RT completely, restoring your Surface to the state it was in when it was new. This is a good idea if you are giving or selling your Surface to someone else.

Before you go through this process, make sure that you plug in your Surface.

1. From PC Settings, tap General.

2. Swipe up to scroll to the bottom of the page.

3. Tap Get Started under Remove Everything and Reinstall Windows.

4. Tap Next.

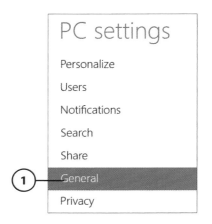

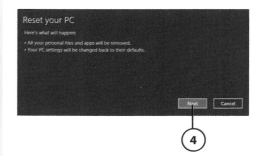

5. To remove your personal files and reset settings while leaving the current Windows RT installation intact, tap Just Remove My Files. This is a good choice if you are giving or selling your Surface to someone else.

6. To fully clean the drive and reinstall Windows RT, tap Fully Clean the Drive.

Use File History

If you use File History to back up your files, you can safely reinstall Windows and then restore your files. For information on using File History, see Chapter 6, "Backing Up Your Data."

7. Tap Reset to reset your PC.

Index

Jim Cheshire

Your purchase of **My Surface** includes access to a free online edition for 45 days through the **Safari Books Online** subscription service. Nearly every Que book is available online through **Safari Books Online**, along with thousands of books and videos from publishers such as Addison-Wesley Professional, Cisco Press, Exam Cram, IBM Press, O'Reilly Media, Prentice Hall, Sams, and VMware Press.

Safari Books Online is a digital library providing searchable, on-demand access to thousands of technology, digital media, and professional development books and videos from leading publishers. With one monthly or yearly subscription price, you get unlimited access to learning tools and information on topics including mobile app and software development, tips and tricks on using your favorite gadgets, networking, project management, graphic design, and much more.

Activate your FREE Online Edition at
informit.com/safarifree

STEP 1: Enter the coupon code: CNGJQZG.

STEP 2: New Safari users, complete the brief registration form.
Safari subscribers, just log in.

If you have difficulty registering on Safari or accessing the online edition,
please e-mail customer-service@safaribooksonline.com